PRAISE FOR
THE GROWTH GAMBLE

"This book is very insightful and also very practical—it provides the practitioner with some real hands-on advice as to what to do differently. We found its contents really helped shape our thinking."
Stephen Ford, Head of Strategy Development, Boots Group plc

"Although I do not agree with all of Campbell and Park's views, this is an important topic addressed in a solid, fact based way, informed by history. Few books meet these tests."
Richard Foster, author of Creative Destruction

"Campbell and Park challenge some well documented views about growth and new business development. Their challenges are not always successful, but they do encourage rigorous thinking about how companies should search and select new businesses."
Robert A. Burgelman, Edmund W. Littlefield Professor of Management at Stanford University Graduate School of Business and author of Strategy Is Destiny

"Campbell and Park address a critical issue—new growth for the firm. Supported by manifold examples from practice, which have been distilled into guidelines for firms that aspire to grow new businesses, *The Growth Gamble* argues for a more cautious view than others, including myself, of how much venturing a company really can accommodate. As a result they provide a valuable antidote to exhortations for growth that drive firms to be overly ambitious."
Professor Ian MacMillan, The Wharton School and author of Corporate Venturing and The Entrepreneurial Mindset

THE GROWTH GAMBLE

THE GROWTH GAMBLE

When Leaders Should Bet Big on
New Businesses and How to Avoid
Expensive Failures

Andrew Campbell & Robert Park

NICHOLAS BREALEY
INTERNATIONAL

LONDON   BOSTON

First published by
Nicholas Brealey International in 2005

3–5 Spafield Street	100 City Hall Plaza, Suite 501
Clerkenwell, London	Boston
EC1R 4QB, UK	MA 02108, USA
Tel: +44 (0)20 7239 0360	Tel: (888) BREALEY
Fax: +44 (0)20 7239 0370	Fax: (617) 523 3708

http://www.nbrealey-books.com

ISBN 1-90483-804-9

British Library Cataloguing in Publication Data
A catalogue record for this book is available from the
British Library.

Printed in Finland by WS Bookwell.

CONTENTS

TAKING THE GAMBLE OUT OF GROWTH

Professor Gary Hamel

Some wag once ventured that second marriages represent the triumph of hope over experience. The same might be said about the millions of dollars, euros, and pounds that companies spend every year chasing the dream of new business creation. As any number of academic studies have demonstrated, the odds of new business success are long—substantially longer than the odds of winning big in Las Vegas.

Yet despite the long odds, companies continue to ante up. Disney bet millions that it could build an internet portal to rival those of Yahoo and Microsoft (MSN)—and failed. Motorola and its partners bet millions that they could successfully scale up a satellite phone business—and failed. Under its former CEO, Jacques Nasser, Ford badly fumbled several attempts to acquire and scale new service businesses— like quick-stop oil-change centers. Hoping to reduce its dependence on the market for computer chips, Intel has, in recent years, dumped millions of dollars into a broad array of new business ventures—and has so far failed to produce a breakaway winner.

With new business success so *im*probable, one might argue that investors would be best served if most companies returned "excess" funds to shareholders, in the form of dividends or share buybacks. Yet I think it is possible for just about any company to dramatically improve its business-building odds. The fact is, there are many

companies that have succeeded spectacularly in growing new businesses—despite the daunting odds. General Electric's business-
building skills have made the company a leader in industries as diverse
as railway locomotives, engineering plastics, medical electronics, jet
engines, and financial services. Founded in 1958 to explore the commercial opportunities for polytetrafluoroethylene, Delaware-based
WL Gore has created a mind-numbing array of new products and
businesses—from advanced dental floss to the world's bestselling gui-
tar strings, from vascular grafts to membrane electrode assemblies for
fuel cells. Over the past couple of decades, Sir Richard Branson's
Virgin Group has created dozens of new businesses and made its brash
founder a multibillionaire. More recently, Dell has extended its low-
cost, direct distribution formula into computer servers, printers, data-
storage products, and flat-screen televisions. UPS, one of the world's
leading package-delivery companies, has recently created a thriving
business that provides logistics consulting and services. And Tesco, the
UK's leading supermarket chain, has parlayed its distribution and
brand power into a fast-growing consumer financial services business.

IMPROVING THE ODDS

Clearly, there are some companies for whom the growth gamble has
paid off—and paid off big. More specifically, there are companies that
have learned how to consistently get more growth for less gamble. A
cursory examination of these exemplary cases reveals some simple lessons for improving the odds of new business creation.

LEVERAGE SOMETHING YOU KNOW HOW TO DO

First, leverage something you *really* know how to do. Although Disney
came a cropper with its Internet portal plans, it has succeeded in
becoming the world's most profitable producer of Broadway and West
End shows, with award-winning productions like *The Lion King* and
Beauty and the Beast. Disney's theatrical triumphs leverage the com-

pany's deep experience in producing live entertainment for its amusement park patrons, as well as its core competence in creating memo-
rable characters and stories. Disney Cruise Lines—essentially an
amusement park at sea—is a similarly direct extension of Disney's deep
competencies. Years ago, in a study of its new business successes and
failures, 3M discovered that new ventures based on long-standing 3M
competencies were dramatically more likely to succeed than those that
didn't leverage core skills. Apparently, this is a lesson some companies
have yet to learn.

In Chapter 5 on the Traffic Lights, Andrew and Robert tackle this
competence issue head on under the section on "value advantage."
They bring some much-needed rigor to the difficult issue of assessing whether competencies are sufficient to give a real advantage.

DON'T BE AFRAID TO PARTNER

Second, don't be afraid to partner. While your company may well have
some world-leading competencies, it may not possess all the assets and
skills necessary to ensure new business success. Partnerships are an
essential tool for taking the gamble out of growth. For example, in
building its financial services business, Tesco partnered with the Royal
Bank of Scotland. Virgin seldom enters a new business without a
strong partner, such as the phone giant Sprint, which is providing the
telecommunications infrastructure for Virgin's US mobile phone venture. In bringing its trend-setting iPod to market, Apple relied heavily
on a US design partner, PortalPlayer, and a Taiwanese manufacturer,
Cheng Uei Precision. Apple is a clever company, but executives there
are humble enough to recognize the limits of its competencies. Today,
new business creation is as much about combining the competencies of
multiple companies—playing the role of orchestrator—as it is about
leveraging one's own unique skills.

Andrew and Robert have not made partnering a central focus of this
book; my bet is that in the years ahead, alliances will become increasingly critical to new business success.

BE BOTH COMMITTED AND TENTATIVE

Third, be committed *and* tentative. It's difficult to get a new business design exactly right the first time. The founders of Pret A Manger, the enormously successful UK sandwich chain, spent five years refining their initial fast-food concept before opening their second store. Perfecting a new business model is a process of successive approximation. Many of the early assumptions one makes around the value proposition, ideal value chain, distribution strategy, and customer response will, inevitably, be proven wrong in the fullness of time. The trick is to be intellectually committed to a broad opportunity, while being careful not to treat initial hypotheses about any particular business model as indisputable facts.

Many managers have a hard time being both committed and tentative. The goal is to be intellectually committed to exploring a new opportunity area, but financially prudent in doing so: to commit additional resources only as additional learning happens. Practically, this means:

- being extraordinarily clear about what you do and do not know. It is the invisible, untested assumptions that undermine success. As Andrew and Robert so beautifully illustrate in some of their examples, assumptions that are based on experience in existing businesses are often the most damaging. They need special attention and testing.
- ranking uncertainties according to their criticality to eventual success. Andrew and Robert propose the Confidence Check in Chapter 9 as one way of ranking uncertainties.
- developing creative, low-cost, low-risk ways of resolving uncertainties such as early customer trials, joint ventures, prototypes, and modeling.
- committing additional resources only as uncertainties are resolved. This turns the traditional "stage gate" into a learning gate, and converts an investment board into a research board, doling out additional funds only as additional learning is accumulated.

Without an explicit learning agenda, it's all too easy for a new business initiative to take on a life of its own: What should have been a little gamble soon becomes a big gamble. A surfeit of resources allows big companies to be impatient and imprudent. "Learn more, spend less" should be the mantra of every business builder.

EXPAND YOUR IMAGINATION AND NARROW YOUR FOCUS

Fourth, expand your imagination and then narrow your focus. New business creation is, at least initially, a numbers game. Take Silicon Valley as an example. For every Cisco, Yahoo, Google, or eBay, there are dozens of failures. That's why the average venture capitalist invests in a portfolio of new business opportunities rather than in a single company. Out of a dozen start-ups, half will fail, three or four will produce modest returns, and a couple, it is hoped, will shoot for the moon. All too often, though, corporate business development executives try to defy these well-established odds. They surrender to the conceit that some combination of analytical horsepower and personal wisdom will allow them to pre-select the one or two sure winners from among a very small number of uninspired and, all too often, relatively unexamined alternatives. As is true for an ageing bachelor, or bachelorette, a lack of attractive alternatives tends to diminish one's discrimination.

A far better approach is to start by throwing the net wide: make sure you've developed a broad range of potential new business concepts. Great new business ideas are few and far between. Hence, the chance of stumbling across an outstanding business concept is directly proportionate to the number of new business ideas that a company is capable of generating. Generating a robust portfolio of truly fresh new business concepts requires an explicit process for nurturing the mindsets and perceptual capabilities that have the power to reveal new opportunities. It requires contrarians, like Michael Dell, who challenged industry orthodoxies with his original direct distribution model. It requires seers, like the founders of Google, who saw an opportunity in the rapidly growing profusion of uncharted websites. It requires empathetic individuals who are able to sense the unarticulated needs of existing and potential customers.

A company that takes the trouble to invest in building a substantial portfolio of new business options will, inevitably, improve its odds of coming up with a new business winner. Yet no company can successfully pursue dozens of new business ventures simultaneously. If a company's new business development priorities are too numerous and too disparate, scarce resources get fragmented and cumulative learning becomes impossible. Luckily, a large portfolio of new business options can almost always be categorized into a much smaller number of opportunity domains. Having done this, a company can select one or two growth domains on which to focus its energies in the near to mid-term. In reconnoitering a new opportunity area, it is nevertheless important not to overcommit to one, overly specific business model. Indeed, it is often wise to simultaneously explore two or three business model variants as alternate routes into an unexplored opportunity arena.

For example Cemex, the highly innovative Mexican cement company, typically focuses its new business development efforts on a small number of opportunity domains—such as developing low-cost housing for the world's poor, or developing building "solutions" for construction tractors. In this sense, Cemex is highly focused. Yet within these domains, it is constantly experimenting with alternate business models: developing new technologies to dramatically reduce the cost of building houses, inventing new financing options that let relatively poor customers finance home construction, and so on. In the same way as companies need to be concurrently committed and tentative, they must also be simultaneously focused and experimental.

Andrew and Robert believe that a careful and meticulous evaluation of new business opportunities will help companies lower the risk of pouring millions down a new business rat hole. And they are right (see Chapter 5, The New Businesses Traffic Lights). But of course, it is not enough to merely avoid investing in a fundamentally unproductive business concept. To create a new business winner, a company must be capable of inventing novel business concepts with the power to positively redefine customer expectations, wrong-foot competitors, and create new wealth. To take an analogy: To run a successful art competition, like the Royal Academy of Arts' famed Summer Exhibition that receives over 8,000 submissions each year, one needs a jury and a set of evaluative criteria. Yet before the jury can set to work, there must first be artists who are possessed of a creative vision. Break-the-rules innovation is essential to new business success. So too is honest and painstaking evaluation of new business options—and it is here that Andrew and Robert make a timely and valuable contribution to our understanding of the challenges of birthing new businesses.

In the pages that follow, you will find a wealth of deep insights, practical advice, and meritorious admonition. I have no doubt that this thoroughly researched and carefully argued book can help your company gamble more wisely on growth.

PREFACE
& READER'S GUIDE

This book feels more like a destiny than a discovery. Much of what we have been doing in the last 10–15 years has been leading us to this.

Andrew has been researching divisionalized companies, diversification, and corporate-level strategy for almost 20 years. During this period there has been mounting evidence that there are limits to diversification and benefits from focus. *Corporate-Level Strategy*, co-authored with Michael Goold and Marcus Alexander in 1994, was designed to help managers grapple with the issue of how much focus. It was aimed primarily at managers in diversified companies seeking to define a focus for their portfolios that would allow them to deliver superior performance. This was the main challenge facing companies in the late 1980s and early 1990s.

Corporate-Level Strategy gave guidance to companies seeking to expand—so long as they had a "parenting formula." The advice was to enter or acquire other businesses that would benefit from this parenting value added. Examples were companies such as 3M, Canon, Emerson, GE, and Rio Tinto. Interestingly, 10 years later, these companies are still building their portfolios based on similar sources of parenting value added.

However, *Corporate-Level Strategy* gave little explanation of why some companies appear to be able to break the rules of Parenting Theory. This theory, the centerpiece of the 1994 book, argued that companies should only own businesses that the corporate parent is good at influencing and guiding: that there should be a fit between the skills of the parent organization and the type of businesses in the portfolio. The problem is that this theory does not explain the many examples of companies diversifying into very different businesses. It did not explain how HP got from instruments to computers, how Mannesman got from engineering to telecommunications, how GE got from aero engines to financial services, or how Nokia got from rubber boots to mobile telephones.

More importantly, *Corporate-Level Strategy* provided limited advice to the manager whose company is maturing, who has no clear parenting formula, and who is struggling to decide what to do next. As the growth decades of the 1980s and 1990s came to an end, maturity and the search for new businesses became more important. It was natural, therefore, for Andrew to lead a project to examine the apparent rule breakers and to consider what advice to give to managers in companies like Barclays Bank, Gillette, Intel, Kelloggs, McDonald's, Philips, and Shell, all of whom have maturing core businesses and a desire to find new sources of growth.

While Andrew's research interests led to the current book, Robert's business activities were heading in the same direction. Through the mid-1990s, Robert was head of strategy at National Westminster, one of Britain's largest banks. During these years NatWest faced some tough strategic challenges. The core UK domestic banking business seemed mature. Opportunities existed for expansion, both internationally and into investment banking. Major corporate banking had become a low-margin business, and investment banking looked the way to make higher returns from NatWest's strong corporate franchise. New technologies, such as smart cards, direct delivery to consumers, and the internet, offered other opportunities and threats. Finally, managers were ambitious to become the leading UK bank by outperforming their main rival, Barclays.

Despite many attempts (Robert counted well over a dozen in a 20-year period), NatWest created only two new businesses of significance—credit cards and treasury—both close to its UK banking core. In the process the company lost hundreds of millions of pounds in failed acquisitions and new ventures. So, despite the successes, the effort was not a success overall. When NatWest announced plans to build a major life assurance and investment business through acquiring Legal & General, the shareholders revolted and the bank fell prey to a hostile takeover bid from its much smaller Scottish rival, the Royal Bank of Scotland.

Robert had been uncomfortable with many of the initiatives taken under his watch, but did not have a hard-edged way of challenging proposals in the face of management enthusiasm and optimistic business forecasts. He was therefore eager to find out if NatWest's experience was bad strategy, bad execution, or bad luck.

To balance out his negative experiences, he volunteered to assemble a database of success stories. The database was biased toward improbable stories, like Mannesman's move into mobile phones. It did not contain parenting formula stories such as Procter & Gamble's acquisition of another food business in a new geography. The database grew to over 60 at one point, but was then culled back to around 50 as some successes turned out to be failures and others were sold by their parent companies.

THE RESEARCH BEGINNINGS

The project that led directly to this book started more than five years ago as a result of a request from Hein Schreuder, vice-president corporate strategy and development at DSM, a Dutch life sciences and chemicals giant. Hein, who was a Member of Ashridge Strategic Management Centre, pressed Ashridge to launch a project on how companies get into new businesses. Moreover, he volunteered DSM as a research site.

DSM has an unusual history. The company had spent most of its life as a coal-mining business—Dutch State Mines. However, in the 1960s the government decided to close the mines, and DSM had to find another business to develop. In the following 10 years it successfully transitioned to petrochemicals. This was not a leap in the dark, since DSM had been making some petrochemicals from coal, but it was still a remarkable transition. In the 1980s DSM developed fine chemicals and performance chemicals businesses and was considering a second major transition from fine chemicals into life sciences.

The research into DSM's transitions was fascinating. It reinforced many of the tenets of Parenting Theory. DSM suffered from the difficulty of matching its parenting skills to the needs of its new businesses and hence made some costly mistakes. The research also pointed to the importance of luck. DSM entered the petrochemical business at the beginning of its high-growth phase. It also over-engineered its initial chemical plants, but in a way that proved invaluable when managers were looking for additional volumes from debottlenecking. The research also demonstrated the power of commitment. DSM's managers did not dillydally. Once the strategic direction was clear, managers moved forward with conviction.

The research also had its frustrations. It was not possible to assess whether the transition had been value creating or value destroying. DSM had entered new businesses, but had it been at the expense of or to the benefit of shareholders? It proved impossible to tell. The company had been a state body for part of the period and had benefited from having the rights to market gas from new fields in the North Sea during its first transition. Nevertheless, the research sparked enthusiasm for more.

THE TEAM

Three other people have been particularly influential in this project. Simon Yun-Farmbrough was head of strategy at Prudential, a UK insurance group, at the time the project was gathering momentum. As an ex-BCG consultant, Simon had experience outside Prudential. He agreed to join the team meetings and share his experiences. He had often found himself with concerns similar to Robert's. He was skeptical about some new business projects, but did not have hard-edged tools for helping managers decide whether to take the risk or not.

Unlike National Westminster, the Prudential had, to the surprise of the industry, launched the most successful internet bank in Europe, Egg. Even against this success, Simon's opinion was that managers are frequently overenthusiastic about new businesses, take inappropriate risks, and overlook the costs of distracting attention from the core.

Andy Morrison had been closely involved with new ventures at BG, Britain's largest independent gas company. He had been part of the team that identified and selected new-venture projects. He had helped some projects through their development stages. He was much more positive about the value of new businesses.

In the research team, Andy took on the challenge of identifying corporate venturing units that had successfully developed significant new businesses for their parent companies. This involved interviews with seemingly successful corporate venturing units. It also involved linking up with Professor Julian Birkinshaw at London Business School, who was running a parallel project on corporate venturing.

To Andy's surprise, although not to Simon's, he failed to find any convincing examples, even when the research was expanded to include corporate venturing units set up in the 1980s. Corporate venturing units have their uses, he and Julian concluded, but they do not generally help companies to develop significant new businesses.

Klaus Volkholz had been head of strategy at Philips's Dutch headquarters from the mid-1980s to the mid-1990s and was now based in California. He was also an enthusiast for new businesses and corporate ventures. He had had considerable experience in both throughout his career at Philips. He had been part of successful and also failed efforts to create new businesses and managed a corporate venturing effort from start to closedown. He agreed to join the team to help us expand our US-based research, to provide some balance to a growing skepticism about the value of investments in new businesses, and to share with us some of the lessons from Philips's experience over the previous 30 years.

With regard to Philips, Klaus summarized 42 significant investments to get into new businesses over three decades, which are part of the public record. Five made major contributions to shareholder value—Integrated Circuits, ASM Lithography, Polygram, Navteq, and BSO/Origin—providing us with some challenging examples to test our theories against; 15 other initiatives, mostly part of divisional new business efforts, were clearly successful additions to the Philips portfolio.

Of all new business initiatives, 18 are still part of Philips, while 24 have been discontinued or sold, including some of the successful ones.

Klaus judged that the total expenditure on new businesses probably outweighed the value of the successes. This was no great surprise, since the period from 1970–1990 was not the most glorious in Philips's history. Many of the new businesses, particularly in computers and communications, suffered from being confined to European national organizations because of the group's organizational structure. While Philips's overall record was extra food for the skeptics in the team, Klaus pointed out that in high-tech industries there is an imperative to develop new businesses to exploit emerging technologies. His understanding of this imperative and his personal belief in the value of the opportunities in new technologies contributed enormously to balancing the team.

The material that follows is, therefore, not just the work of Andrew and Robert. We take the blame for any failings and omissions, but need to give credit to those who have helped our journey.

HOW TO READ THE BOOK

This book is for a mix of audiences: senior managers, business development executives, consultants, academics, and students. Each group may want to take a different path through the book.

We suggest senior managers read Chapters 1 and 2, which describe the growth challenge, using Intel and McDonald's as examples, and summarize the main messages. Based on their interest, they can then read any or all of Chapter 5 (tool for screening new business proposals), Chapter 7 (advice on what processes to set up to increase the flow of good projects), Chapter 8 (the value of corporate venturing units), and Chapter 9 (how to look after and control a new business after its early beginnings).

Chapter 4 (When Low Growth Is Better than Gambling) is a chapter we would like all managers to read, because it helps them understand that growth is not an absolute requirement. It is a matter of choice. This understanding will help managers be wiser when they start looking at new businesses.

Business development executives will probably want to start with Chapter 5 (the screening tool), Chapter 8 (advice on corporate venturing units), or Chapter 9 (advice on how to look after a new business as it develops). They will then enjoy reading Chapter 3, which explains why so many mistakes are made, and Chapter 4, which shows them why their job is not indispensable.

Academics will want to take a different path through the book. Many will want to dive straight in at Chapter 5, to understand the screening tool we have developed, or Chapter 6, which places this tool in its academic context. The latter chapter discusses, in particular, the advances we think we have made over previous theory. Academics will also want to browse through Appendix A, in which we compare our views to that of a number of other prominent thinkers in the field.

Consultants will want to spend a good deal of time on Chapter 5, to understand the screening tool, and Chapter 9, to understand how to support a business as it starts out. For those with a little more time, a gradual browse through the book from the beginning will pay huge dividends in helping consultants position themselves with the client. In the area of helping companies with growth and new businesses, many consultants do their clients more harm than good. This book has many subtle differences from current received wisdom that can only be fully absorbed by following through all the chapters.

Students will want to get their bearings with Chapters 1 and 2 and then focus on Chapters 5 and 6, which contain the main intellectual work. They will then want to read Appendix A to find out more about what other writers have said. If they have time, they will be well rewarded by reading Chapter 3, which explains why failure is so common, and Chapter 4, which explains why growth is optional.

We hope you enjoy your read.

CHAPTER 1

THE CHALLENGE OF NEW BUSINESSES

Imagine you are a senior manager at McDonald's or Intel. Both companies have had very successful histories. Intel was started in the 1970s as a producer of integrated circuits for memory products. In the 1980s it focused on microprocessors and by 2000 the company was worth nearly $400 billion. McDonald's was founded in the 1950s. Since then it has become the world's best-known fast-food chain, and in 2000 had grown to a market capitalization of over $60 billion.

Both companies face a tough challenge: the future does not look as good as the past unless you, as one of the senior management team, can help find some new avenues for growth. Fortunately, both companies are positioned in industries that are growing. The demand for both semiconductors and good-value restaurants is expected to continue to expand. But the segments that Intel and McDonald's are strongest in—microprocessors and hamburgers—are weak. In fact, recent performance has been poor. In 2003 McDonald's published its first quarterly loss for 40 years and Intel's net income for 2002 was a third of its peak. Furthermore, both companies have devoted significant resources to the quest for new growth businesses, with little success to date. So as a senior manager at either company, what should you do? Should you launch a number of small initiatives? Should you take a big gamble on some major acquisition or greenfield investment? Should you be more cautious?

THE INTEL STORY

Intel has made many attempts in the last 10 years to enter new businesses. Some have been successful, but most have not. Fortunately, Intel's efforts have been carefully studied by one of the most well-regarded academics on the subject of new business development—Professor Robert Burgelman—and summarized in his book *Strategy Is Destiny*.[1]

Intel began life in the 1970s using integrated circuits to produce electronic memory products. It was the early leader in this market as a result of superior technology and design skills. As the memory market exploded, Intel began to lose share to more aggressive competitors focused on volume rather than superior technology. However, as a result of a chance request from a Japanese customer, Intel began designing microprocessors. As margins in the memory market began to fall, more attention was given to higher-margin and higher-technology product areas like microprocessors. By the early 1980s, Intel had become a microprocessor company in terms of profits and technical commitments, even though the chief executive, Gordon Moore, still described it as a memory company. In fact, it took a change in leadership from Moore to Andy Grove to complete the transformation and to exit the memory business.

Intel then entered a golden period of around 15 years during which its dominance of the microprocessor market for PCs and servers powered the company's growth and extraordinary profitability. During this period, there were many attempts to enter new businesses. Some were intended to help extend the core microprocessor business into new areas, while others concerned growth opportunities outside the core business strategy. Intel managers even labeled these two types of initiatives Job 1 (extending the core) and Job 2 (beyond the core). In practice, it was not easy to define objectively whether a new initiative was Job 1 or 2. But the way the effort was treated inside Intel depended strongly on whether top managers viewed it as Job 1 or 2.

In 1993 Frank Gill took charge of Intel Products Group (IPG), the organization unit with responsibility for most of the Job 2 initiatives. It included new businesses such as motherboards for PCs, LAN adapter cards, fax modems, PCMCIA cards, video conferencing, and massively parallel supercomputers. Gill, as recorded by Burgelman, was trying to create a significant new business for Intel. "My main challenge in coming to IPG was to find opportunities for Intel to develop a significant business without competing with our customers." One of Gill's subordinates, Jim Johnson, explained: "Andy [Grove] wants a second product line to balance microprocessors."

By 1999, however, little progress had been made. Burgelman concludes:

> Despite the emergence of many new opportunities across the computing industry, and the emergence of many new ideas within the company, Intel had had difficulty turning these opportunities into successful stand-alone businesses. ... Grove enumerated some fifteen non-microprocessor initiatives and observed that only chipsets, motherboards, networking and Intel Capital had been successful.

In fact, his criteria for success were limited. Only Intel Capital had earned a decent return on invested money. Intel's lack of success was in part because the core microprocessor business was growing so fast and was demanding so much support that initiatives without a justification in terms of Job 1 were viewed with suspicion. Despite the stated intention of growing a significant new business, the follow-through was weak. This caused Craig Barrett, Grove's successor, to refer to the microprocessor business as a "creosote bush," comparing it to the desert plant that weeps creosote onto the ground, killing anything that grows near it.

Another reason for the run of failures was the difficulty Intel had in managing businesses with a different business model. The successes tended to be close to microprocessors and "predictable." Intel's culture, functional structure, and managerial rules of thumb were driven by the needs of the microprocessor business, with its largely predictable technological progress. In businesses with different rules and technical judgments that depended on insights about the future, Intel struggled. Frank Gill commented:

While the functional organization worked great for our core micro-processor business, it was very difficult for my group who depended on the functional groups for support.

Overall, Andy Grove concluded that he had failed in his ambition to develop a significant new business. After he had passed the CEO's mantle to Craig Barrett, he admitted to an MBA class at Stanford:

The old CEO knew that this [slowdown in the microprocessor business] was coming. He tried like hell to develop new business opportunities, but they almost all turned into shit.

With Craig Barrett came a new energy to push Intel into new businesses. His first action was to define a direction of development. Intel's mission, he decided, was to change from being a microprocessor company to being an internet building block company. The focus was switched from computers to the internet. The urgency was reinforced by a clear slowdown in sales growth. Revenues in 1998, the year Barrett took over, grew by only 5%.

THE MCDONALD'S STORY

McDonald's has had around 40 years of exceptional performance. Founded in 1955, the company was driven forward by Ray Kroc, whose passion was value for money and consistency. McDonald's went public in 1965 and powered ahead of its rivals by opening restaurants fast. The company then drove growth by going international. By 1995, nearly 50% of its operating income came from outside of North America, and in 1997 70% of new restaurant openings were outside North America.

By 1998, McDonald's operated 25,000 restaurants in 115 countries. In that year Jack Greenberg became only the fourth CEO in McDonald's history. In his first annual report he was able to point to a 10-year record of 21% compound annual total return to shareholders.

However, he was worried about the company's ability to continue its long performance record. Growth potential in the core hamburger business was becoming limited, its strong position in the US market was being threatened, growth opportunities in international markets were reducing, and customers were raising concerns about beef and/or fatty foods. In fact, financial results in 1996 and 1997 had not been satisfactory. Quinlan had opened his 1997 shareholders' letter with an apology: "1997 was a disappointing year."

Greenberg's first initiative was to focus on reviving performance in the US with the launch of Made For You. This required some investment in every US restaurant, a special cost that hit 1998 figures. He also reduced the number of new restaurant openings from around 2,500 per annum to fewer than 2,000. At the same time, he began to look for opportunities to enter new businesses. In 1998 he acquired a minority stake in Chipotle Mexican Grill, a 14-restaurant chain in Denver, as part of a strategy to "create additional franchising opportunities for our McDonald's franchisees." In 1999 he acquired Donatos Pizza, a 143-restaurant chain in the US, as an opportunity to "learn about how McDonald's competencies in real estate, restaurant operations, marketing, … [and] unique global supply infrastructure can be leveraged." He also acquired a small coffee chain with some 30 sites in the UK, Aroma Café.

Jim Cantalupo, CEO of McDonald's International, explained the strategy in terms of McDonald's share of the quick service restaurant (QSR) industry. These new brands enhance "our ability to serve more customers across the QSR industry."

> We owe it to our shareholders, owner/operators, employees and suppliers to carefully explore selected, complementary opportunities to capture more of the total meals-away-from-home market.

In 2000 and 2001 a number of other initiatives followed:

❏ The acquisition, from Chapter 11 bankruptcy, of Boston Market, a chain of nearly 900 restaurants, some with potential for converting to McDonald's or to its Donatos or Chipotle Partner Brands.

❑ An investment in Food.com, a company known for its internet food takeout and delivery service.

❑ A joint venture with Accel-KKR to launch eMac Digital, a vehicle for creating trading exchanges and business service platforms that leverage McDonald's strengths.

❑ A minority stake in Pret A Manger, a UK sandwich chain.

❑ The testing of two new McDonald's concepts: McDonald's with a Diner Inside, providing table service and a 122-item menu, and McCafe, offering gourmet coffee and related products.

❑ Finally, in 2002, McDonald's signed a letter of intent with Fazoli's, a 400-site fast-casual Italian restaurant, to jointly develop the concept in three US markets. The letter of intent also gave McDonald's an option to purchase the company.

This rash of initiatives was partly boosted by a decision in 1999 to give a remit for new growth initiatives to the then strategy director, Mats Lederhausen. He now became responsible for new businesses and for stimulating innovation (excluding Partner Brands). His thoughts included the following:

> We are very humble about our growth challenge. We realize how hard it is to identify new paths of growth. I wish we had more answers to the question you are asking but I don't. All we know is that we have to try to keep growing. We know that the misery of uncertainty is far better than the certainty of misery. If we don't try to grow we will fail, and at least if we try we have a chance of sustained growth.

> The pipeline of new businesses must be dynamic and vibrant. There must be initiatives at different stages of development. When a big business hits a stall point it takes time to develop new initiatives. So these projects must already be in the pipeline. This does not mean that you should let 1000 flowers bloom. I hate this. But it does mean that you should not let the pipeline dry up.

RECENT HISTORY AT INTEL AND MCDONALD'S

In early 1999, Craig Barrett decided to focus Intel's commitment to new businesses. This was in response to a groundswell from executives who had been on an internal management program titled "Growing the Business." This program had labeled Intel's microprocessor businesses as "blue" businesses and all new businesses as "green" businesses.

Barrett put Gerry Parker, one of two executive vice-presidents, in charge of the green businesses under the heading New Businesses Group. The New Businesses Group contained one big initiative, Intel Data Services, Intel's entry into the web-hosting business, and a number of smaller ones. "We're focusing on two areas, the internet and appliances," explained Parker.

However, despite setting up the New Businesses Group and Craig Barrett's decision to free up his own time by appointing Paul Otellini "in charge to a large extent of the core business," Intel's efforts were still not solving the problem. Burgelman comments that, in early 2001, when John Miner was taking over the responsibility for new businesses from the retiring Gerry Parker, "top management seemed to have concluded that it was difficult to develop businesses that were not related to the core business." Moreover, the "internet building block" vision was now being toned down to "PC Plus," implying that Intel would in the future focus on businesses that were closer to its PC/microprocessor heartland.

In 2003, Intel announced that it was withdrawing from web hosting and wrote off around $1 billion. However, undaunted by the continuing failures, in 2004 it committed to another bold set of diversification moves. The focus was chips, but the ambition was to dominate additional segments of the chip industry. Intel had over 80% of the market in PCs and servers. Its ambition was to enter and dominate the markets for chips in flat-panel displays, handhelds, personal media players, Wi-Max, a new wireless technology, and cellular phones. At the time of writing, progress on these ambitions is mixed. In August 2004, Intel announced that it was holding back its plans to enter the projection television business because of delays in its next-generation computer chip. Working models of the Pentium 4, the next generation, created too much heat. Moreover, Intel was losing market share and technical leadership to its smaller rival, Advanced Micro Devices.

In early 2005 Paul Otellini, due to replace Craig Barrett in May, announced a reorganization around user platforms. "The new organization will help address growth," he explained. At the same time, Advanced Micro Devices issued a profits warning due to aggressive pricing by Intel in flash memory products.

McDonald's most recent experience has been somewhat similar. Between 1999 and 2002 the core hamburger business performed even less well than expected, and in 2002 Jack Greenberg was replaced by Jim Cantalupo. In the reshuffle, Mats Lederhausen, already in charge of strategy and innovation, also became responsible for Partner Brands.

The message from McDonald's was that greater management attention would be focused on improving the core business and that continuation of some of the Partner Brands and other new initiatives would be reviewed. Dow Jones reported that McDonald's had contacted several leveraged-buyout firms and financial sponsors to gauge their interest in buying a 51% stake in the Partner Brands portfolio (Boston Market, Chipotle, Donatos, Pret A Manger, and Fazoli's).[2]

In January 2003, McDonald's announced its first ever quarterly loss as a result of plans to close 700 underperforming restaurants and cut costs. Cantalupo also declared that the historic gospel of 10–15% growth was no longer sustainable. Instead of opening new stores, he would focus on "getting more customers in our existing stores." The back-to-basics medicine worked. By 2004 McDonald's was announcing double-digit growth in its US business and planning to revitalize its European business.

At the time of writing, McDonald's still retains some of its new businesses, but its ambitions have been reduced. Pret A Manger, for example, abandoned most of its international expansion plans, changed some of its top managers, and announced plans to refocus its energies on the UK market. Along with the four other remaining new businesses, Pret has been placed in McDonald's Ventures. Mats

Lederhausen, managing director of McDonald's Ventures, has been charged with deciding whether any of these businesses can become significant for McDonald's without distracting from the core. For those that cannot achieve this difficult objective, Lederhausen will develop an exit strategy.

If McDonald's exits all of the businesses in McDonald's Ventures, it will have failed to develop any significant new businesses despite a 10-year effort. However, its search for growth has not been a failure over-all. The core business has revived. The new focus on healthy menus was in part stimulated by consumer insight work carried out in the search for new growth. The retailing of DVDs at McDonald's stores is an idea that came from the portfolio of new initiatives, as is the Wi-Fi access that is now available at many sites. According to Lederhausen, the difficulty McDonald's had with its new businesses made managers realize that there was unlikely to be any alternative to reviving the core. This helped in the revival. Moreover, Lederhausen is still hopeful that some of the Partner Brands will become significant new businesses.

McDonald's has also had to cope with unexpected deaths. Jim Cantalupo died of a heart attack in April 2004. His successor, Charlie Bell, was diagnosed with cancer weeks after taking over and died in January 2005. No organization can face two such public tragedies without being deeply affected.

WHY DID THEY FAIL?

To many, the failures at Intel and McDonald's seem most peculiar. Surely McDonald's, a powerhouse of fast-food retailing, must have many opportunities. Its skills in supply chain management, franchising, branding, and international expansion must be of enormous value to any new restaurant concept looking to expand. Yet it has consistently found it difficult to make a growth success out of its portfolio of Partner Brands; and Pret A Manger, one of its most successful Partner Brands, appears to be rejecting McDonald's help and refocusing on its core.

Moreover, Intel and McDonald's are not alone. According to *Business Week*, Microsoft has invested billions in its new businesses—games, MSN, business software, and software for mobiles and handhelds—with little success in terms of growth or profit.[5] Or consider Kodak, a classic case of a 20-year effort to get into digital photography that has until recently been plagued by failure. The oil companies have also tried many other businesses with little success. In fact, the experiences of McDonald's and Intel are the norm. Despite huge resources, despite management commitment, despite taking big risks, large companies with maturing core businesses find it very hard to develop new growth businesses.

Klaus Volkholz, a member of our research team, long-time watcher of the semiconductor industry, and an ex-head of strategy at Philips, found Intel's failures particularly hard to understand. He pointed out that Intel has strengths in manufacturing and design, which should be a huge advantage in many of the adjacent semiconductor businesses. He speculated that the problem must be Intel looking for businesses that earn returns as good as microprocessors—a hurdle that is impossible to leap.

We were so surprised by Intel's failures that we located a manager who had first-hand knowledge of the Intel experience. He explained that the failures, as seen from the inside, were even more significant. He pointed out that it was not from lack of trying. In his view, the problem was the management mindset baked into every Intel manager. This mindset is the microprocessor mindset: a virtual monopoly business, where paranoia about competitors, refusal to double source, technical arrogance, a lack of customer sensitivity, and many other mental habits dominate. These habits work in the peculiar environment that is the microprocessor business. They are just plain wrong for most other businesses.

We even observed the ramp-up at one of Intel's new Fabs (fabrication plants). Everything about Intel's unique way of doing things was confirmed. Managers were working battlefield hours with a total dedication to driving yield and making the Fab the best in the Intel family. But, we could see that these habits—the work hours, commitment to yield regardless of cost, fanaticism about safety, and so on—might well be a disadvantage in other businesses where Intel has less control of the market.

It is this observation, in Intel and in many other companies, that gives us our cautious position about new businesses: the strengths of the core business are often weaknesses when applied to other, even adjacent businesses.[3] Moreover, these strengths and weaknesses are so ingrained in the minds of managers that they are not easily changed, even when you take the managers out of the company.

Take Paul Allen, co-founder of Microsoft. He has had the same difficulty developing new businesses outside Microsoft as Bill Gates has had inside. *Business Week* reported that he has "burnt through" $12 billion following a vision of a "wired world." His idea was that the technologies lying behind the convergence of entertainment and communications would be gold mines.

> But the strategy crashed along with the tech boom, its demise compounded by Allen's missteps. Often he paid wild prices for harebrained schemes. Other times he bought too soon.[4]

We believe that companies like Intel and McDonald's can only find significant new businesses under two circumstances. Either they discover a business that "fits with" their existing businesses and responds well to the habits and rules of thumb that apply to the core. Or they go through a crisis that breaks their commitment to the old habits and rules of thumb, and brings in new leadership and new ideas at the top and in the middle.[6]

IBM is an example of a company that has transitioned from its core twice. Both times required wrenching changes. The first occasion, the move to computers, was driven by a unique manager, Thomas Watson Jr, at war with his father. The second time, the move to services, IBM had to go through one of the biggest crises in US industrial history. We rarely see companies solving the problem with the middle-ground solution that many authors propose: more innovation, more support for new businesses, and more separation of new ventures from the core. Hence, since this book is not primarily about how to engineer a crisis, it is aimed mainly at helping managers at companies like Intel and McDonald's find those few businesses that will fit with their existing core.

CHAPTER 2

BEATING THE ODDS

Intel and McDonald's illustrate an important reality: most companies fail to find new growth businesses when the core businesses mature. Over 15 years for Intel and nearly 10 for McDonald's, these companies have not found a significant new business that will enhance their future growth prospects. And they are not alone.

If we take the most pessimistic statistics, as many as 99% of companies fail to create successful new growth platforms. The Corporate Strategy Board's study of growth restarts concludes that less than 10% of companies manage to restart growth once it has slowed. Only 3% sustain a restart for more than three years. Less than 1% do so by creating new growth platforms.[1]

Yet nearly every company tries. There are only a tiny percentage of management teams who settle for sticking to their core businesses and declining gracefully as the business matures. Chris Zook, a consultant from Bain & Co., points out in *Profit from the Core* that 90% of companies aim for growth rates more than twice that of the economy, while less than 10% succeed for more than a few years.[2]

This is why we have labeled the challenge of finding new businesses a growth gamble. To even take on the challenge is to bet against the odds. This is also why you will find a rather sober approach to the challenge in the following pages. We will not be suggesting that there are any easy answers. You are not going to be advised to set up a corporate venturing unit or to let 1,000 flowers bloom. You are not going to be told that the solution lies in creating a more innovative culture. In fact, you are going to learn that much of the received wisdom is dangerous. You will discover that entering new businesses is highly risky and should be avoided unless the circumstances are clearly favorable. You are going to be encouraged to focus on existing businesses first. You may end up less enthusiastic and more cautious about entering new businesses. You will understand why the odds are against you and learn when they are likely to be in your favor. You may even decide that McDonald's or Intel or your company would be better advised to stick to its existing businesses for the next few years rather than risk major investments in new areas. Importantly, you will be armed with some tools for helping your company make the right decisions. You will be able to help it enter new businesses when the circumstances are right and avoid them when the circumstances are wrong.

As you read on, you should remember that we are talking about new businesses, not new products. This book is about the challenge of creating new legs for a portfolio that is beginning to mature, not new products or new markets that extend the franchise for an existing business. Sometimes this distinction, between new businesses and extensions to existing businesses, is blurred. McCafe and McDonald's with a Diner Inside are examples on the borderline. Our definition of a new business is "a separate business unit that has a business model different from that of the existing businesses." Go, the low-cost airline, was a new business for British Airways. Keebler, the cookie company, was a new business for Kelloggs. While this book may help managers wrestling with extensions to existing businesses, it is primarily aimed at those looking for new businesses that can be grown into whole new legs to the company's portfolio.

A SHORTAGE OF OPPORTUNITIES THAT FIT

Much of the current literature argues that the high failure rate of new businesses is due to poor processes and skills.[3] Companies are advised to become more entrepreneurial, to copy some of the approaches used in the venture capital industry, and to build a process for developing new businesses.

Our view is different. We have observed that established companies have established managerial habits, rules of thumb, and mindsets.

These mindsets are normally well tuned to the needs of the existing businesses, but get in the way when the company tries to enter new businesses. Success comes when companies select new businesses that respond well to these mindsets. Failure is often the result of trying to do things that do not fit. Moreover, for many companies there are very few opportunities that fit. In other words, the main difficulty that managers face is the fact that there are likely to be very few good opportunities for their company to enter new businesses.

This shortage of opportunities explains the low success rate and implies a different way of approaching the problem. It suggests that efforts to generate additional ideas and experiment with a portfolio of new ventures are likely to be fruitless. It suggests also that a screening tool that helps managers identify opportunities with a reasonable fit is likely to be more useful than a series of process steps for developing new businesses. In fact, trying to make dramatic changes to managerial mindsets, as suggested by those authors who encourage companies to set up a separate new businesses process, is also unlikely to succeed. Short of changing many senior managers and challenging the company's ways of working—the crisis solution—the inherited mindsets and rules of thumb will continue to influence success.

We recognize that our view can be criticized for being defeatist. However, we will show that it is not. Managers who face up to the reality of "few significant opportunities that fit" will find they are better armed to help their companies succeed than those who believe that more experimentation and more new ventures are the answer. But first we need to share our research data.

OUR RESEARCH

We shadowed for a number of years managers in companies like BG, the major British gas company, McDonald's, and Shell. In every case, we concluded that these managers were investing in too many projects, most of which had little chance of success. In one case 24 significant ideas were identified and examined and 11 were launched as new ventures. However, when put through a screening process developed by the research team only one small venture passed the screen; two others were marginal. In the three years since, eight of the projects have been closed down, some with hundreds of millions in losses. The remaining three are either small or still high risk and, in aggregate, do not make a profit. In other cases there were many more new initiatives (one manager referred to 361 proposals his department had processed), but only a few passed our screen.

Our second research avenue involved assembling a database of successes. It is evident from this database that most successes are a result of careful strategic choice rather than multiple experiments or portfolios of initiatives. Of the sample of more than 50 successes, which was biased toward examples of diversification rather than extension, more than 70% originated from a process of strategic planning: thinking through the options and choosing a few new businesses to invest in.

Centrica, a British retailer of gas that had previously been part of a nationalized industry, is a good example. Faced with new competition in a previously protected market, Centrica forecast tighter margins and reduced volumes. This spurred managers into a major review of what the company should do. The review was divided into an upstream project focused on gas supply and storage and a downstream project focused on retailing and customer relationships. Many new business opportunities were considered, such as call center outsourcing building on the company's experience servicing its 17 million customers.

The review concluded that the company should expand its gas asset interests, enter the business of retailing electricity, explore retailing telecoms, and look for acquisitions of companies with business models that involved a mobile workforce and large call centers. The latter thought led the company to acquire AA, the UK motor rescue and financial services business. While some of these strategies have not progressed as well as hoped, the overall result turned a company with declining prospects into a top-quartile performer.

Hewlett-Packard's move into computers, IBM's success in business consulting, and GE's development of financial services are also examples of decisions that were driven by careful strategic choice. In all three cases, the company already had some activity in these new areas that could be built on: in-house sourcing of CPUs at HP, an unloved consulting and services activity at IBM, and customer financing at GE. However, these seeds were not sown deliberately. They were resources these companies could build on that, at a certain point in time, presented a good opportunity and fit with the company's managerial approach.

None of the examples in the database started out as part of a corporate incubator, as a result of an internal program to create a "third horizon," as a cultural change effort aimed at generating new businesses, or as a deliberate program of investing in a portfolio of promising new ideas. About 20% of the examples were more opportunistic than planned. For example, Royal Bank of Scotland's decision to invest in Direct Line, described in more detail in the next chapter, was clearly opportunistic. Peter Wood was looking for a company to back his idea. He happened to know the manager who had become finance director of Royal Bank of Scotland. One day, when he was "playing golf" with this manager, he suggested that Royal Bank support the project. Twenty years later Direct Line is one of Royal Bank's most successful businesses.

Our third research avenue involved surveying, together with Professor Julian Birkinshaw of the London Business School, the successes and failures of corporate venturing units. These units operated under different rules from their parent companies. In fact, they were often set up to avoid the mindset constraint of the existing businesses. During the second half of the 1990s, most companies launched one or more corporate venturing units or corporate incubators. Normal rules of corporate risk aversion were suspended. Corporate funds and third-party venture funds were available for all promising projects. Many of these units mimicked the processes and methods of the venture capital industry. In other words, they were following current advice. They were investing in more projects, taking more risks, and trying to create the seeds that would lead to significant new businesses.

Yet out of a sample of more than 100 units, the number of significant new businesses that was created for the parent company was fewer than five. Moreover, it was apparent that the total costs far exceeded even optimistic estimates of the value created. Our conclusion was that these units were not an appropriate way of trying to tackle the growth challenge. It turns out that corporate venturing does have a place, but not as a process for developing new growth businesses.[4]

SIX RULES FOR NEW BUSINESSES

In contrast to the advice that fills most of the pages of most books and articles, we have concluded that it is the shortage of significant opportunities that fit that is the biggest challenge for managers seeking new growth. This has led us to some different recommendations. To guide managers in companies like Intel and McDonald's, we have developed six rules about new businesses.

CONTINUE TO INVEST IN THE CORE

The first rule is to continue to invest in the core businesses. Writing in a business column for the *Independent on Sunday* titled seductively "My biggest mistake," Sir Peter Walters, a former CEO of British Petroleum, described attempts by his company to enter new business areas. Driven by concerns about the future of the oil industry following the 1970s oil shock, BP entered nutrition, IT, minerals, and other businesses either because of the similarity of the skills required (minerals) or because of their growth potential (IT software). After describing the failures, Sir Peter concluded:

> If we had put even half the effort into our core businesses that we put into new businesses, we would have come out ahead.

We have heard the same story again and again from companies that have lost faith in their core businesses. John Steen, a manager from British fibers company Courtaulds, described it as a "strategic round trip." He explained:

You decide that the core is not growing fast enough. You invest in new businesses. They underperform; and seven years later you are worse off than when you started having closed or sold the last of the new initiatives. I have seen my company do this three times.

In *Profit from the Core*, Chris Zook has made much of this point.[5] Yet most companies have still not got the message. Oil companies, tobacco companies, bulk chemical companies have all tried to find new businesses to invest in. For most the costs have been high and the benefits hard to find. Moreover, during their campaigns to diversify, they have given too little attention to their core businesses. As Sir Peter pointed out, the real cost of investing in new businesses may be a distraction from the core, rather than money lost from a failed venture. Moreover, if there are no new business opportunities that fit, the company's future will depend on the performance of the existing businesses. Unless management's first priority is to maximize the potential from these businesses, the future challenge may be survival rather than growth.

What we are suggesting is that senior managers need to have their feet firmly on the ground when they decide in which new businesses to invest. One sure way of shortening the life of their company is to invest unwisely in new businesses.

For many companies patience is a virtue. For a period of years, it may be best to focus on their core businesses, even if they are not growing fast. At intervals during this period the company will want to review its opportunities for new businesses and it will want to keep an opportunistic watch at all times. However, it may take 5, 10, or 15 years for the right opportunities to come along. Trying to force the pace can speed rather than stem decline.

Kelloggs spent 20 years on many fruitless initiatives before it found a way, with the acquisition of Keebler, of moving successfully beyond branded cereals into convenience foods. Crown Cork and Seal, which we will describe in more detail in Chapter 4, is an example of a company that kept focus on its core for 40 years while its competitors chased new businesses in the evolving packaging industry. Their new businesses created poor performance and led them first into the hands of break-up specialists and then into the arms of Crown. Often a company can survive longest by focusing on its existing businesses and exploiting the occasional opportunity to step into new businesses.

We say more about focusing on the core in Chapter 4.

DON'T BE SEDUCED BY SEXY MARKETS, BUT RECOGNIZE RARE GAMES

The second rule is to beware sexy markets. In one company, the head of the corporate development division was focusing on telecommunications and internet opportunities because these were the only industries that were growing fast enough to allow for the creation of large amounts of value in a short period. The result was more than $600 million in write-offs.

In another company, the focus was on diversification into biodegradable products. Growth in this sector was expected to accelerate as legislation tightened. A suitable acquisition was identified by the business development team, but rejected by a cautious board. Subsequently, the target company was forced to close when too many competitors entered the market.

The attention given to growth markets is understandable. Managers are looking for growth. But so are all their competitors. To create value, managers should be focusing on markets where they have an advantage, rather than markets that are growing. In fact, it may be easier to create value in less popular areas than in "businesses of the future" that attract every growth-hungry manager. What managers should look for are opportunities where their company can bring some special resource or competence to the game.

There are only two exceptions to this advice: "dog markets" and "rare games." Dog markets are ones where most competitors currently earn less than their cost of capital or are likely to do so in the future. Airlines and steel are good examples, as were semiconductors in the 1980s. They normally occur because the competition has become too intense. Dog markets should be avoided whether the company has advantages or not.

Rare games are markets where even average competitors are likely to do well. They normally occur because a new market suddenly opens up, creating more demand than supply. Those companies that get in early have an advantage in terms of written-down assets or stronger brands. Internet service provision and fiberoptic networks were examples in the early 1990s.

Another reason for rare games is the behavior of competitors. Sometimes they price high, making room for new entrants. Sometimes they are so hampered by legacy processes and habits that unencumbered competitors have an advantage. These conditions have existed in financial services in many countries, allowing new entrants such as GE Capital and even supermarkets to enter the business and do well.

A company can enter a rare game without an advantage because it is an easy environment. To be sustainable, however, the company needs to create an advantage during the first few years. This normally comes from early-mover benefits.

We say more about how to identify dogs and rare games in Chapter 5.

LOOK FOR ADVANTAGE, DON'T PLAY THE NUMBERS GAME

Many authors argue in favor of creating a portfolio of new business initiatives. The logic is as follows. Investing in new businesses is risky. Failure rates are high, with estimates of 80%, 90%, and even higher numbers being quoted. Statistics from the venture capital industry are often used. To get one significant success, companies need to screen 1,000 business plans, investigate 100, and invest in 10. Gorilla Park, a new business incubator, is an example. In the two years up to the end of 2001, the incubator had looked at 2,000 proposals and invested in 16. As Kirby Dyess, a former senior Intel executive, put it: "In order to get a home run, we need to go to bat multiple times."

It is argued that companies need dedicated venturing units in order to process this volume of work and manage the large number of investments that need to be made. Moreover, since the one or two successes will take a number of years to emerge, companies need a pipeline of new initiatives. In the same way that companies have a new product development process and dedicated staff, they should also have a dedicated new businesses development process. In fact, we started our research with this hypothesis.

We now believe that the numbers game is a losing game. Our third rule, therefore, discourages managers from having multiple tries and from even thinking with this mindset. If the presumption is of many failures and few successes, each new initiative will get back-of-the-hand support from the organization because it will be expected to fail. A numbers game mentality is not only a bad gamble, it contributes to failure rather than success.

The alternative is to be selective: to invest in opportunities only when the company has a significant advantage. Sometimes this may mean no new initiatives. At other times it may mean two or three. But for a particular level in the organization, it should never be 10 or 12 or, as in one company, 44.

Take the analogy of new product launches. Every marketing manager knows that the failure rate is high. Yet each new product launch has the full support of the organization. As a consequence, businesses rarely launch more than two or three new products a year. If you are going to give something your full support, you cannot do it to more than two or three at a time. This forces managers to weed through the ideas for the very best, and then to try to make them work.

In opposition to this selection thesis are authors who point out the difficulty of picking winners. If the venture capital companies cannot pick winners, why will Intel or McDonald's be able to? Moreover, there are many stories of success by accident and of successes with counter-intuitive business models that would be unlikely to pass any screen.

Having studied many new business projects and shadowed many managers in the process of choosing which projects to support and which to reject, we believe that wise selection is possible.

So, when does a company have a significant advantage? The answer is when it believes it can serve the market and earn 30% better margins than competitors. When Rentokil, a company in pest control, considered entering the office plants business, its advantage was its business model. Managers believed they could charge a 30% premium by offering a higher-quality service. All other things being equal, this would translate to a 200% increase in profits.

When Kelloggs considered buying cookie company Keebler, managers knew that they could drive significant additional volume through Keebler's distribution system: they could add Nutrigrain and other products to Keebler's portfolio. In addition, they knew that Keebler's strong direct sales and merchandising force would increase the sales of these Kelloggs products. All other things being equal, these changes could add 50–100% to Keebler's profits.

However, for most new business projects, the 30% challenge is too great. Either an existing competitor has many of the same advantages or it is possible to imagine other likely competitors with similar advantages. When British Airways launched its low-cost airline Go, it had some advantages. The parent company could give the new business some landing slots and help with operational support. But when compared to established competitors such as Ryanair and easyJet, these advantages would not have met the 30% hurdle. Go struggled as a new business under BA's wing, did better as a management buyout, and ended up being acquired by easyJet. Optimists can persuade themselves that they have a 10 to 20% advantage, but a 30% hurdle is high enough to require more than optimism.

We say more about the numbers game in Chapter 3 and about advantage in Chapter 5.

BE HUMBLE ABOUT YOUR SKILLS

The fourth rule is to be humble about the current skill set, at least with respect to the new business. One of the reasons the advantage hurdle needs to be set at 30% or greater is because managers are frequently overoptimistic about their skills. The Rentokil or Keebler advantages only turn into 100% increases in profits if all other things are equal.

Normally, however, all other things are not equal. Competitors have advantages that are difficult to observe. Moreover, there are learning costs in a new market. In unfamiliar situations, managers make mistakes: they invest too much in marketing, overdesign products, mismanage suppliers, and more. Acquisitions are often used to overcome learning costs. But acquisitions involve premiums. This is why the advantage for the new company needs to be at least 30%. If the learning costs or the premiums are likely to be high, the expected advantage needs to be even higher, 50% or 100%, to make sure that there is a significant residual advantage.

It is the learning costs that explain why, for any specific company, there are few opportunities. This is obvious in sport. We would expect a team skilled at soccer to perform pretty poorly playing American football, and we would expect the Olympic table tennis champions to fail to qualify for the tennis event. Yet we often expect similar leaps of skill in business.

Learning costs are an unknown that upset many plans, but they can also suggest one type of new business idea to look out for—saplings. Saplings are operating units that already exist within the company. They are often unloved or ignored, but exist for historical reasons or reasons connected with the core businesses, which have the potential to be grown into new legs for the company. Their special feature is that they have, for whatever peculiar reason, especially strong managers with insights about how to grow the activity. Their other big selling point is that most of the learning has already been done.

Hewlett-Packard first started manufacturing processors for its instrument business in the 1960s because it did not want to rely on third-party suppliers. In the 1970s the unit started selling mini-computers for technical applications. Around 1980, after many requests, the unit's strong management team was allowed to enter the market for commercial applications. Now, after the addition of servers, software, and personal computers, HP is one of the world's largest computer manufacturers.

Hotel company GrandMet acquired the IDV wines and spirits business in 1974, along with its bid for a brewer called Trumans. Management tried to sell IDV to pay down debt, but failed. Twenty years later, under the guidance of a uniquely talented manager, Anthony Tennant, IDV had become the largest business in GrandMet.

The most dramatic example of a sapling in our database is IBM Global Services. Now accounting for nearly 50% of IBM's revenues, and in itself the world's largest computer services company, it began life in the late 1980s as a sapling. Some maverick vice-presidents persuaded a reluctant IBM to respond to requests by some major customers such as Eastman Kodak to bid for their IT operations on an outsourced basis. A small arm's-length operation was set up, which developed its own life well away from the core business, and was largely ignored until Louis Gerstner became IBM CEO at a time of crisis in 1994. Even then he left IBM Global Services well alone for two years, waiting until he had started to turn around the core hardware and software businesses before bringing the growing services business center stage.

By understanding the impact of learning costs, managers can discover good prospects for new businesses where much of the learning has already been done, as well as avoid potential disasters where the learning cost is likely to be larger than any advantage the company possesses.

We say more about learning costs in Chapter 5 and about saplings in Chapter 6.

SEARCH FOR PEOPLE AS MUCH AS POTENTIAL

The venture capital industry has a saying that there are only three things to think about when selecting projects to support: management, management, and management. The same applies to new businesses inside larger companies.

Large companies are lulled into presuming that somewhere, within the huge pool of talent, managers can be found to lead projects. The challenge, they believe, is to find good projects for them to lead. While this approach works within an existing business, it does not work when the challenge is new businesses. Within an existing business there are many managers who understand the products, the markets, and the essence of the business model needed to make a profit. In new businesses all three of these areas of knowledge may be absent.

Exercises that focus on identifying opportunities can be dangerous. They build enthusiasm for some new opportunity before the management that can exploit the opportunity has been identified. Often this leads to projects starting out with the wrong leadership. A company may have a huge advantage in technology or brands or customer relationships, but if it does not have the managers with the talent, experience, and will to exploit these advantages, no value will be created.

In all of our research sites management was an issue. In some, like Egg, the internet bank created by Prudential, management was the key to success. Mike Harris, hired in to run the bank, was about the only manager in Britain who had had the experiences needed to make a success of the opportunity. He had previously run First Direct, Britain's first major direct-to-consumer bank. He had also been involved in other technology-driven start-ups.

In other research sites, management was the scarce resource. "We had great ideas, but we did not have managers with the right entrepreneurial skills to exploit them" was a common theme. In one case, the company launched two new businesses and the head of business development became chief executive of both. A year later this manager was moved to run a larger division. In another company, the chief executive confided that his failure to succeed in mobile telephones was greatly affected by not having a "strong enough leader" for the business. He explained:

> It is not just a matter of technical talent. You need someone with the will to win, someone who can get the rest of the organization to support the project. These people are rare.

It is the rarity of these people that drives the need to focus on people as much as potential. Any process to search for new business ideas should be complemented by a search for managers with the experience, talent, and passion to lead. In fact, since these managers are likely to have their own ideas about what sorts of new businesses they want to create, it is often better to start with a search for talent rather than a search for opportunities. As Larry Bossidy, president and CEO of AlliedSignal, puts it: "At the end of the day, you do not bet on strategy, you bet on people."

We say more about identifying opportunities and the importance of people in Chapters 5 and 7.

BE REALISTIC ABOUT AMBITIONS

Our sixth rule is to set ambitions in the light of opportunities. There is a macho attitude in management thinking that argues for setting high targets. In *Built to Last*, Jim Collins refers to BHAGs (Big Hairy Audacious Goals).[6] Managers, he argues, achieve more dramatic advances when they set audacious goals. Leaders of companies, like Intel and McDonald's, who are facing a big growth challenge are advised to set a big goal: "Create a billion-dollar business within five years" or "Raise our growth rate from 10% to 15% in the next three years."

Our view is that the successes managers have had using stretch goals to power performance in their existing businesses cloud them from realizing that the same techniques cannot be used to drive the creation of new businesses. Stretch goals work in existing businesses because managers get stuck in ruts and stretch goals can unlock their thinking. Moreover, their knowledge of the existing businesses enables them to be wise about which breakthrough ideas are foolish and which are gems.

In the search for new businesses, managers have no ruts to break out of. Moreover, they have much less instinct about which new ideas are acorns and which are rabbit droppings. Stretch goals just distract them from thinking rationally. Hence, in our view, goals should be set only after the opportunities for new businesses have been screened, not before.

One director of corporate development was asked to generate $500 million of operating profits from new businesses in five years. He made the target more manageable by setting himself the objective of creating 10 new businesses, each with $50 million of profit. But the target pushed him into risky investments that resulted in $500 million of write-offs rather than $500 million of new profit. While this was a particularly bad outcome, similar stories emerged from most of the other companies.

The need to avoid setting ambitious goals has major implications for the way that efforts to get into new businesses should be organized. If managers create a new businesses division or even a development unit, pressure will mount from bosses and subordinates to set targets and define objectives. This was an issue in most of the companies shadowed in the research. Where targets were set, they were more of a hindrance than a help, interfering with objective assessment of the opportunities rather than stimulating additional ideas. The task should be to identify opportunities and see if any of them are worth supporting—to explore the potential rather than fill a growth gap. The task of exploring new businesses is, therefore, likely to be better done as a project team with a finite time frame rather than by setting up an organizational unit.

In addition, managers need to be prepared to discover that there are no new businesses that the company should invest in at the moment: that the project team may come up with a blank. Fear of this outcome is one of the reasons managers set up new businesses divisions. The expectation is that there will be a stream of new projects or acquisitions to invest in. Our research suggests that this is irrational. Most companies only have a few new opportunities that fit their capabilities. Hence there is no need for an incubator or new businesses division.

The alternative—giving money back to shareholders—may feel defeatist. But it can still be the right thing to do, at least until an opportunity that is likely to succeed emerges. Moreover, it is possible to produce acceptable performance for shareholders so long as growth performance is not significantly lower than expectations. Over the last 10 years IBM has grown in line with the economy, but, by buying back more than 25% of the company's stock, it has produced a total return to shareholders in the top quartile.

We say more about setting targets and organizing the new businesses effort in Chapter 7.

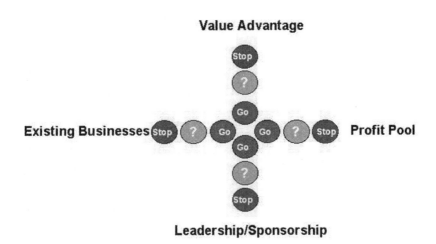

Figure 2.1 The New Businesses Traffic Lights

THE STRATEGIC BUSINESS CASE

We believe that managers can use the power of basic strategic analysis to help them find those opportunities that fit. At Ashridge Strategic Management Centre we have developed a screening tool: the New Businesses Traffic Lights (see Chapter 5). The tool can be applied to an idea before a business plan has been developed. It can also be applied alongside a business plan to assess the strategic logic for the proposal. It can even be applied to an existing investment that is failing to meet its short-term targets to see if the strategic logic is still sound.

The Traffic Lights are a distillation of good strategic thinking. There are four lights: the size of the value advantage, the attractiveness of the profit pool, the quality of the managers running the new ventures and their corporate sponsors, and the likely impact on existing businesses (see Figure 2.1). Each element is scored red, yellow, or green. Red implies that we have a significant disadvantage, or that the market segment has little available profit, or that our managers and sponsors are inferior to those of the competitors, or that there is a big negative for existing businesses. Any one red light signals that the probability of success is too low, even if some of the other lights are green.

Green implies that we have a big advantage, or that the market segment is an easy one to make money in, or that our managers and sponsors are clearly superior to competitors in this market, or that there are big benefits for existing businesses. Any one green light (without any red lights) suggests that the probability of success is favorable: the company should invest so long as a viable business plan can be developed.

Situations that have all yellow lights are marginal. Ideally, managers should be asked to reformulate their proposal so that at least one light can be green. Alternatively, an experimental investment can be made in the hope that experience will show that one of the yellow judgments should be green.

Applying this screen to a typical portfolio of new business investments results in red lights for many projects. Our conclusion is that most companies are taking too many risks in search of new growth businesses. Either they are driven by a commercially irrational concern about survival, or they have been encouraged to make too many investments by the current literature. The potential for improvement is huge. Not only can significant money be saved from the "new businesses" budget, but extra resource can be focused on improving the core businesses, an activity that is likely to give good rewards. By reducing the amount they gamble, managers can improve their existing businesses and keep some powder dry until better projects emerge.

HOW OUR ADVICE DIFFERS FROM OTHER AUTHORS

There are several excellent books on the subject of growth into new businesses (see Appendix A for our analysis of the advice these books give).[7] None takes exactly the same focus as this book—achieving growth by developing significant new businesses, especially in companies whose core is slowing down. However, they all throw some light and some confusion on our topic. The difficulty is that many of the authors are addressing innovation and growth in general, including innovation to improve the core, innovation to extend the core, innovation to create significant new businesses, and innovation to create smaller new businesses. This confusion between innovation in general and the creation of significant new businesses is, we believe, the cause of some misunderstandings about our topic that need to be corrected.

We have already commented on two points of disagreement with the current literature: the advice that managers should play the numbers game, and the suggestion that companies need to set bold targets for their new businesses effort. In addition, we want to alert managers to two other messages in the literature that can easily mislead the unwary.

1 Success is about creating a supportive environment for entrepreneurs, for "purposeful accidents," and for exploring the periphery

A common theme in the literature is about releasing potential. Corporate cultures are viewed as risk averse and blinkered; good ideas are killed off before they get a chance to develop. If companies could only create the sort of supportive environment that occurs in Silicon Valley, growth problems would surely be solved.

This view of the world presumes that there are many good opportunities and many managers with latent entrepreneurial skills. The solution is to run "ideation workshops" to tease out the natural creativity and knowledge in managers. An internal market needs to be created between entrepreneurs and providers of funding that mirrors the external marketplace. Systems need to be changed to promote and reward risk taking. Cultural change through training and selection is required.

In our view, there are very few situations where good ideas and good entrepreneurs combine with good operators and good luck. This is because there are few good ideas, fewer good entrepreneurs, and a limited amount of luck. Hence the probability of it all coming together is low. To some degree this is why so many successes seem more accidental than planned. The late 1990s, when conditions were most favorable to entrepreneurs with ideas, spawned many thousands of would-be Bill Gates, but did not greatly increase the number of successes. In the same way, the suggestion schemes that many companies have tried can generate a large number of ideas without creating much additional value.

We therefore believe that most good projects (the few "accidents") will shine brightly enough to be identified by managers using appropriate screening criteria. Thus companies need to put more effort into the process of top-down screening: eliminating all but the most exceptional ideas, entrepreneurs, and "accidents." In our experience, at least half of the new business projects that companies launch could be screened out before any significant investment is made.

This rational view contrasts somewhat with the more emergent and even mystical view taken by some. Mats Lederhausen of McDonald's, for example, stated:

> I believe the mysticism surrounding growth is why there are so many books written about it and why so few seem to get it right. Growth is situational, it is contextual, it is philosophical and yes it is even spiritual. The quest for growth is a marathon not a sprint. It is a journey not a destination. It is culture not strategy. Ultimately it is less about where you want to go and more about who you are.

Mats was referring to growth in general rather than new businesses in particular, but also argues that the distinction is less than useful. He points out that McDonald's new business activities have succeeded. They did not create a significant new business, but they contributed to a rebirth of the core business and McDonald's is now growing again—the main objective in the first place.

We acknowledge McDonald's turnaround of the core business, but are committed rationalists. More rationality and less attention to preparing the conditions for "purposeful accidents" will, we believe, bring better results.

In addition, human beings are biased in favor of positive thinking and optimism. This is especially true of managers. A philosophy toward new businesses that is excessively negative is no more use than one that is foolishly hopeful. Managers need to believe that they will find new businesses that they can exploit. However, they need to search for these opportunities recognizing that the task is not like seeking a needle in a haystack, implying that you will find it if you look hard enough, but is more like looking for the lights of a rescue ship when at sea. Sometimes when you look there are definitely no lights, and sometimes you think you see a light in the distance but are not sure. When finally a ship does appear, the lights are unmistakable. If you wait for this moment, you will not have used up your flares on mirages, and you will have plenty of energy left to attract the ship by ringing bells, shouting, and waving.

For many, the analogy of looking for the lights of the rescue ship is much too passive. We agree. However, it is a useful contrast to the desperate search we see many companies involved in. Using the needle in the haystack mindset, they examine every piece of straw, even taking some of the stronger pieces to see if they will act as needles. Another benefit of the sinking ship analogy is that this is often how it feels for managers, who become increasingly worried that the core business is sinking under them. Like ships, existing businesses normally sink much more slowly than managers predict. Moreover, holes below the waterline can often be repaired. The rule, therefore—with sinking ships and with core businesses—is to focus first on making them as seaworthy as possible and to abandon them only when you are confident you have something safer to board.

2 Success is about learning the disciplines of new business creation and integrating them with the disciplines of running the core businesses

Some companies are continual creators of new businesses—new boat builders! Famous examples are 3M, Corning, Canon, and Virgin. These companies have a track record of spawning new businesses again and again, and they have management processes, competencies, and a culture that support this. In addition, in Silicon Valley and elsewhere, there are venture capital companies and technology incubators whose whole reason for existence is to nurture and develop new businesses.

Many authors have therefore concluded that the answer to the new businesses challenge is for companies to learn the skills possessed by 3M or the venture capitalists. They observe that these skills are rather specialist and are often very different from the skills of running McDonald's or Intel. Hence they argue that companies need to develop these skills in parallel with those required to run the core businesses. Over time, they should meld the two sets of skills together into an integrated management approach that will allow the company to drive hard in its existing businesses and, at the same time, innovate and nurture new businesses.

In our view this is unrealistic. There are so few examples of companies that succeed in achieving the combination of continuous new business creation and dedication to the core that this is, for most, an unrealistic objective. Some companies devote all their energies to new business creation and, as a result, often exit businesses that were previously core—tapes for 3M, music for Virgin, consumer products for Corning. Most, however, focus on driving their core businesses and successfully adding new businesses only when the needs of the new business fit with the management approach that is required to run the existing businesses.

Moreover, our database of successes demonstrates that companies can successfully add significant new businesses to an existing portfolio without developing and integrating the skills of continuous new business development. In fact, many of our successes would not be considered to possess the skills of new business creation that are so frequently described in the literature. Admittedly, some have been lucky. But most—like GE in financial services, Mannesman in mobile telephones, or Prudential in internet banking—made a strategic decision to expand in a certain way and were successful.

Rather than advise companies to develop the skills for continuous new business development, we believe it is more realistic to encourage them to focus on a less ambitious objective. They should maintain a watchful eye for promising new businesses through careful selection processes, and then focus their efforts on making a success out of the few promising opportunities that can gain the commitment of the organization.

GAMBLING ON NEW BUSINESSES

All companies need a strategy for new businesses. In this book we are focusing particularly on a subset of companies—those, like McDonald's and Intel, that have a growth challenge. These two companies are concerned that their core businesses are running out of steam, and they feel the need to find major new revenue streams. We feel confident that the advice we have for companies like McDonald's and Intel is also relevant for others. But we are cautious. Our research has focused on companies that have successfully entered significant new businesses or are trying to do so.

Many authors present the world as one of plentiful opportunity. They see a changing world with opportunities in many directions: new types of demand, new technologies, and new business models. Companies, they argue, need to create a supportive environment for entrepreneurial activity, learn new skills, stretch their imagination, and try a number of new initiatives.

Our research leads to a different conclusion. We believe there are few significant opportunities: it is a world of scarcity rather than plenty. Significant opportunities are rare because so many factors need to fit for the probability of success to be high: a large market, advantages over competitors, managers capable of exploiting the market and the advantages, and minimum disruption to the existing businesses. Therefore our advice is more about caution than encouragement, more focused on selection than experimentation, and more linked to patience than activity.

The lack of opportunities and the inherent risks make the growth gamble difficult. However, it is made more difficult than it need be because of the way many approach the challenge. Some of this is the fault of managers, who tend to overcommit to unrealistic objectives and overestimate their capabilities. But some is the fault of consultants and academics, who have given managers well-intentioned but misleading advice and encouragement. We say more about this in the next chapter.

We hope this book will help managers develop more realism in their strategies for entering new businesses. We hope it helps them avoid taking risks when the odds are stacked against them and encourages them to invest with confidence when the odds are in their favor. Overall, managers can gamble and beat the odds, but only once they fully understand the game they are playing.

CHAPTER 3

THE DIFFICULTIES OF BUILDING NEW LEGS

We have established that most companies fail when they try to enter new businesses. Moreover, when companies gamble and fail, it is often at huge cost both to shareholders and to management.

Clayton Christensen, author of *The Innovator's Dilemma* and *The Innovator's Solution* and one of the world's top strategy gurus, uses AT&T to illustrate the problem. During the 1990s AT&T, America's leading telephone company, lost more than $50 billion trying to get into new businesses. It made three big attempts: computers with NCR, mobile telephony with McCaw Cellular, and cable broadband with TCI and MediaOne. They were all disasters.

Christensen concludes:

> We could cite many cases of companies' similar attempts to create new-growth platforms after the core business had matured. They follow an all-too-familiar pattern. When the core business approaches maturity and investors demand new growth, executives develop seemingly sensible strategies to generate it. Although they invest aggressively, their plans fail to create the needed growth fast enough; investors hammer the stock; management is sacked; and Wall Street rewards the new executive team for simply restoring the status quo ante: a profitable but low growth core business."[1]

The same statistics are recognized by every author on the topic. Intel reputedly lost $1 billion on its web-hosting business. Even companies that succeed often do so at the expense of long-term shareholder value. Richard Foster and Sarah Kaplan, authors of *Creative Destruction* and deep thinkers about long-term company survival, provide chilling data.[2] They identified 18 companies that remained in the Forbes top 100 between 1917 (the first year the data was compiled) and 1987. These remarkable survivors, companies like General Electric, DuPont, and Procter & Gamble, might be expected to be the exemplars other companies should copy. However, Foster and Kaplan conclude the opposite. As a group, these survivors underperformed the market by 20% over the 70 years. They may have survived but, as a group, they destroyed value.[3]

In order to understand why managers often destroy value when they try to build new legs, we shadowed executives responsible for helping their companies find new businesses. Over a period of four years we shadowed 10 managers. Shadowing involved speaking to the manager every three months or so to find out what issues he or she was working on and what successes and failures had occurred in the previous period. Most of these efforts did not survive the time of our research and only two of the efforts survived the full period of our shadowing. Three of the managers were encouraged to leave their companies as a result of failure. The research, however, gave us invaluable insights into the problems managers face and the mistakes they make.

In addition to the shortage of opportunities, described in the previous chapter, there are two reasons investments in new businesses often destroy more value than they create. First, managers are trying to do something that is inherently risky. Like prospecting for oil, a high failure rate is to be expected. This occurs because each project contains many risks that cannot be managed away. This source of failure makes any decision to enter a new business a gamble, at least in part.

The second reason for failure is more avoidable. It stems from the way that managers approach the task. Without a firm theoretical framework for thinking about new businesses, managers find themselves following guidance and thought patterns that cause them to make mistakes. The fault lies primarily with the managers responsible for the new businesses effort, but it is also partly shared with their bosses and the advice they get from consultants, academics, and current received wisdom. In other words, the second reason for failure stems from the way these managers think about what they are doing.

In this chapter we will focus primarily on the avoidable reasons for failure. Before that, however, we will first describe the context in which these managers are working and the inherent risks involved in new businesses.

THE CORPORATE LIFE CYCLE

The companies we were researching were all mature businesses: a major oil company, a utility, a consumer products company, a hospitality company, a chemicals company, a restaurant chain, a high-tech company. The companies had been built many years before by managers no longer involved in them.

These companies had all succeeded in their industries. Based on superior technology, superior management skills, or a superior business model, these companies were all leaders. But, like Intel or McDonald's, they were facing a slower-growth future. To maintain their track record or meet the ambitions of their managers, they needed to grow or acquire some new businesses.

Intel and McDonald's were first timers. Their efforts to develop into new businesses were the first both companies had made. The core business had been kind to managers, providing plenty of opportunity over the previous 20 or 40 years. Inevitably, however, managers were steeped in the management attitudes and processes needed to make a success of the core and less sensitive to the demands of different businesses. Some of the other companies we shadowed were second, third, or fourth timers. Previous attempts had not all been unsuccessful. Some had faced periods of underperformance and retrenchment. These managers were inevitably less dominated by one way of doing business and more sensitive to the demands of different businesses.

Whitbread, for example, had started life as a beer company, and expanded into pubs as part of its beer strategy. It then began converting its pubs into restaurants and hotels. It also acquired some restaurant and hotel businesses, such as Pizza Hut and Marriott in the UK. In the late 1990s, it sold its beer business and entered the leisure industry through the acquisition of David Lloyd tennis clubs. There had been plenty of failures along the way and the total value created by this transformation was not obviously positive. However, some painful lessons had been learnt and managers approached the task of creating new businesses with a good deal of caution.

Whitbread's experience of new businesses over a period of 30 years can be contrasted to that of a gas utility company that had been "privatized" a few years earlier. After privatization the company had invested aggressively in international exploration, channeling money from its home-base monopoly to the new area. At the time we were shadowing the business, management had just consolidated its reasonably successful international operations and concluded that additional growth was still required. Managers had successfully exploited the obvious growth opportunity and, buoyed with their success, were now eagerly looking for another growth platform.

The traditional business life cycle of early-stage development, high growth, maturity, and decline was only partly evident in the companies studied. Most were past the high-growth stage, at least in the businesses that had launched the company. Most had some mature businesses and some growth businesses, but still found the combination insufficient for their ambitions. Most had already exploited the obvious adjacent opportunities—restaurants in Whitbread and international exploration in the gas utility. They were therefore facing a tough challenge: What should they do next?

INHERENT RISKS

One story from our research illustrates well the combination of chance events that needs to occur for a new business to succeed. One of the most successful parts of the Royal Bank of Scotland Group, the second-largest UK-based bank, is a business called Direct Line. It sells motor insurance, motor rescue, and general insurance products direct to the public and through partner relationships with intermediaries, such as supermarkets.

In 1980 two managers, Mike Flaherty and Roy Haveland, were working in the IT department of Alexander Howden, an insurance brokers. Mike reported to Roy, the head of IT, and Roy reported to Peter Wood, who was the head of group services. Explained Mike Flaherty:

> At the time there were some important changes in technology happening—relational databases, a major shift in mainframe technology which meant that mainframes, that had previously cost £2 million, were now available second hand for £20,000, changes in drive technology, the arrival of laser printers and the development of software for composing documents. This was making it possible to have multiple indexes. If there was a train strike and you wanted to identify all of your employees in the affected postal addresses, it would previously have taken days if not weeks. It could now be done in a day.

In an attempt to justify a large computer, exploit these new technologies, fulfill the entrepreneurial instincts of the managers involved, and prove the value of the IT department to a skeptical management, the department started to sell services outside. This involved manipulating databases and printing low-volume documents. They did internal catalogs for the BBC and the electoral register for the Borough of Croydon.

> It was probably one of these rare situations where you have a combination of people with technical and commercial skills. We had all been detailed systems programmers. We were all more fluent in Assembler language than we were in English. We could write the machine code that made our computers sing. But we were also commercial.

In 1982, the team was approached by two people who had worked in an insurance brokers, selling motor insurance. "They originally asked us if we could print rate books for them a couple of times per year." As the relationship developed, the motor insurance brokers, who had also been in IT, recognized Mike and Roy's capabilities. The brokers explained that up until that point the rate books only allowed £5 step changes. Because of the competitiveness in the industry, it was felt that it would be a big advantage to be able to quote rates between these numbers. Their idea was to produce more fine-grained rates and download them for a fee onto "midi" computers that they would sell to insurance brokers.

> At the time, the brokers' systems asked 16 questions and gave rates with step changes of £5. Their idea was to ask 21 questions and give step changes of 50 pence. We were capable of doing this number crunching because we had this huge, under-utilised computer.

The business proposition was to sell midi computers and software to the brokers at cost and then make money by selling them the ratings. But the cost of midi computers meant that they were not able to produce a package that was attractive enough for the brokers and the whole idea fell apart.

The big pay-off from this experience was that Mike and Roy learnt about producing rate cards. They considered producing rate cards for Alexander Howden's motor insurance department, but at the time Alexander Howden had just been acquired by Alexander and Alexander. The acquisition had unearthed some funny accounting and the whole company was in turmoil. Costs were being cut and Peter Wood, along with other administrative staff, was worried about his job. As a result, Peter suggested that Mike, Roy, and he try setting up an independent motor insurance service using this new technology.

Peter and Roy knew some ex-Howden individuals who had set up as independent brokers. Working with them, a business plan was developed. The plan was to set up as a direct insurer to avoid the commissions to brokers of 20–30%.

We had seen that people were beginning to book theatres and things over the telephone with credit cards. We just thought of it as a processing task. We could have been just a panel on the AA platform. But we decided to set up a whole business, with the underwriters as suppliers.

The team spent 18 months looking for a backer for this idea, while they were still working for Howden. Then they got a break. One of the jobs they had carried out earlier was data entry of Time Life invoices. The person they had been dealing with at Time Life became finance director at the Royal Bank of Scotland (RBS). Peter Wood was talking to this person about doing printing work for RBS and one day, when he was playing golf with him, Peter said that he had this idea for a new business.

The Royal Bank decided to back the idea and, 20 years later, the business is worth around £2 billion. As Mike Flaherty reflected:

If you had 40,000 people in the UK who knew about relational databases and motor insurance, the chances of one of them coming up with what turned out to be Direct Line is about as close to zero as you can get. The number of chance events that had to come together to get this to happen was mind numbing.

In particular, chance had a big impact on the combination of people and experience necessary for this business to work. The excess computer capacity in the hands of entrepreneurially minded IT experts who were under pressure to demonstrate their value. The chance encounter with the insurance brokers who could see the opportunity to produce fine-grained rate cards. The commitment of Peter Wood to this unpromising project because of internal cost cutting.

In addition, Mike Flaherty commented about the importance of the balance of skills and power among the three founders:

We were a unique combination of people with the right balance of skills. Roy and I had agreed that we would share whatever we got out of it. As a result we were the ideal counter balance to Peter.

Without the deep IT knowledge, the motor insurance knowledge, the "seniority" that Wood brought to the team, and the balance between the team members, the business would never have succeeded. In fact, even after the Royal Bank's investment, it had a difficult first three years, only avoiding closure because of Wood's negotiation and persuasion skills.

The Direct Line story is important because it can be contrasted with those of the 10 or 20 other UK financial institutions that tried to build large direct businesses at about the same time. Spotting the opportunity evident from Direct Line's early successes, these companies set up projects, ventures, and divisions aimed at the direct market. But as Mike Flaherty explained, the chances of any of these companies assembling the unique skills and experiences that fueled Direct Line were zero. Inevitably, there were other paths into this market and some succeeded. However, none has come close to the success of Direct Line.

Not all of our examples were dominated by so many chance events. Some, like IBM's decision to get into the PC business, were businesses waiting to happen, and were previewed by a number of earlier attempts. Others, like the decision by the electrical retailer Dixons to set up PC World, were entrepreneurially opportunistic. The CEO noted the success of a new start-up, acquired the business, and built on its business model.

However, anyone who has studied new businesses is struck by the large number of different things that need to come together to make the business a success. Even if the probability of each element coming good is 80%, the overall probability of five elements coming good is 32%, and 10 elements is 11%. In other words, new business ventures are inherently risky.

AVOIDABLE CAUSES OF FAILURE

In addition to the inherent risks of any initiative to enter new businesses, we have observed some common and avoidable problems that lead to value destruction. They are problems that stem from the way managers think about the task (Figure 3.1).

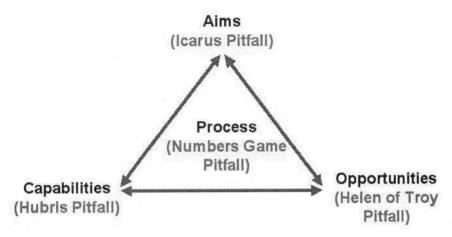

Figure 3.1 Avoidable causes of failure

THE ICARUS PITFALL

Icarus, according to Greek myth, was trying to escape from the island were he was held captive. He and his father glued feathers onto their arms and used them to fly. However, Icarus became overambitious and tried to fly too high. The heat of the sun melted the glue holding his feathers, and he fell to the ground. The efforts by some of the managers we shadowed felt rather Icarus-like.

There are a number of reasons managers try to fly too high. The first comes from the way strategic plans are developed. Managers, developing a strategy for a company like Intel or McDonald's, will start with the plans of the major businesses. These are aggregated into a corporate plan and an assessment is made about whether the company has sufficient capital to support the plans of the businesses and whether the performance that will result is good enough.

Good enough for an ambitious management team normally means top-quartile performance among a peer group of similar companies. Double-digit annual growth in earnings is not an unusual ambition. When the existing businesses cannot deliver this desired growth level, managers consider that the gap needs to be made up with new businesses. Hence, companies often derive their ambition for new businesses from an analysis of the gap between their likely performance and their ambition. This is like a traveler in the desert deciding how much he would like to drink based on his level of thirst rather than the amount of water he has available. The alternative approach, the one we recommend, is to develop the ambition from an assessment of the opportunities.

BG plc was a classic example of this. In the late 1990s the company consisted of two businesses: a UK domestic gas-transmission business that owned pipelines and storage facilities and an international gas-exploration business that owned gas reserves. Both businesses required focused attention. The domestic business was regulated and management needed to focus on driving costs down faster than the regulator had predicted. The international business was created out of a merger between a pure exploration business and a downstream business involved in gas terminals, pipelines, and power stations. The international business needed to focus on making this merger work.

The holding company managers, including the previous head of the international distribution business, were reducing central costs and decentralizing functions and decisions to these two divisions. However, when the central team produced a corporate plan, they concluded that the combined performance of the two divisions would fall well short of their ambitions.

As a result, they set up a corporate development division, incorporating a property development activity, a central research function, some shared services, and responsibility for new businesses. The head of the division, Stephen Brandon, commented:

> We have set ourselves a very big ambitious target. We want to be in the top quartile of the FTSE 100 in performance. Based on the CFO's analysis this means that we need to create an additional £500 million of net income or the equivalent in value within five years.

> I have to find businesses that create value at a phenomenal speed. There are only two ways. Either major acquisitions, like the BP/Amoco deal, or something new in an area that can deliver huge increases in

value. In the current environment (1999), this probably means the Internet or telecoms.

Moreover, the ambition was not just hope. The bonuses of the top managers were linked to the "top-quartile" goal.

The development division screened some 24 new business ideas and decided to take 11 to the next stage. One, investing in the telecoms industry, was the most attractive, in part because it had the most potential of achieving the ambition. Within a year, the 11 ideas had been presented to a management conference in the form of a "growth fair." All but one of the ideas attracted a sponsor, the telecoms project being the most significant. Two years later, part of the telecoms investment had been closed or sold at a cost of £350 million, and none of the other new business ideas had made significant progress.[4]

Undoubtedly the size of the ambition influenced the thinking and efforts of the development team, but not in a beneficial way. It caused them to look at other companies, such as Vivendi and Enron, which had created new value quickly. It encouraged them to consider industries where BG had little experience. It also encouraged them to do things quickly, reducing the amount of time they had to test and learn. They tried to fly too high because of a focus on the gap rather than the opportunity.

The second reason for flying too high is pressure from the financial community. The BG story is an example of the pressure that is applied both directly and indirectly by the financial community. At BG, the top team were clearly influenced by the performance that they thought was expected of them by "the city."

Unfortunately, at certain periods the financial markets are influenced by fashion. When some companies are growing by acquisition, all companies are asked what their acquisition plans are. When some companies are setting up e-commerce incubators, all companies are asked to describe their e-commerce plans. The combination of comparative target setting and the pressure of fashion can easily combine to encourage managers to set goals that are overambitious.

The third motivation to fly too high is the belief in the power of stretch goals already discussed in the previous chapter. Unhappily, as with the BG case, a stretch goal is less than useful. When managers are doing something they are familiar with, a big goal will help raise their heads and encourage them to consider changes to their routine. But when managers are doing something they have not done before, they do not need to be jolted out of a routine, they need to be cautious.

The fourth reason for flying too high is a concern for long-term survival. We will address this more fully in the next chapter, but it is well captured by the quote from McDonald's: "the misery of uncertainty is less than the certainty of misery." Managers believe that they have an obligation to find new businesses for their companies almost regardless of the risks. Without these new businesses, they worry that their company will mature and ultimately become obsolete. This fear can override the caution that normally controls management action.

We believe that companies should resist these pressures. Instead of setting high ambitions for new businesses, they should set targets only after they have reviewed the opportunities. There is something flat footed about using gap analysis or survival pressures to set targets. It implies that managers have a goal that is independent of their environment. It suggests that a company, with many opportunities, can stop investing in them once the goal has been met. It also suggests that companies with few opportunities can conjure up new ones until the goal is met. It is much more sensible, we believe, to set targets only after understanding what the opportunities are.

THE HELEN OF TROY PITFALL

Helen, according to myth, was the beautiful wife of the king of Macedonia. She fell for the prince of another country and went with him to his home city, Troy. Her husband assembled an army and besieged Troy for some years in an attempt to get her back. He only finally succeeded with the deception of a hollow wooden horse in which he concealed soldiers. He pretended to abandon the siege, offering the horse as a sign of his good intentions. When it was brought inside the gates of Troy, the concealed soldiers sneaked out of the horse and opened the city's gates to the attacking army.

The myth is probably more famous for the Trojan horse than for Helen. However, it was the pursuit of her beauty that caused all the damage in the first place. In a similar way, we have seen managers, obsessed by the attractions of a market opportunity, become blinded to its risks or its appropriateness.

The Helen of Troy pitfall stems from a combination of the seductiveness of "sexy" markets and a failure to apply the available tools of objective analysis. When analyzing new business opportunities, we have noted that managers devote a lot of energy to searching for large, growing, and profitable sectors. By definition these are relatively rare, so that when one is identified it has a magnetic pull that is hard to resist.

Take the example of British Sugar, one of two suppliers of sugar in the regulated UK market. Faced with a mature market and possible changes in the regulated structure, the company (a division of ABF) was actively seeking new business ideas. The head of the development unit was looking at opportunities with some connection to the core skills of the business: the processing of agricultural raw materials. Unfortunately, there are few large, profitable, growing sectors in primary agricultural products.

However, the team identified that automotive companies faced legislation requiring them to produce vehicles with a greater percentage of recyclable or biodegradable parts. One area where biodegradability was being considered was the interiors, using natural fibers such as hemp. Armed with the prospect of a fast-growing market, the team looked closely at the industry and identified one of the leading hemp companies as a prospect. This company was in a poor financial condition and was looking for a partner.

Excited by the growth prospects, the team pitched the idea to senior management on more than one occasion. They abandoned it only when an external consultant reported on the poor prospects for the company and the sector. In their enthusiasm, the team had overlooked evidence suggesting that the hemp industry traditionally had low profitability, that this growing segment would be selling into an industry with the toughest buying policies in the world, and that there was little technical connection between hemp and sugar.

Another force driving the hemp proposal was the feeling that environmentally friendly solutions are part of the future. British Sugar, the team implied, should be investing in this kind of project because it would provide more long-term security for the company. Similar thoughts influenced many of the other teams we were shadowing. "We should be moving into services." "We need to be in China." "We must be in the faster-growing sectors." "Something to do with the internet." All these are thoughts built round a belief that companies should invest in the next big trend or even catch onto the current trend.

The awkward part of this thinking is that it is hard to dismiss. "You mean we should be investing in yesterday's ideas?" "Are you suggesting that we do not try to look into the future?" These are common responses to a suggestion that chasing the next wave is unlikely to deliver the desired result.

The next wave, we argue, will attract more interest and investment than other businesses. Hence, all things being equal, the next wave is likely to be less attractive than other opportunities, unless certain conditions exist: unless the company has some special advantage over rivals; unless there are exceptional benefits to be gained from being an early investor; or unless the opportunity is one of the rare situations where demand is likely to exceed supply for a few years. Hence, unless these conditions exist, chasing the next wave is likely to destroy value, not create it.

The second reason for the Helen of Troy pitfall is management's failure to use appropriate tools of analysis. Too much attention is given to growth rates and business model economics (whether the service costs less than the customer is prepared to pay), and not enough attention is given to what Michael Porter calls the Five Forces.[5]

We shall say more about the Five Forces in Chapter 5. However, the main point of Five Forces analysis is to predict the future profit levels in an industry sector. The prediction depends on judgments about five forces: bargaining power of customers, bargaining power of suppliers, threat of new entrants, threat of substitutes, and intensity of rivalry between competitors. Each of these forces can be favorable to or damaging to high profitability. Companies will find it harder to make profits in sectors where one or more of the forces is against profitability.

The power of Porter's tool is that it excludes the one measure that so easily seduces the inexperienced—growth. The tool helps pinpoint declining sectors that are likely to provide more profit potential than growing sectors. It also helps managers distinguish between those growing sectors that are likely to reward companies that invest, and those that are likely to punish companies.

Despite the tool being widely taught and included in every textbook on strategy, it was not formally used by any of the teams we shadowed. This does not mean it was completely ignored. Issues such as the power of customers and the likelihood of competitor response were often discussed. But in our view, because the tool was not used formally, the seductiveness of a growth sector and of businesses of the future frequently crowded out Five Forces thinking. Without such a tool, it is hard for managers to resist the temptations of the Helen of Troy pitfall.

HUBRIS

Hubris is the inappropriate self-confidence that can develop in successful management teams. The *Concise Oxford Dictionary* defines hubris as "insolent pride or security" or "overweening pride that leads to nemesis." Nemesis was the goddess of retribution. She made sure that those whose pride caused them to challenge the gods suffered.

Unfortunately, the outcome of many new businesses is so disappointing that one could be forgiven for thinking that Nemesis was taking her revenge on the insolence that caused the managers to believe they could beat the odds.

One manufacturing company had two such experiences. The company was involved in a processing activity that generated excess heat and excess carbon dioxide. As managers looked for ways to use this excess, they came into contact with the tomato industry.

In temperate climates, tomatoes are often grown in heated glasshouses. Moreover, they grow better in a carbon dioxide-rich environment. The company therefore tried to link up with a tomato grower to sell its spare heat and carbon dioxide. However, the tomato growers were not very profitable and had little cash for investing in new capacity. Attempts to persuade a grower to build glasshouses near the company's factory failed. This spawned the idea of using the manufacturing company's strong cash position to finance the glasshouses and, at least in part, enter the tomato-growing industry.

The company's management was, however, very risk averse. Knowing that it had little experience in tomatoes, the board insisted on a plan that would reduce risk to a minimum. This involved signing a contract with one of the major growers to sell all the tomatoes at an agreed profit margin. This was sufficient to provide a respectable return on the investment in building the glasshouses.

Inevitably, there were start-up problems. But after a year the project seemed to be going well. However, unknown to the company, there were big changes going on in the tomato industry. Supermarkets were changing to a new variety of tomato with a better shelf life. Customers were responding favorably to these new tomatoes—ones that could be grown successfully only in hotter climates. In the second year, there was such a glut of the old variety that prices only just covered transport costs. Moreover, it seemed likely that the market would deteriorate further.

At the time of writing the project is still in operation, but its future is in doubt, especially when the contract with the grower expires. Looking back, management had considered some negative scenarios, but none that involved prices that left no margin over transport costs.

About the same time, the company decided to invest in a combined heat and power plant. This would save energy costs in its processing operation and generate electricity that could be sold into the local electricity grid. The project was low risk. The technology was mature. The cost savings were known. There were buyers for the electricity happy to sign long-term contracts. Furthermore, the initiative provided the opportunity for the company to experiment in the power industry, an area that had been considered as a diversification.

In the final approval process, some senior board members argued against the long-term electricity contracts. They believed that it was unnecessary to eliminate all risk. They argued that the contracts were overly favorable to the buyers given the stability of the electricity market. The project therefore went ahead with only the minimum of long-term contracts.

The market, however, did not remain stable. As the company was building the unit, other companies were building similar units and electricity companies were constructing gas-powered generators of their own. The result was a glut of electricity capacity.

As with the tomato experiment, the price of electricity fell precipitously. For a period, it was below the cost of the gas needed to generate it, and the project was losing money even before deducting the cost of capital.

With two such improbable disasters on their hands, the management of the company could well conclude that Nemesis was taking revenge on them for attempting to get into different businesses.

The primary cause of hubris is the lack of a framework for deciding whether the company has the appropriate capabilities, experience, and knowledge for the new business. The problem stems from focusing primarily on areas of fit rather than taking a balanced view of a company's full set of skills.

There are three common tools for assessing fit. The first views fit in terms of technology or market. The product/market matrix[6] (Figure 3.2 overleaf) has market and product (or technology) as its two dimensions. Development teams using the matrix ask "What other products can we sell to our current customers?" or "What other markets can we enter with our existing technology?" If a new initiative only involves changing one of these two dimensions, it is considered to offer sufficient fit.

A second approach involves defining a company's core competencies.[7] These may be broad functional skills, for example Honda's skill at small-horsepower engines or McDonald's skill at managing its supply chain. The skills may also be narrow technical competencies, such as 3M's thin film coating technology, or special market relationships, such as Shell's relationships with certain governments. If the new initiative involves one of these core competencies, it is considered to fit.

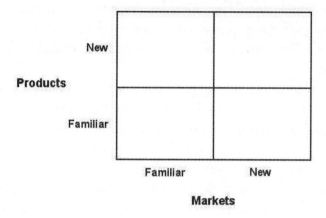

Figure 3.2 The product/market matrix

A third tool of analysis is the "adjacencies steps test."[8] This defines six dimensions of adjacency: customer, competitor, channel, geography, cost structure, core capability. When any dimension is different from the company's core business, it is recorded as one step away. If all six are different, the new business is six steps away and the probability of success is miniscule. The more steps, the lower the probability of success (Figure 3.3).

The first two approaches to fit analysis suffer from giving too much attention to what fits and not enough to what does not fit. In contrast, the adjacencies steps test focuses only on what does not fit. In our view managers need a balanced understanding of what fits and what does not fit.

There are two levels in the organization where fit issues need to be analyzed: the business unit level and the parent company level. The key questions managers need to ask are:

1 Does our company have some contribution to make to this new business that is more important to success than the contributions of current or likely future competitors?
2 Will the managers we put in charge of this new business, taking account of the habits, instincts, and experience that they already

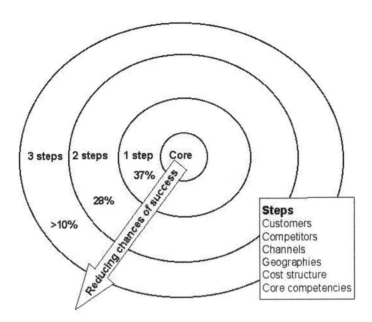

Source: Zook and Allen, *Beyond the Core*, p 88

Figure 3.3 Adjacency steps

have, understand the business as well and be as capable of making a
success as their current and likely future competitors?

3   Will the managers this business reports to, taking account of their
habits, instincts, and experience, understand the new business and
be as capable of helping the new business as the parent companies,
venture capitalists, or other financiers of competitor businesses?

Time and again we were told stories of misjudgments and mistakes
caused by the inexperience of business-level managers. Mars's move
into ice cream in Europe is an example. After a successful test market,
Mars followed its normal strategy of producing easy-to-wrap bars.
This fit the company's manufacturing skills and its desire to be the low-
cost producer. Concerns were raised about whether consumers would
accept ice-cream bars without sticks. But evidence from the UK suggested that they could be persuaded.

As it turned out, consumers, especially in France and Germany, did
prefer sticks in their ice creams and were slow to try the new products.

Without long experience of consumer preferences in this market, it was easy for Mars's managers to misjudge the reaction.

We have also been regaled by complaints that parent company managers do not understand a new business. Inappropriate policies and misdirected guidance are imposed from above in a way that makes it hard for the business to succeed. For example, when the tobacco company BAT entered the financial services industry, parent company managers believed they could apply the marketing skills of the tobacco industry in financial services. One of the core concepts in tobacco marketing is relative market share. Hence BAT encouraged its newly acquired financial service businesses to analyze relative market share. This exposed potential for increasing share and, over the next three years, the new businesses aggressively gained share. However, in the fourth year the businesses announced huge insurance losses, and a few years later BAT exited financial services and refocused on its tobacco interests.

Unfortunately, in financial services market share is not always profitable. In its aggressive drive for share, BAT had inadvertently encouraged its new businesses to take on high-risk customers. When the management team of the financial services business was asked why they had agreed to this policy, when they knew it involved highly risky transactions, they replied that they had been concerned, but felt they ought to give their new parent's policies a try. "We thought they probably knew something we did not. After all, they had bought us."

We will explain in Chapter 5 how we believe managers can reduce the risk of hubris. However, it is hard to eliminate altogether. Whatever framework or analysis structure is used, it can be polluted by excessive optimism. The good news is that a cautious mindset and careful use of screening methods can greatly reduce the tendency for managers to misjudge their capabilities.

THE NUMBERS GAME

The numbers game is the final cause of avoidable error. We mentioned this in Chapter 2. Many managers believe they will succeed only if they have many attempts. This encourages them to devote considerable resources to generating and nurturing ideas, running incubators and venture capital units, and supporting a portfolio of new ventures.

This approach to developing new businesses is encouraged by most textbooks and partly supported by Gary Hamel in his Foreword to this book.[9] The argument is compelling. Progress comes from a process of variety followed by selection. If a company is to progress, it needs to generate sufficient variety to give it a chance of finding an exciting new business. Once this has been found, it can then select and commit to this new opportunity. Because only a small percentage of new business ideas turn out to be substantial opportunities, the company needs to invest in a large number to be confident of finding at least one.

The venture capital industry, it is argued, is proof of the need to play the numbers game. Venture capital companies invest in a large number of projects before they come up with one real winner. Companies, it is claimed, need to recreate Silicon Valley (the place where venture capital is most vibrant) within their organizations.[10]

Unfortunately, despite the power of the logic, the numbers game does not appear to work. None of the companies we shadowed was successful with the approach of launching a large number of ventures. This was a surprise to us. As a result, we extended the research to include a sample of corporate incubators and venturing units. We even combined our research with work that was happening in parallel at the London Business School.[11] This gave us a sample of over 100 corporate incubators and venturing units: vehicles set up by their parent companies to promote, nurture, and invest in new ventures.

The vast majority of these units were unsuccessful, even in achieving the limited objective of earning a return on the money invested. Less than 5% of them achieved the more demanding objective of successfully spawning one or more significant new businesses for their parent company. Moreover, there is little disagreement about these results. Research by Bain & Co. and by Strategos reached similar conclusions.[12]

The common response to this dismal record is to accuse companies of failing to implement the venture capital model effectively. If the venture capitalists in Silicon Valley can succeed, runs the argument, then companies should be able to do as well so long as they effectively copy the Silicon Valley model.

In our view this is the wrong conclusion to draw. We will explain more about why the incubation/venturing approach does not work in Chapter 8 and we will propose a different approach based on rigorous selection in Chapter 5. We believe that the only way to beat the odds is to reject the numbers game and develop a much more demanding selection process.

WHY DO NEW BUSINESSES FAIL?

One of the objectives of our research was to find out why developing significant new businesses is so difficult. In previous work we had done, we had observed that companies with a spread of businesses were only successful when the skills and resources of the parent company fit well with the needs of the businesses (see Chapter 6 for more on parenting theory). The simple logic of parenting theory directs managers to enter new businesses if they have appropriate parenting skills and to avoid businesses where the parenting skills do not fit. We believed that this logic for being in different businesses is quite widely understood. Hence we were somewhat puzzled by the high failure rates of managers tasked with extending their portfolios.

This chapter goes some way to explain why managers have not followed the simple rules of parenting theory. The pressures on them, their managerial instincts, the advice they are getting from other quarters, the role models they have, and the approach to the task that seems appropriate are all part of the problem. To improve, managers need to be given guidance they can believe in and a tool or a theory that is built on the basic factors involved in business success. The following chapters are an attempt to provide the necessary frameworks and guiding thoughts.

CHAPTER 4

WHEN LOW GROWTH IS BETTER THAN GAMBLING

The story so far is that most companies fail when they try to enter new businesses. The main problem is that there are few significant opportunities that fit the specific set of resources each company possesses. A secondary problem is that managers are driven by some inappropriate motivations and beliefs. Our conclusion is that managers should be more selective rather than more energetic in their approach to new businesses. They should assess opportunities to enter new businesses with a tough set of criteria, only investing in those that pass a strategic business screen.

The implication of this advice is that some companies will, at some points in time, screen out all ideas for new businesses. This will condemn the company to a rate of growth determined by its core business. If the core market is growing slowly, the company is likely to be low growth, at least until the screening process identifies some promising opportunity. If the core market is in decline, the company is likely to be in decline.

This chapter will address this low-growth challenge. It will not offer solutions that will help a company become high growth. Rather, it will address the issue of whether low growth is such a bad thing, and help managers decide when they should choose low growth rather than gamble on new businesses.

Most managers believe growth to be an imperative. It feels natural to have an ambition to grow. Growth is like a virtue, something of unquestioned value. But growth is also a dilemma. As Clayton Christensen, Harvard's leading business strategist, points out:

> Most executives [in low-growth businesses] are in a no-win situation: equity markets demand that they grow, but it's hard to know how to grow.

In this chapter we are going to challenge the managerial presumption that growth is necessary. We are going to argue that, in some circumstances, it is acceptable to choose to be a low-growth company. Before we present our thinking, however, it is worth first summarizing the arguments in favor of growth.

THE ARGUMENTS FOR GROWTH

There are two sets of arguments for growth: value driven and moral. The value-driven arguments are powerful. First, the value of a company, in terms of market capitalization, is greatly affected by its growth rate. For companies with modest growth rates, each percentage point of growth will add around 10% to market capitalization.[1] If a decision not to grow reduces expected future growth rates, the value of the company will decline, sometimes dramatically. For example, the average market capitalization decline for companies that hit a "growth stall" is over 50%.[2]

Second, success breeds success. A decision to stop growing may break the magic of momentum, allowing managers and employees to lower their sights and encouraging them to be satisfied with less. Sir Clive Thomson, CEO of Rentokil Initial for 20 years and nicknamed "Mr 20%" because of his growth record, explained:

> Managers began to believe that this was the norm, that they could do it every year, and they achieved much more as a result.

Third, growing companies attract the best talent because they can provide more interesting career opportunities. Once growth slows the opportunities for advancement decline, and capable younger managers are likely to look elsewhere. A manager at Kerry Foods described her feelings when the company reduced its growth target from 15% to 10%:

> I felt cheated. I felt that we were no longer ambitious to be a top company. I was proud of our 15% record. Now I do not know what to be proud of.

The moral arguments are often deeply held, but strike us as less powerful. The assertion is that, if everyone stopped investing in new businesses, progress would slow down. Therefore, companies have a duty to society to innovate and develop new businesses. Moreover, societal benefit can result even if the efforts of a company do not create shareholder value. As economists point out, all commercial activities create a consumer surplus (the value to consumers that exceeds the cost of the product) as a well as a producer surplus (the net profit that the producers make after deducting the cost of capital). It is possible to create a surplus for society even when the producer surplus is negative. Hence, the moral argument is that companies should innovate even if the producer surplus is questionable.

It may seem implausible that managers might make a moral argument in favor of new businesses, but it is not. At least half of the managers we shadowed used the moral argument in one form or another at some point in our relationship. With hindsight, this is not surprising. Managers who get selected to promote new businesses are those who believe it is important and who get turned on by creating new things. One head of new businesses described the excitement she felt when driving up to one of her new ventures and compared it with driving up to the company's headquarters. The new venture was on a bumpy road. It led to some buildings in poor repair. Inside, managers were working alongside front-line employees with a passion for their product. Managers have values and emotions just like the rest of us, and those who are excited by new businesses are as comfortable making a moral connection with their work as anybody else.

One manager drew an analogy with the efficient market hypothesis. Fewer companies investing in new businesses would, he argued, reduce the volume of new businesses being launched, which would reduce the "liquidity" of the new businesses market.

Another manager argued that companies are living organisms that have value separate from their economic role. They are part of the rich tapestry of diversity and are communities that provide satisfaction for their members. It may be appropriate, therefore, for companies to make value-destroying investments in pursuit of survival.

Another manager, an ex-CEO of a major European company, was concerned about competition from Asia. He argued that Asia is more committed to new businesses and more comfortable betting against the odds. He would like to see similar determination being exhibited by European companies:

> If we do not match their appetite for risk, we will create an economy
> with a permanent underclass with no prospect of getting jobs.

These moral arguments are inadvertently supported by most authors. Explicitly or implicitly, they presume that companies should seek to survive over the long term. Since all businesses have finite life expectancies, the only sure way to survive is to migrate to new businesses with better prospects before the existing ones die. In fact, research into companies that have survived for more than 100 years demonstrates this. They all radically changed their portfolio of businesses at one or more points in their history.[3]

This recognition of the fragility of existing businesses suggests that companies must develop the skills needed to get into new businesses. It is not a question of *whether* to get into new businesses, but *how* to get into new businesses. As Hein Schreuder, corporate vice-president, corporate planning for Dutch chemicals company DSM complained:

> If you argue that our company should stick with its existing businesses
> and cut back on its new businesses, you are asking us to commit pre-
> mature suicide.

Mats Lederhausen of McDonald's expressed the same thought when he declared that "the misery of uncertainty is less than the certainty of misery."

In this section we will address these moral arguments. In the rest of the chapter, we will tackle the value-driven arguments.

The moral arguments are deeply felt and cannot be rejected out of hand. But they are, we believe, based on a presumption that better selection is not possible, that managers must be driven by hope rather than by strategic logic.

We counter the moral argument in three ways. First, initiatives to create new businesses have societal costs as well as benefits. A new business that fails creates problems for society in the same way that a failing old business does. Hence we are looking at the balance of cost and benefit. A company that starts many new businesses, most of which fail or underperform, is not benefiting society even if it survives a few years longer than it would otherwise have.

Second, given the odds of creating new businesses, a strategy of careful selection between alternative new business projects is likely to create more value than one of ambitious expansion. This is not only more value for the company, helping it to survive, but more value for society, both in reducing the number of failures and in helping apply resources to their most productive uses. Companies that try to get into new businesses indiscriminately are gamblers squandering society's resources. They are as immoral as those who have resources and do not use them. If better selection could lead to fewer failures and more successes, we would all be happy. So the question comes down to an issue of whether it is possible to eliminate some of the losing projects before they are started.

Third, the existing managers of an existing business are not necessarily the managers best able to exploit some new opportunity, even though it may draw on links with their existing business. For example, in flat-panel displays Philips had a technical lead. However, it also had a location and managerial disadvantage. The cluster of capabilities needed to support the business was most available in Asia, not Europe, giving Japanese and Korean competitors an advantage. Moreover,

Philips did not have a team of managers with all the skills needed to champion the flat-panel business. Faced with a location disadvantage and only adequate management, Philips struggled. After a few years, it merged its flat-panel business with LG. In this situation, investing in the flat-panel business in Europe, even with commitment, was the equivalent of chasing rainbows.

Instead of encouraging managers to deploy resources to enter new businesses, society might benefit more by encouraging them to select between those battles they can win and those where they will do better by selling existing resources to a third party. In our view, those who do not know how to turn their spare resources into successful activities have a responsibility to give the resources back to the market so that others who do know what to do can use them. This is unlikely to happen unless we have a rigorous way of screening opportunities and a philosophy of growth that makes it acceptable, in certain circumstances, to choose *not* to grow.

Clearly, there are non-economic benefits for the continuing existence of some business organizations. If so, it is better that these organizations are funded by the communities gaining the benefits. There are many governance structures, such as partnerships, trusts, charities, and cooperatives, that can legitimately give credit for non-economic benefits. Companies funded by capital markets are not well placed to take on this role. They are best advised to act rationally, choosing to invest when the probability of success is high and choosing to avoid new businesses when the odds are stacked against them.

HOW COMMON IS LOW GROWTH?

Turning to the value-driven arguments, the rest of this chapter will explain that a decision to reduce growth or even not to grow at all may be the right choice. We show that low-growth companies and even negative-growth companies can still produce acceptable financial results. Low growth, we argue, is the norm, not the exception. Managers need to recognize that many companies at many points in their history will be able to grow only slowly, if at all. Managing low growth wisely may be a skill that most managers still have to learn.

The world economy grows in real terms at less than 5% per year and, even if the commercial sector is growing faster than the government sector, the average real growth of the commercial sector in most economies is below 5% per year. Even high-growth economies, such as China, do not sustain growth rates of more than 7–8% for many years. In Europe, real growth in the last decade has been less than 3% for many countries. With underlying economic activity growing at these sorts of rates, most companies must perform similarly. In some economies and some industries inflation can come to the rescue. Companies can grow revenues at above 10% even when their underlying volumes are growing at less than 5%. However, inflation only masks the truth. It may make it easier for managers to accept low real growth rates. But it does not change the fact that low real growth is the norm.

There is, of course, huge variation. Intel and Microsoft sustained growth rates of over 30% per annum for much of the 1990s, even in an industry where prices were declining. At the other end of the scale major industrial companies, like Britain's chemical group ICI, suffered decline, with gross revenues falling by 36% in money terms, let alone real terms, between 1994 and 2003. The one-time US industrial giant USX performed similarly, with revenues falling by 32% from 1990 to 2000. Between these extremes, stalwarts of the world economy, like Ford, Procter & Gamble, or Nestlé, have grown on average at less than 5% per annum in real terms, and have not always kept pace with GDP growth. Between 1989 and 2003, Ford clocked up an average of 2% per annum real growth in total sales, when the US economy grew by an average of 2.84% per annum in real terms.

The Corporate Strategy Board's research on growth stalls is instructive in this regard.[4] It showed that 95% of companies that were at some point part of the Fortune 50 hit a growth stall. Following the stall, 83% of companies had growth over the following 10 years of less than 2%. In other words, nearly 80% of companies that enter the Fortune 50 have faced periods of 10 years when their average growth was less than

2%. Moreover, nearly 50% of companies experienced long periods of negative growth. In an age where growth is everything, this may seem incredible. Most of the years covered by the analysis, the last half of the twentieth century, were good years for business. Yet half of the most successful companies in America experienced long periods of negative growth. Only 8 companies out of a sample of 161 avoided a growth stall. Only six companies (Chase Manhattan, Coca-Cola, Fleming, Johnson & Johnson, Merck, and Motorola) experienced a growth stall and were able to recover to average growth rates of more than 6%. In other words—at least for America's most successful large companies, the companies in the Fortune 50—high growth is not the norm. Low growth and real decline in revenues are not uncommon.

The Corporate Strategy Board also documented the growth rates (deflated by the growth in the economy) of companies before and after entering the Fortune 50. In the years immediately prior to entry, growth rates between 9% and 15% faster than the economy were not unusual. But the average growth rate 2 years after entry was 2% faster than the economy, 5 years after entry minus 1%, 10 years after entry plus 3%, and 15 years after entry minus 4%. If you exclude the year of entry, the highest average growth rate achieved was only 5% faster than the economy (Figure 4.1 overleaf). Companies do have long periods of high growth; both Intel and McDonald's are examples of this. However, once the core businesses start to slow down, the norm is for the corporate growth rate to slow despite efforts by managers to find new growth businesses.

Maybe the Corporate Strategy Board's research does little more than document one stage in a corporation's life cycle: the transition from high growth to low growth. It appears to be a painful stage and one that many managers do not seem good at managing: 28% of companies lost 75% or more of their value following a stall, and only 5% lost less than 25% of their value. This stage, the one when managers are looking for new growth businesses because the core businesses are maturing, is the focus of this book. This chapter is therefore designed to help managers prepare for periods of low growth and manage them well.

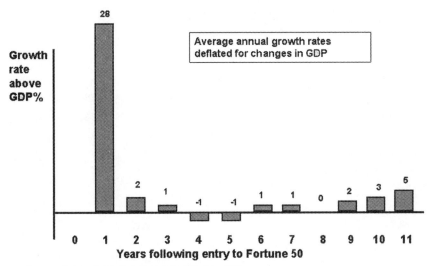

Figure 4.1 Fortune 50 growth rates

THE FINANCIAL CONSEQUENCES OF LOW GROWTH

The reasons for growth given at the beginning of this chapter—fall in stock price, loss of momentum, and loss of talent—are presumed to be very detrimental to financial performance. Most managers assume that low-growth companies are failing companies that cannot generate decent returns for shareholders. Moreover, the catastrophic declines in market capitalization of companies that hit a growth stall serve to reinforce the message that low growth is bad. However, this fear of low growth is a misunderstanding of the way the market anticipates performance. The challenge of producing decent returns for shareholders year on year is no different for low-growth companies than for high-growth companies, so long as this is what the market expects.

Some simple modeling will help (Box 4.1 overleaf). This compares two companies with steady growth rates, one at 10% and another at 3%. The stock price at the beginning of the period is calculated to take account of the different growth rates, the faster-growing company obviously having a much higher stock price.

Box 4.1 Simple modeling of high and low growth

Suppose we have two companies, A and B, and both pay out dividends of $100 million per annum. A is expected to grow earnings at 10% p.a., but B at only 3% p.a. The respective annual returns on these two companies (total shareholder return or TSR%) will be the growth in value of the company over the next year plus the dividends as a percentage of the original market value of the company. Suppose also that shareholders can expect an average return on their market investments of 12%. The following calculations show that TSR% will be the same for both companies, namely 12%.

	Company A	Company B
Dividends ($m)	100	100
Expected annual earnings growth in coming year (%)	10%	3%
Market capitalization at start of year ($m)	VA	VB
Expected increase in market cap over year ($m)	10% of VA	3% of VB
So:		
Expected total annual return to shareholders is increase in value plus dividends ($m)	0.10*VA+100	0.03*VB+100
Suppose shareholders can earn average of 12% on their stock market investments. So the total annual return required by shareholders will be ($m)	12% of VA	12% of VB
The market will value companies A and B so that the expected total annual return to shareholders equals 12% of what they would have to invest, i.e., what they require on their investment	0.02*VA=100	0.09*VB=100
Hence market capitalization ($m) is	VA = 5000	VB = 1111
TSR%, or total annual return to shareholders as a percentage of market value, is thus	0.10*5000+100 as % of 5000	0.03*1111+100 as % of 1111
So TSR% is	600/5000	133/1111
So TSR% is the same in both cases	= 12%	= 12%

NB: The same result would apply for a company in decline. If Company C had an expected decline in earnings of 5% p.a., the equation for calculating market capitalization (VC) would be:
$$-0.05*VC + 100 = 0.12*VC \text{ or } 100 = 0.17*VC \text{ or } VC = 588$$
TSR% would then be (100 - 0.05*588)/588 = 12%.

What Box 4.1 demonstrates is that the slow-growth company, assuming all else is equal, produces a total return for shareholders identical to that of the high-growth company. The return is the same even with negative growth. This may seem counter-intuitive. However, the explanation lies in the different starting valuations. These differences exist because the market anticipates performance. Companies can only produce a superior total return for shareholders if they outperform shareholder expectations. If they perform according to shareholder expectations, they will deliver an average total return. If they perform less well than expected, the return will be below average. In other words, the problem of low growth is less about the annual performance challenge and more about major shifts in market perceptions. If a company suddenly moves from high growth to low growth, perceptions will change and the shares may decline by 50% or more. If, however, a low-growth company remains low growth but earns returns better than the cost of capital, it will perform better than the average.

SHAREHOLDER INDIFFERENCE

Managers have a choice about how to spend their earnings. They can either distribute earnings to shareholders, or retain earnings to invest in new activities. However, more simple modeling (Box 4.2 overleaf) shows that if the new investments only earn the cost of capital (i.e., what shareholders could earn on the market through reinvesting distributed earnings), then shareholders should be indifferent. They will expect to have the same result whether the company invests and continues to grow, or distributes and forgoes growth (assuming the investments bear a similar risk profile to that of the market). Shareholders are only interested in supporting growth ambitions if the new businesses are likely to outperform the average company on the stock market.

Simple modeling also demonstrates that the total return for shareholders is the same whether the low-growth company uses its spare cash to buy back shares or pay additional dividends (Box 4.3).

Box 4.2 Shareholder indifference: growth vs. dividends

Take two companies, A and B, both with post-tax earnings of $500 million. Suppose they have different strategies on dividend distribution. Company A distributes 90% of post-tax earnings and Company B distributes 10%. Though Company B will grow faster than Company A, the return to shareholders will be the same if the return from the new assets matches the cost of capital.

	Company A	Company B
Post-tax earnings ($m)	500	500
Dividend distribution (%)	90%	10%
Dividends ($m)	450	50
Retained earnings ($m)	50	450
Post-tax return on new investments (%)	12%	12%
Additional post-tax earnings in first year ($m)	6	54
New level of earnings ($m)	506	554
New level of dividends ($m)	455.4	55.4
Dividend growth rate (%)	1.2%	10.8%
Cost of capital (%)	12%	12%
Market capitalization ($M) on basis of dividend growth model, i.e.:		
Market cap = Dividends/(Cost of capital − dividend growth rate)	450 / (0.12 − 0.012) = 450 / 0.108	50 / (0.12 − 0.108) = 50 / 0.012
So market capitalization ($m) is the same	= 4166	= 4166
As is TSR%		
= Growth in capitalization + dividends Market capitalization	(4166*0.012+450) 4166 = 12%	(4166*0.108+50) 4166 = 12%

These areas of shareholder indifference are not just theory. In July 2004, Microsoft announced the biggest ever program of returning cash to shareholders. Dividends were increased to nearly 40% of current earnings, a special dividend of $3 amounting to 10% of the market capitalization was paid, and share repurchases of up to $30 billion were

---

Box 4.3 Shareholder indifference: dividends vs. buybacks

Take two companies, A and B. Suppose both have a policy of full distribution of earnings, and so have no growth from retained earnings. However, Company A pays out 100% of post-tax earnings as dividends, and Company B uses earnings to buy back its shares. In both cases it is assumed that earnings are retained through the year, and the share price rises accordingly in the expectation that earnings will be distributed at the end of the year.

	Company A	Company B
Market capitalization at start of year ($m)	150	150
Expected post-tax earnings in first year ($m)	15	15
P/E ratio	10	10
Number of shares at start of year (m)	100	100
Share price at start of year (cents)	150	150
Share price at end of year just prior to distribution (cents)	165	165
Dividends per share (cents)	15	0
Number of shares repurchased (m)	0	9.1
Number of shares at end of year (m)	100	89.9
Expected earnings in second year ($m)	15	15
Market capitalization at start of year two ($m)	150	150
Share price at start of year two immediately post distribution/repurchase (cents)	150	165

TSR%
= (Increase in share price + Dividends) / Share price at start of year

	Company A	Company B
	(150 − 150 + 15) / 150	(165 − 150 + 0) / 150
	= 10%	= 10%

declared over the next four years. In total Microsoft announced that it would return $75 billion to shareholders. Yet the share price moved very little. It had more than halved from $55 in late 1999 to $26 in mid-2004, and it continued in the $25–30 range.

Managers might have presumed that a cash handout of this size would be interpreted as an admission that Microsoft had few growth prospects outside its core business. No doubt they agonized about the risk of a further share slump. Evidently, the shareholders had figured out that Microsoft was not going to be able to use this cash in its growth plans (the $25 price presumed growth at about 10%) and had factored this into their calculations. They appeared to be indifferent as to whether the cash was returned to them or Microsoft was allowed to manage it.

LIVING WITH MARKET EXPECTATIONS

HIGHLY RATED COMPANIES

The main problem that managers need to consider when expected growth rates change—when a company hits a growth stall—is the shift in value that occurs. A company with a growth track record is likely to be highly rated, maybe with a price/earnings (P/E) ratio well in excess of 20. This can present a particularly difficult problem. The current value is likely to be based on an assumption of continued growth, at least in the medium term. A decision by management to abandon attempts to get into new businesses could cause the market to downgrade its assumptions about growth, leading to a significant fall in the stock price. Rather than taking the pain of a stock price fall today, managers are tempted to launch additional new businesses that at least have a chance of maintaining the growth path and hence, if the shareholders believe the story they are told, maintaining the share price. We call this problem the "overvaluation trap."

In the short term, while market expectations remain fixed and a company's P/E ratio stays more or less constant, a company will increase shareholder wealth so long as the post-tax return on retained earnings exceeds the reciprocal of the P/E ratio. When P/E ratios are high, companies can invest in relatively low-return investments and still increase shareholder value. Take a simple example, of Company A with a P/E ratio of 30 investing $100 million of retained earnings in a new business. To justify spending $100 million of shareholder value, the company need only earn 3.3% post-tax on a earnings multiple of 30 to match the original $100 million invested. Any new business earn-

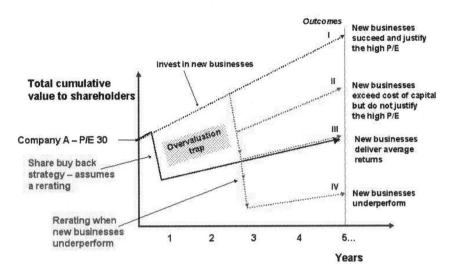

Figure 4.2 Company A: Overvaluation trap

ing over 3.3% will add to shareholder value on a multiple of 30. This gives management a considerable incentive in the short term to invest in new projects to maintain earnings growth.

The position is illustrated by Figure 4.2.

If the new businesses succeed to such an extent that high earnings expectations are met, then the share price will have been justified and the company will continue to prosper—Outcome I. However, if the new businesses only meet the cost of capital, then in due course the market will rerate the company downward—Outcome III. In terms of cumulative shareholder value, Outcome III will be the same as if the company did not invest in the new businesses, but instead returned funds to shareholders. The difference between investing in new businesses that match the cost of capital and deciding to return cash to shareholders lies in the timing of the share price adjustment. If cash is returned to shareholders, the adjustment is likely to happen immediately. If cash is invested in new businesses, the adjustment is likely to be delayed while shareholders decide how well the new businesses will perform.

If the new businesses perform well and produce returns that exceed the cost of capital, there may still be an adjustment downward. In fact, there will be an adjustment downward if the new businesses earn a return greater than the cost of capital but less than that required to support the original P/E of 30. This is Outcome II—shareholders will see a decline in share price, but they will be better off as a result of the new businesses when compared with having the cash returned to them.

If, however, the new businesses fail to earn the cost of capital, the fall from grace will be more precipitous—Outcome IV. The long-term result will be worse than it would have been under the less risky policy of returning the cash to shareholders.

For managers who know that growth in their core businesses is likely to slow down sometime soon—for the managers in charge of Intel and McDonald's—the overvaluation trap presents a real dilemma. Should they signal to the market today that growth will slow in the future and face a significant, and possibly career-threatening, decline in the share price? Or should they invest in new businesses, in a bid to find new sources of growth, and risk a much more calamitous share price decline if the new businesses fail?

The rational answer to the trap is to pursue new business projects only if they have a reasonable chance of earning above the cost of capital. If insufficient new businesses pass the test, managers should signal the change in growth expectations and aim for Outcomes II or III. Given the failure rate of companies seeking additional growth from new businesses, it is irrational to risk a calamitous share price decline (Outcome IV) by making investments with a low probability of success.

However, managers are not wholly rational: they frequently fall into the overvaluation trap. Both McDonald's and Intel chose the high road of aggressive investment in new businesses. Both efforts failed and contributed to calamitous falls in the share price. McDonald's appeared to learn from the experience, announced lower growth ambitions and a determination to focus on the core business, and was rewarded with a significant improvement in the share price. Intel managers also announced a more cautious new businesses policy—PC plus. However, by 2004 the strategy had again become ambitious, with plans to enter four or five new silicon businesses such as chips for flat panels and mobile phones.

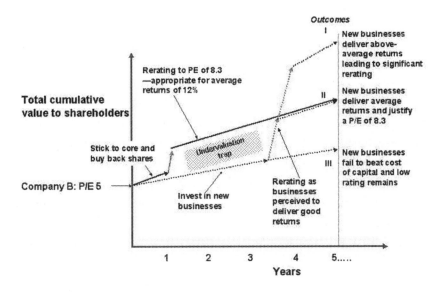

Figure 4.3 Company B: Undervaluation trap

LOWLY RATED COMPANIES

Companies that are lowly rated because of low growth expectations face other issues. In many ways, theirs is the more enviable position, it being easier to exceed low rather than high expectations.

So long as the P/E ratio remains the same, new investments will only increase shareholder value if they earn more than the reciprocal of the P/E ratio. Suppose Company B has a P/E ratio of 5 and invests $100 million of retained earnings in a new business. To gain $100 million of market capitalization the new business needs to earn $20 million, assuming the P/E remains at 5 (5 times 20 is 100). Any new business earning over 20% will add to market capitalization. A new business earning less than 20% will reduce market capitalization. This gives management a considerable hurdle in the short term. Thus, when the P/E ratio is low, companies need to earn returns well above the cost of capital in order to increase capitalization.

Figure 4.3 illustrates this position. Managers in Company B will be tempted to try to rectify the undervaluation through greater distribution of earnings via dividends or share buybacks. This ought to result in a rerating of the company as an income stock. If the average return shareholders can earn elsewhere is 12%, then, as an income stock, Company B should be rerated upward to a P/E ratio of 8.3—Outcome II.

Investing in new businesses may delay the rerating because the new investments will not prove their potential for a year or two. The delay will only be worthwhile if the return on the new investments is in excess of the cost of capital—Outcome I. The "undervaluation trap," therefore, is that managers can feel trapped into low-growth, high-distribution strategies, even though there may be good opportunities to invest in new businesses.

If the new initiatives only meet the cost of capital, then the final outcome will be the same as distributing the reinvested funds to share-holders—Outcome II—but with a delay in its achievement. However, if the new businesses fail to meet the cost of capital, then Company B can expect to remain lowly rated—Outcome III.

The rational answer to the trap is to invest only in new businesses that have a reasonable chance of earning above the cost of capital. However, managers often choose the low-risk path: they announce a back-to-basics strategy with a high dividend or share buyback as a way of restoring confidence. Then, once the company is fairly valued, they consider investments in new businesses. Choosing not to invest, and opting for greater distribution, delivers a very attractive immediate total shareholder return; in the case of Company B, a TSR of 20%. With earnings of $100 million and a P/E ratio of 5, the company will have a market capitalization of $500 million. Buying back $100 million worth of shares, or distributing the full $100 million in dividends, gives a 20% return. Whereas it is easy to criticize managers for mishandling the overvaluation trap by overinvesting in risky projects, it is harder to criticize them for choosing the risk-averse strategy when faced with the undervaluation trap. However, if the company does have good new business opportunities, the value lost can still be significant.

WHEN IS LOW GROWTH THE RIGHT CHOICE?

Low growth is the right choice for companies under two conditions:

❑ When there are few opportunities for the core businesses to grow.
❑ When there are few new businesses that have a good chance of out-performing the average company on the stock market.

Companies following a low-growth strategy under such circumstances will minimize their risks of value destruction and increase their chances of value creation.

When deciding on a company's growth policy, the following principles should guide the choice:

❑ Companies can only add to shareholder value if their growth exceeds market expectations—just growing is not enough. High growth is an expectation treadmill.
❑ When new business opportunities earn the cost of capital (roughly the average return on the stock market) shareholders are indifferent between making the investment or returning the cash through dividends and buybacks. Thus investments in new businesses need to have a good chance of exceeding average returns to justify management attention.
❑ If a company cannot find new business projects that are likely to earn more than the cost of capital, surplus funds should be returned to shareholders.
❑ Low-growth companies can still produce good returns to shareholders.
❑ So long as there are no tax differences between income and capital gains, shareholders are indifferent between dividends and share buybacks.

We have also looked at the particular dilemmas faced by companies with high and low P/Es. Companies with high P/Es face an over-valuation trap:

❑ In the short term, highly rated companies may do better for their shareholders by making new investments that make quite low returns. However, unless the returns are sufficiently high to warrant the original high rating, the share price will eventually adjust downward to reflect the returns actually received.

❑ So long as the returns from new businesses exceed the cost of capital, shareholders will be better off if the company invests: even though the share price may fall, it will fall less than it would without the investments.

❑ The fall in share price will be even greater if the new businesses fail to earn the cost of capital.

❑ Thus the rational stance for companies that cannot see ways of maintaining high expectations of growth is to pursue new business projects only when they are likely to earn more than the cost of capital and manage a decline in their share price to reflect the appropriate value.

Companies with low P/Es face an undervaluation trap:

❑ In the short term, new business investments will need to earn considerably more than the cost of capital to add to immediate shareholder value.

❑ Increasing distributions, whether by dividends or share buybacks, is a tempting, low-risk option that can give very good immediate shareholder returns, and could lead to a rerating upward as a good income stock.

❑ However, shareholder value should be increased if the new businesses outperform the average, and exceed the cost of capital.

❑ Nevertheless, the low rating will remain if the new businesses fail.

❑ Thus the rational stance for undervalued companies that see good opportunities is to pick only those projects that have a high chance of success, recognizing that paying back funds to shareholders will be a more attractive alternative than making average investments.

CAN LOW GROWTH BE A WINNING STRATEGY?

Despite the logic of this chapter, most managers remain unconvinced. Growth has been seen as a necessary objective for so long that managers find it hard to accept low growth. They feel certain that low growth will lead to problems that simple financial theory has overlooked. They feel insecure without a growth plan.

To support our view that low growth is not only sensible for many companies but also financially attractive, we would like to offer some examples.

CROWN CORK AND SEAL

Probably the most famous example of a company succeeding by taking a lower-growth, more focused strategy is Crown Cork and Seal.

In 1891, a manager in a Baltimore machine shop hit on an idea for a better bottle cap—a piece of tin-coated steel with a flanged edge and an insert of natural cork. The new product was a hit and the company prospered until patents ran out in the 1920s. In 1927, Crown Cork was bought by a competitor, Charles McManus.

McManus steered the company to a dominant position in the world market for bottle caps. He also anticipated the rise of the beer can and built a one million square foot plant in Philadelphia. McManus's success, however, did not survive his death in 1946. The Philadelphia plant proved to be a failure because it was not close to its customers, and his successor invested unsuccessfully in other new businesses such as plastics and bird cages.

By the mid-1950s the company was in distress, and John Connelly, a local businessman, shareholder, and previous unsatisfied customer, became president. Connelly's plan was "just common sense." He removed layers of unnecessary management, cut staff functions in half, closed central research, shut down the Philadelphia facility, invested in plants close to customers, and gave each plant manager responsibility for profitability, quality, and customer service.

Faced with much larger competitors—American Can and Continental Can—Connelly decided to focus on crowns, where he was still market leader, and specialist segments of the canning industry. He developed a strong position in motor oil cans and in cans for "hard-to-hold" liquids, such as soft drinks and aerosols.

As the market for cans matured in the 1970s and 1980s and large companies, like Campbell's and Coca-Cola, began to make their own cans, Crown's competitors invested in new packaging solutions with new materials such as fiber-foil, paper, and plastic. Their vision was to convert from being canning companies to becoming packaging solutions companies. Connelly, however, chose to go firmly in the opposite direction.

Crown focused on crowns and cans, expanding internationally using secondhand equipment, helping customers convert from steel to aluminum, and investing in plants close to customers' canning lines. Since the business was highly profitable, Connelly was quickly able to pay off the debts he inherited. He then paid off all the preferred stock and, from 1970 onward, he used spare cash to buy back shares.

In the 1980s margins came under pressure. However, Crown's high levels of depreciation generated sufficient cash to support a modest level of real growth and buy back significant numbers of shares. In 1970 there were over 20 million shares. By 1987, Connelly had repurchased more than half. Not surprisingly, earnings per share performed especially well, rising from $1.41 to $9.28 in 1987. Similarly, the share price rose from less than $5 to nearly $50.

In the meantime, Crown's competitors had concluded that cans were a mature market. Not only did they expand into other growth areas of packaging, but they also invested in other growth sectors, including insurance and oil. Unfortunately, both kinds of diversification produced low returns. There was excess capacity in the growth areas of the packaging industry because most packaging companies were entering the new markets. In addition, the non-packaging businesses performed poorly, due in part to the lack of experience of managers schooled in the canning industry.

By the mid-1980s, American Can, National Can, and Continental Can had all been the target of aggressive acquirers looking for underperforming businesses to turn around. In 1985 American Can was acquired by Triangle Industries, who also acquired National Can the following year. In 1988 the integrated company, American National, was sold to Pechiney, a French aluminum company.

The Continental Group was acquired in 1984 by Peter Kiewit, who sold most of the non-packaging businesses as part of a program to restore focus and profitability. When Kiewit was looking for a buyer of the improved business, an obvious candidate was the best-performing company in the can industry: Crown Cork and Seal.

Having avoided diversification outside metal crowns and cans for more than 20 years, Crown, with one huge deal, not only became one of the largest metal packaging companies in the world, but also added plastic, glass, and foil packaging skills. Its timing was both good and bad. The deal was completed near the top of the 1980s boom, causing Crown to pay a full price. However, the company's entry into other areas of packaging was timed to suit its skills. By the early 1990s the "new packaging materials" were beginning to mature into predictable businesses that would respond well to Crown's cost-conscious, decen-tralized, customer-centric management style.

If the tale could be ended at this point, Crown Cork and Seal would be the ideal example: a company that ended up dominating its industry while its competitors became distracted with new businesses. However, the story did not stop there. The growth pressures of the 1990s seduced even this focused management team. Crown continued to make acquisitions, adding further businesses in Europe and other parts of the world to become a leader in metal containers and one of the world's top packaging companies. In the process it paid too much for its acquisitions and the business began to get out of control. Toward the end of the 1990s the company's profits collapsed and its market capitalization fell by 90%. In the end, the pressure to grow and the ambition to become the world's leading packaging company undid much of the work of John Connelly's low-growth strategy.

IBM

Metal packaging is a mature industry and Crown's experience demonstrates the value of focus in an environment that is not growing. IBM, on the other hand, has been in a fast-growth, high-tech industry. Yet like Crown, IBM has demonstrated the benefits of limiting growth ambitions.

Under Louis Gerstner IBM delivered good returns to shareholders through modest growth combined with aggressive share buybacks. Between 1993 and 2003, it delivered a cumulative total shareholder return of 22% per annum while distributing nearly all its earnings back to shareholders.

Gerstner joined IBM on 1 April 1993 at a time of extreme crisis, when its share price dropped below $50 compared to over $175 in 1986. That summer it fell further to an all-time low of $41. Dividends had been cut drastically in 1992, from $4.84 to $2.16, and then by Gerstner himself to $1 in July 1993. Yet by March 2004 the share price had risen to an equivalent of $367 (taking account of two intervening 2:1 scrip issues). Over that period total revenue grew by an equivalent of only 1.9% per annum in real terms, well below US GDP, which grew by an average 3.2% over the same period.

How did Gerstner do it? First, he offset the decline in the hardware business by building a major services business. But this did not give him significant growth. He therefore needed a second strategy to get earnings per share and the share price rising. This was his share buyback program.

IBM had bought back shares previously. Between 1986 and 1989 it bought back around 6% of issued shares, spending over $4 billion. However, Gerstner made share buybacks a central strategy. Between 1995 and 1998 he bought 29% of outstanding common stock, spending a net $22.2 billion. This was more than 100% of post-tax earnings over that period of $21.9 billion. Dividends were also increased, but only from $1.00 to $1.88 per share. In all, from 1995 to 1998, IBM distributed on average 114% of earnings to shareholders by way of dividends and share buybacks.

By decreasing the number of shares, a 33% increase in earnings from 1995 to 1998 turned into an 87% increase in earnings per share.

The share price increased by 152%, being boosted by a rising P/E ratio over the period, from 13.2 to 17.8. The pace of share purchase and retirement eased slightly after 1998. Even so, over the 10 years 1994 to 2003, revenue increased by an equivalent of 3.6% per annum, earnings by 11.1% per annum, earnings per share by 15.1% per annum, and the share price by 21.4% per annum.

During this period IBM did not stop developing its businesses, making two significant acquisitions: Lotus Corporation for $3.2 billion in 1995, and the consulting arm of PricewaterhouseCoopers in 2002 for $3.5 billion. It also continued to invest in its core businesses, not least through its significant spend on R&D and engineering. This averaged a pretty steady $5.1 billion per annum. Thus over the period 1993–2003, IBM spent $56.2 billion on R&D, earned net of tax $51.4 billion, and spent $52.6 billion (gross) buying back its own shares ($44.3 billion net).

Would shareholders have been better off if IBM had invested more of its earnings in new businesses rather than its own shares? Many commentators advised this over the period, not least during the heady dot-com days. IBM, after all, was close to the center of a technological revolution. Gerstner's view was different. He credited much of his success to the businesses he did not enter. He told a *Business Week* journalist:

> If life was so easy that you could just go buy success, there would be a lot more successful companies in the world. There were few PC companies that we weren't offered at some point. Telecommunications companies all over the world proposed joint ventures. There were people who suggested we get into the content business. We turned them all down.[5]

Instead of investing in these new opportunities, Gerstner chose a lower-growth path. As we have outlined, he continued to invest heavily in IBM's core businesses through R&D, made two significant, but not huge, acquisitions that added to existing growth businesses, and distributed over 100% of earnings back to shareholders. The result was a performance well ahead of most of his growth-driven rivals. He argued:

> The value that some analysts put on revenue growth versus what they put on profit is out of whack. There is a huge difference between what we hear from our owners and from analysts and the media. Every time I met with owners they said "Please don't take the cash and invest it in stupid acquisitions or ventures."

With the handover to Palmisano, IBM has become more growth oriented. The Emerging Business Opportunities program described in Chapter 7 is one process that Palmisano has put in place to try to accelerate growth. We believe that this has helped remove some of the cultural and structural barriers to new businesses inside IBM and may make some small addition to the company's growth rate. But we are concerned that IBM's increasing focus on growth will cause managers to be less selective about which businesses to invest in. Because Palmisano's growth goals appear to be driven more by ambition than by a realistic assessment of prospects for new businesses,[6] we are concerned that IBM may make the same mistake as Crown: drive for growth without sufficient caution.

DO LOW-GROWTH COMPANIES EVER BECOME HIGH-GROWTH COMPANIES?

Part of the reason managers are so uncomfortable setting low growth targets is that they fear the long-term implications. They fear that once their company settles for low growth it will never be able to change gear and become a high-growth company. So far as Fortune 50 companies are concerned, this appears to be true. As we have noted, only 4% succeed in restarting growth after a stall.

Armed with this knowledge, the Corporate Strategy Board decided to see if the same were true in smaller companies.[7] They looked for companies whose "revenue growth performance began a sustained and meaningful positive inflection from its past performance," a phenomenon they called "growth restart." From a sample of 1,487 large mature firms, they identified 490 whose three-year revenue growth most outperformed competitors; 174 of these companies also had growing margins. Of these 174, 30 were labeled "continuous growers" and 144 "growth restarters." In other words, some 10% of companies do successfully restart growth following a period of slower growth. This is a more promising number than the 4% in the Fortune 50, but it is still a small percentage. While it may depress many managers of mature companies, it underlines the importance of being cautious about investing in new growth ventures when the core businesses are mature. Since most companies try and less than 10% succeed, the net accumulated effort is likely to be value destroying.

Further analysis by the Corporate Strategy Board should cause managers to be even more cautious. Of the 144 growth restarts only 42 were "sustained restarts." These were companies that managed to sustain their growth rate at levels higher than the industry average. In other words, less than 3% of mature companies were able to restart growth and sustain rates above the average of their industries.

Unfortunately, the statistics get even worse: 60% of these sustained restarts achieved their success by revitalizing their existing businesses. Only 40% succeeded by developing new businesses, and less than half of these, only 11 companies, succeeded by developing new businesses outside their core. In other words, less than 2% of companies restart growth through developing new businesses and less than 1% do it by finding opportunities outside their core.

While these statistics reinforce management's desire to avoid letting their companies reach maturity, they also underline the main message of this book: that there are few opportunities for mature companies to create significant new businesses. Managers who attempt to develop new businesses need to recognize that their success does not depend on the amount of effort they put in. It depends on whether the combination of market opportunity, competitor behavior, internal skills and resources, and leadership that is needed for success exists at a particular point in time. For many companies at many points this combination does not exist, and these companies would be better keeping their powder dry. For some at some points, the combination does exist, and these companies should invest with confidence.

CHAPTER 5

THE NEW BUSINESSES TRAFFIC LIGHTS

T he central message of this book is that managers need to be more selective about the investments they make in new growth businesses. In our view the pressures to grow, the natural optimism of managers, the over-reliance on the financial business case, along with a number of the reasons given in Chapter 3 cause managers to be insufficiently thoughtful and rigorous when selecting new businesses in which to invest. The numerous failures of both new business initiatives and acquisitions by many of the major corporations around the world attest to this. Much shareholder value has been needlessly destroyed. This chapter, which describes our selection screen, is therefore the most important in the book. If managers understand the logic behind the Traffic Lights and use its criteria to choose projects, they will invest only in those projects that have a reasonable probability of success.

This chapter alone is not enough. Managers also need to have read Chapter 4 on low growth. Without understanding the financial consequences of low growth or acknowledging that many companies have long periods of low growth, managers will not be comfortable using the Traffic Lights to screen out most of their projects. Believing that low growth is unacceptable, they will either be deliberately optimistic about some of the Traffic Lights or decide to invest in a new business even when the Traffic Lights suggest that the chances of success are too low. Unless managers understand that low growth is acceptable, they will be tempted to gamble.

The Traffic Lights have been developed out of our research. We examined the criteria managers use to evaluate new businesses. We

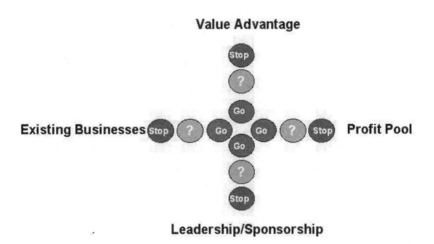

Figure 5.1 The New Businesses Traffic Lights

shadowed managers in the process of screening new business ideas. We studied the criteria suggested by other authors. Finally, we applied pure logic. The tool (Figure 5.1) has taken nearly three years to develop and test.

The Traffic Lights involve making red, yellow, or green judgments about four questions:

❑ Do we have a significant advantage (green), small or uncertain advantage (yellow), or significant disadvantage (red) in this new business?
❑ Is the profit pool for this new market average (yellow), a "rare game" (green), or a "dog" (red)?
❑ Do we have leaders of this new business (and sponsors in the parent company) that are clearly superior to (green), similar to (yellow), or less strong than (red) competitor businesses?
❑ Is the impact of this new business on existing businesses likely to be significantly positive (green), uncertain (yellow), or significantly negative (red)?

The purpose is to decide whether the project should go ahead or not.

We have found that any one green signal can be enough to make the project into a go, so long as there are no red signals. One red signal is enough to stop the project. A project with all yellow signals is marginal.

When HP considered entering the personal computer business in 1981, for example, three traffic lights were green:

❑ HP had reason to believe that it could gain a technical advantage in large computers for commercial applications because mainframes were threatened by the new client-server model, IBM was closing down its RISC development effort, and HP could acquire IBM's RISC team. By moving to RISC technology, HP could leapfrog incumbents focused on the CISC software used by their installed base.

❑ The profit pool looked exciting: most manufacturers were making attractive returns.

❑ HP also had a strong team running its computer business and suitable sponsors at the corporate level. It had been manufacturing minicomputers for many years and selling them mainly into technical applications. By chance, the management team in charge of the business was particularly strong. On several previous occasions they had proposed entering the market for general-purpose commercial applications and had been turned down.

On the other hand, when British Sugar, a company focused on processing sugar beet, looked at the opportunity of entering the hemp processing business, four traffic lights were red:

❑ An advantage would be hard for British Sugar to create. The company British Sugar was thinking of acquiring was not the best player in the market and British Sugar had limited skills to bring to this new area.

❑ The market appeared to be a "dog." The auto industry and matting customers who bought most of the hemp had a history of providing low margins. Even if changes in legislation caused significant growth (the main reason for considering this opportunity), the prospect of earning good returns was limited because the main customer would be the auto industry, the toughest of all buyers.

❑ The team British Sugar could assemble from the acquisition and internal appointments would be less experienced and less customer led than competitors.

❑ Finally, the impact on the existing business would be likely to be negative. The project would involve some of the most able managers from both the processing and technical sides of British Sugar at a time when these managers could be much more profitably employed in the sugar business, driving costs down and developing new service offerings for customers.

The New Businesses Traffic Lights cover many of the criteria that are commonly used to screen projects. For example, Tim Hammond, then corporate development and group marketing director at Whitbread, used a simple matrix (Figure 5.2) to screen 30 ideas for new leisure businesses. Whitbread is a restaurant, hotels, and leisure group and was exploring opportunities in new restaurant areas, movie cinemas, spas, wellbeing services, sports clubs, and other leisure activities. In fact it was from Tim Hammond that we picked up the idea of a traffic lights system. He defined criteria for each axis of the matrix and graded each

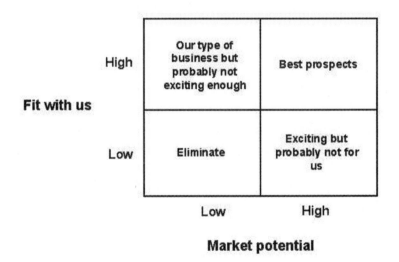

Figure 5.2 Potential/fit matrix

criterion red, yellow, or green. By eliminating all those with a red signal, he reduced the number of options to six. Further investigation identified only two with multiple green signals.

The difference between the Traffic Lights and the criteria used by most managers, such as Tim Hammond, is in the detail. The Traffic Lights are built on some fundamental insights about the circumstances that lead to value creation and the mistakes that managers make when evaluating new businesses. In total there are five insights, ranging from the realization that managers often underestimate learning costs to the observation that they often overlook the costs of distracting attention from existing businesses. Box 5.1 summarizes these five insights. Their impact is to highlight some negative criteria that are often ignored or given insufficient weight. The result is that the Traffic Lights reject more projects than most normal screening processes.

The rest of this chapter examines each of the Traffic Lights in more detail. To illustrate how the tool can best be used we will focus on two situations: whether a chocolate confectionery company such as Mars or Cadbury should enter the ice-cream business in Europe using its brands and its experience with snack products; and whether a retailer of health and beauty products, such as Boots in the UK or Neiman Marcus in the US, should set up a chain of eye-care shops using its branding and retailing skills.

This is a long chapter. It is, therefore, worth providing some guidance to readers. Those who want to focus on the unique ideas in this chapter need only read the five insights (in bold) and the text that relates to each—about 11 pages in total. Those who have a new business idea that they want to assess will need to read enough under each heading to be confident that they understand the criteria being used and how to make the assessment—probably more than half of the pages that follow. Finally, those who already have some criteria for selecting new businesses and want to see whether the Traffic Lights contain additional ideas should focus on those sections that are unfamiliar to them—probably a third or a quarter of the chapter. In other words, it is unlikely that any reader will want to work through all of the next 50 pages in sequence. Box 5.2 overleaf provides an overview of all the criteria used in the Traffic Lights.[1]

Box 5.1 Five insights that inform the Traffic Lights

Insights

1. Managers do not normally consider the tradability of their unique value when assessing new businesses (page 102).

2. Managers do not normally assess the likely costs, at both the operating level and the corporate level, of learning a new business (page 110).

3. Analysis of markets should focus on identifying extreme situations that are either so good that even a competitor with disadvantage can earn a good return or so bad that even an advantaged player may earn less than the cost of capital (page 117).

4. Managers do not normally give sufficient attention to the issue of who is going to run a new business and, particularly, who the new business is going to report to (page 130).

5. Managers often underestimate the loss of performance in the core businesses that occurs when attention shifts to new businesses and some of the most energetic managers are allocated to new business projects (page 142).

Reasons

The value reason for entering a new business is the extra value that can be created. Hence managers should deduct from their calculations that part of their unique contribution that can be turned into value without enter- intg the new business.

Because learning costs are hard to quantify they are usually left out of the equation. Fit analysis, one way of identifying likely learning costs, is normally focused on what fits rather than on what does not fit.

Strategy analysis demonstrates that in most markets companies with an advantage will earn above-average returns. Hence detailed analysis of growth rates and likely margins, while neces- sary for a financial plan, is often unnecessary for making a strate- gic decision.

Managers, especially in large companies, believe that their managerial resources are consid- erable or that good talent can be hired from the marketplace. They also presume that they can learn most new businesses.

Once managers have decided that the core is not enough they often switch too much of their attention to the new. Moreover, new growth businesses often offer more attractive careers for the company's better managers.

Implications

Since many types of unique value, such as brand or patent, can be licensed or "cashed" through a joint venture, the value advantage equation is often neu- tral (yellow) or negative (red).

Since learning costs are rarely less than 10% of profits and can be 50% or more at least for a few years, the value advantage equa- tion is often neutral (yellow) or negative (red).

Since most markets are at neither extreme, they score yellow on the Traffic Lights, offering no infor- mation for or against the strate- gic decision.

When an objective assessment is made of the quality of the pro- ject's managers and sponsors compared to those of current and likely competitors, it is often evi- dent that they are inferior (red) or at least not superior (yellow).

Most new businesses create some distraction from existing busi- nesses. Distraction costs become significantly negative (red) when the new business competes with existing businesses for scarce resources or skills.

Box 5.2 The New Businesses Traffic Lights

Value advantage
- ❑ Our unique contribution (at operating and parenting levels)
- ❑ Less % of our contribution that is tradable
- ❑ Less unique contribution of competitors
- ❑ Less cost of learning the new business (at operating and parenting levels)

Profit pool potential
- ❑ Business model potential for high margins (value relative to cost, break even as % of market)
- ❑ Industry structure potential for high margins (five forces taking account of likely growth rates)
- ❑ Opportunity for us to be a leader in this market
- ❑ Cost of trying relative to size of profit pool (taking account of time to commercialization)
- ❑ Business model vulnerability (number of enablers, sensitivity to key variables)

Leadership/sponsorship quality
- ❑ Relative quality of MD/leadership team of the unit
- ❑ Significance of MD/leadership's personal insights about the business
- ❑ Status of sponsor within main parent

Impact on existing businesses
- ❑ Size of positive or negative synergies
- ❑ Risk of distraction costs

   ## DO WE HAVE A VALUE ADVANTAGE?

One of the truths of business is that a superior return on capital is normally the result of some area of advantage. Success is hard to achieve without an advantage. Michael Porter captured this thought compellingly in his book *Competitive Advantage*.[2] Business strategy, he argued, should be about how companies can achieve advantage over their rivals. Advantage, he proposed, comes either from superior costs or from superior products.

Box 5.3 Value Advantage Equation

Unique value we bring (from the operating and parent level)
Less   Percent of value we could trade (through sale, license, or joint venture)
Less   Unique value our competitors bring
Less   Cost of learning the new business, at the operating level and at the parent level, relative to competitors
Equals **Our value advantage**
        (green if significantly positive, red if significantly negative)

Many managers, consultants, and academics have built on Porter's ideas and defined hundreds of different ways of creating advantage, including the design of the business model, market share, special competencies, close relationships, market positions, and unique assets.

In particular, the resource-based view of strategy, developed about the time of the publication of Porter's book, focuses on the resources that companies possess as the main explanation for performance differences. The most important resources, the theorists argue, are those that are valued by customers, rare and difficult for rivals to acquire or imitate. Competencies that are "path dependent," meaning that managers need to have had a certain set of experiences to have developed the skill or knowledge, are often especially valuable because they are hard for others to acquire or copy.

So how does a management team assess whether it is likely to have an advantage in a new business situation? Clearly, this is difficult. It can be especially difficult if the advantage is based on competencies that are hard to understand. As a result, we have developed the Value Advantage Equation to help managers make the right judgment (see Box 5.3).

WHAT UNIQUE VALUE DO WE BRING?

The equation starts with an assessment of what the company can contribute to this new business that has special or unique value. Figure 5.3 overleaf lists some of the areas of special contribution that we

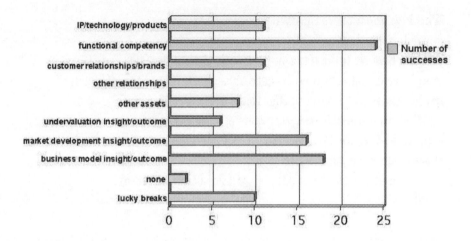

Figure 5.3 Sources of unique value

identified from our database of success stories. Most of the successes were based on more than one source of unique value, the average being two. Just under 20% of the successes were also influenced by luck. In these cases the sources of unique value were fewer, averaging only 1.5.

We considered trying to develop a checklist that managers could use to define their unique contribution, but decided against it. The checklist could never be complete and it might encourage managers to tick boxes rather than think through their unique situation. Managers, we decided, need to define as precisely as possible what special contributions they believe they can make to the new business and how valuable the contributions are. It is the judgment about value that is the hardest.

For example, the health and beauty retailer considering eye care might have a list of special contributions like this:

❑ Trusted health and beauty brand.
❑ Excess retail space in some locations.
❑ Knowledge of the health and beauty consumer.
❑ Distribution system to every significant retail location.
❑ Retailing skills.
❑ Employee loyalty.

The key question is "How unique?" How much advantage does each contribution deliver?

The brand could clearly be an important contribution. If the brand could drive extra sales volume to each site compared to existing brands in the market, it could significantly increase profitability.

The excess retail space might be a valuable contribution, if it were especially valuable to the eye-care business. Unless we are confident that the company has a number of sites that are especially good for eye-care retailing, we would have to assume that the spare retail space would be useful but not a significant contribution.

Knowledge of the health and beauty consumer could be important, but again it is unlikely to be a unique contribution. Other competitors have been in the market for many years. Unless the health and beauty managers believe they possess some insight about this consumer segment that eye-care competitors do not have, the knowledge is unlikely to be a significant contribution.

The distribution system could be a significant contribution if it would enable the new eye-care business to have fewer lines out of stock or have lower supply costs than competitors. Given the maturity of the existing industry and the availability of third-party distribution services, this is unlikely to be a source of significant advantage.

Retailing skills and employee loyalty could be a major contribution. This would depend on whether the application of these skills would be likely to enable the business to serve more customers, attract more customer loyalty, operate at lower cost, or sell at higher prices than competitors. The company might well believe that this would be a significant contribution.

In summary, the health and beauty managers might have concluded that they had an advantage in branding and in retailing skills, which might enable them to earn significantly higher margins than most competitors, assuming all other aspects are equal.

To make best use of the Value Advantage Equation, managers need to convert judgments like "significantly higher margins" into a number they feel is realistic, such as 50%. When faced with a number, vague words like significant become less misleading. In ideal circumstances, the analysis would involve reverse engineering the business models of important competitors. These would then be compared to the business model of the proposed new business to see how big the value advantage is likely to be. With some detailed reverse engineering, it is possible to make quite fine-grained judgments, distinguishing for example between a 30% and a 40% advantage.

Assessing the unique contribution and putting some value on it, such as "50% higher margins," is easier when talking about an existing market, such as eye care. When the business is a new market, for example internet service provision in the early 1990s or outsourcing auto safety testing in 2000, the task is harder. Managers need to compare their special advantages with those of likely future competitors and try to identify those unique resources that will be a significant source of advantage in five years' time. Guesswork comes into play along with the biases of the person doing the guessing. Nevertheless, laying out the value that managers believe is unique and assessing its significance to relative profitability forces managers to make the necessary strategic judgments.

WHAT VALUE CAN WE TRADE?

Insight 1: Managers do not normally consider the tradability of their unique value when assessing new businesses.

The branding and retailing skills of the health and beauty company may be valuable resources. One way to turn these resources into value is by entering the eye-care business. However, there is another way for the health and beauty company to turn these resources into value. It can try to sell or license them, either to existing competitors in the eye-care business or to some new entrant.

For example, if the brand increases sales by 10%, resulting in an increase in margin from 10% to 15%, then it ought to be possible to go to one of the less successful players and offer to license the brand. While it would not make sense for the competitor to pay as much as a 5% royalty, it might be possible to earn a 2.5% or 3% royalty just by licensing the brand. In this way, the health and beauty company could get a proportion of the value of its resource without any of the risks and costs associated with entering a new business. Disney, for example, routinely licenses its brand and characters to other companies.

In the Value Advantage Equation, we deduct the tradable proportion of the unique value from the original contribution to arrive at a non-tradable contribution. The reason for this deduction needs careful explanation.

We are trying to assess the logic for entering this new business. As will become clear later in the Value Advantage Equation, there are costs and risks associated with entering a new business. In order to justify the costs and risks, we need to believe we have a contribution to make that can only be turned into value by incurring these costs. If we can get value for our contribution without incurring the costs, we have no reason to enter the new business. We would be better advised to cash in our contribution, saving ourselves the costs. In other words, it is the size of the non-tradable portion of our unique contribution that is the key reason for going ahead. The focus on non-tradable contribution is supported by our sample of successes. The vast majority had significant sources of value that could not be traded (Figure 5.4 overleaf).

Another example might help. Transco, a gas pipeline business, had underground channels and rights of way that were valuable to any company in the business of laying fiberoptics for the internet and telecoms industry. The channels and rights of way reduced the costs and increased the speed of laying communication fiber. This valuable resource was causing Transco to think about entering the telecoms business: Transco could lay fiber and sell the communication capacity to its existing gas customers.

An alternative option for Transco would be to lease the channels and rights of way to an existing telecoms company, either for a fixed fee or for a share of the revenues. When deciding whether to enter the business, Transco managers needed to compare entering the new business with the alternative of leasing the resource to someone else. At the time, they concluded that they could not get full value from leasing the rights of way and chose to enter the business. With hindsight this may

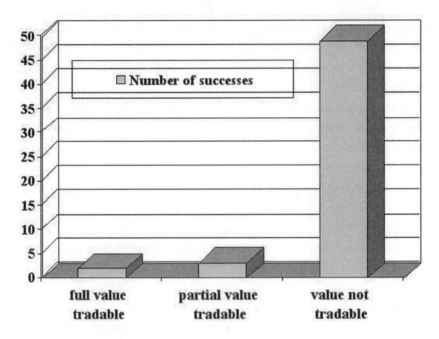

Figure 5.4 Tradability of unique value

have been the wrong judgment, since Transco lost a significant amount of money when the telecoms industry collapsed. Williams, a US gas pipeline company, faced the same choice and made the same decision. However, because Williams could lay fiberoptic cable at a cost 20% below the industry average and because this source of advantage would have been hard to trade for value, Williams probably made the right decision.

In practice, of course, there are many alternatives, including different kinds of leases and different kinds of joint ventures, involving different parts of the business. For example, the pipeline company could lay the fiber under an agreement with a telecoms company who would lease the fiber. The price paid could be on a sliding scale dependent on the volume of traffic. An agreement could be made to lease back some capacity for use by the pipeline company and for selling on to gas customers.

In an ideal world all these different options would be defined and evaluated. However, options normally come on the table one at a time. In practice, the managers in Transco put together a proposal for entering the telecoms business in joint venture with an experienced telecoms company. At this point the deal on offer needed to be assessed. Rather than sending the managers back to lay out all the other possible options, we have found it best to deduct from the unique value the amount that managers believe they could release through a licensing or trading relationship. Discounting the value is a realistic way of taking account of the alternative options.

Returning to the eye-care example, we should deduct something for the tradability of the brand. If managers believe that it would be possible to license the health and beauty brand to one of the current competitors, we should deduct the value of a likely license fee, say 2.5%. We should also consider deducting some of the value attributed to retailing skills and employee loyalty. However, experience suggests that the company is unlikely to be able to trade its retailing skills and employee loyalty for any significant value. Even if it were successful in offering these skills as consultants, it is unlikely that it would create any significant value contribution.

The non-tradable contribution, therefore, is the additional value the company could get by using the brand itself plus the value it can add through its retailing skills and employee loyalty. If the previous estimate was a 50% higher margin, the non-tradable contribution might be more like a 25% higher margin.

Managers often criticize our process at this point, arguing that it is impossible to put figures on something as qualitative as non-tradable contribution. Our response comes in two forms. First, we point out that in acquisition situations these issues have to be quantified in order to arrive at a price the buyer is prepared to pay. The unique value in an acquisition is the "synergy." If it is possible to estimate synergies in an acquisition, it should be possible to estimate the equivalent in a new business situation. Our second response is that accurate quantification is not necessary. All that is necessary is to judge whether the non-tradable contribution is larger than the combined value of the other terms in the Value Advantage Equation. We recognize that the judgments required are hard, but we believe that the format of the Value Advantage Equation helps.

WHAT IS COMPETITORS' UNIQUE VALUE?

The flip side of assessing our unique value is to consider what unique value the competitors bring to the business. The analysis can focus first on the existing competitors, but should focus also on potential competitors.

The list of contributions of existing competitors in the eye-care business might have been:

❏ Low rents in some locations due to leases signed some years before and/or property purchased at lower prices.
❏ Established locations and knowledge about location advantage.
❏ Volume advantages in purchasing costs and other costs not connected to the site.
❏ Brand strength, customer loyalty, and switching costs.
❏ Knowledge of customer preferences.

In the same way as before, these contributions need to be assessed in terms of their worth: how much advantage these contributions give.

The low rents will give a calculable cost advantage. However, should this cost advantage be taken into account? The competitors ought to be assessing their property costs against market values (the rent they could get if they sub-leased the property), hence their central property company ought to be charging a market rent for the sites. If so, these sites would have no property cost advantage. But overall, the competitor is still benefiting from these lower costs and can use the money to strengthen its business. Hence it should be part of the Value Advantage Equation.

Knowledge about locations will enable the competitors to choose better sites, at least for a few years. We could assess the likely impact of this based on a typical comparison between better sites and average sites in the health and beauty company's current portfolio. We might give this a value of an average of 5% extra sales per site.

The volume advantages could also be estimated. Let us suggest that these might amount to a lower cost base of 2% of sales.

Box 5.4 Net non-tradable contribution in eye care

	% of margins
Unique contribution	50
Less tradable portion	25
Less competitor advantages	
– Site selection	20
– Scale benefits	2
– Marketing costs	3 (for 5 years)
– Cost per sale	3 (for 5 years)
Net non-tradable contribution	–3

Brand loyalty is hard to put a number on. However, we could make a guess at the discounts or extra marketing a new company would need to give (and for how many years) in order to build up market share. We might estimate that this would lead to an extra 3% on the cost base for five years.

Finally, the knowledge of customer preferences will enable competitors to fulfill customer needs more often than a newcomer. This would reduce their cost per sale. It may also enable the competitors to successfully sell customers more expensive solutions more often. We could guess at the impact of this temporary advantage as being a further 3% per year over five years.

Putting this all together, we need to judge whether the unique contribution that the competitors are able to make is significantly greater than, roughly equal to, or significantly less than the non-tradable contribution the health and beauty company can make. The judgment is about whether there is a net non-tradable contribution (Box 5.4).

At this point the judgment involves trying to weigh both quantifiable and qualitative parts of the different contributions. We should not pretend that it is easy or that it can be done on a calculator. However, in our experience, managers who understand the business and who have worked through the details normally come to the same answer. In this case the net non-tradable contribution is probably about zero. In other words, there is no strong value advantage logic for the health and beauty company to enter this business.

ICE CREAM IN EUROPE

If we do the same analysis about whether Mars or Cadbury should enter the European ice-cream market, we come to a similar conclusion. They clearly had some important contributions to make to this new business:

❏ Their confectionery brands.
❏ Knowledge of snack products and European markets.
❏ Manufacturing skills.
❏ Branding skills.
❏ Sales and distribution.
❏ Ice-cream experience in North America.

Most of the value that the brands contribute could probably be traded through licensing or joint-venture agreements, without involving the companies directly in the risks of the ice-cream industry. The other contributions, however, would be much harder to trade.

When compared to the main competitors, nevertheless, the other contributions are not so unique. Both Unilever and Nestlé have direct knowledge of the ice-cream business in Europe, good branding skills, established sales and distribution, as well as experience in North America. Where Mars has an advantage, if any, is in manufacturing. Most observers would argue that Mars's manufacturing skills are superior to those of its consumer product rivals.

A proposal, for example, that Mars enter the ice-cream business would need to rest on a belief that Mars is much better able to exploit the value of its brands by entering the business directly, and that its manufacturing skills are a significant advantage. In addition, Mars managers would need to believe that the incumbents, Unilever and Nestlé, have no significant offsetting advantages.

Since the incumbents have much greater knowledge of consumer preferences, established relationships with retailers, proprietary distribution units in some retailers, as well as significant economies of scale in purchasing, manufacturing, and distribution, it is unlikely that Mars has any positive "net non-tradable contribution." More probably, if Mars chose to enter the business through a greenfields operation, it would have a significant disadvantage.

If, on the other hand, Mars were able to enter the business through a major acquisition, say Nestlé's business, the net non-tradable contribution could be positive. Mars would be bringing its brands and its manufacturing expertise to a business that already had the other advantages. If the premium Mars had to pay for the business were less than the value of the non-tradable part of its brands plus its manufacturing skills, the net non-tradable contribution would be positive.

The judgment about net non-tradable contribution is therefore dependent on the precise nature of the proposal. It may be possible to change the judgment by choosing a way of entering the business that makes the balance of contributions more positive. For example, if Mars could do a deal with Nestlé that involved merging Mars's North American ice-cream business with Nestlé's mainly European business, it might have been possible to avoid paying a premium and hence create a large positive net non-tradable contribution.

If a project has a negative net non-tradable contribution, it is not necessary to look at the remaining terms in the Value Advantage Equation. The project can be rejected without further analysis. If the project has a positive net non-tradable contribution, however, it may still not be supportable. The last term in the equation—cost of learning the new business—may be sufficiently negative to outweigh the positive.

WHAT IS THE COST OF LEARNING THE NEW BUSINESS?

Insight 2: Managers do not normally assess the likely costs, at both the operating level and the corporate level, of learning a new business.

As every manager knows, it takes time to learn a new business. During this period of learning, the management team makes mistakes that impose extra costs on the business and misses opportunities that could bring in extra revenues. The benchmark here is the competition. The new management team is likely to underperform the competition during its learning period. Of course, if the new management team is experienced in the industry, either because the managers have been hired from the industry or because the new team is part of an acquisition, this learning cost is likely to be low. If the new team is from a different industry where different rules of thumb guide the major decisions, the learning costs can be quite high.

In our sample, which was biased toward situations where the company had much to learn, we found very few successes where the company had lots to learn compared to competitors. When the business is new to the world every competitor has lots to learn, hence the relative position is more even (Figure 5.5).

In addition to the learning that needs to take place at the operating level, there is also learning required at the corporate level. The new business will have a reporting relationship with its parent company and will share resources or functions with some other businesses. A new eye-care unit in the health and beauty retailer might report to the business development director, who in turn reports to the CEO. In Mars or Cadbury, a new ice-cream business might report to the head of Europe, who in turn reports to the worldwide CEO.

These reporting relationships are influential: the management team in the new business is significantly affected by the signals, guidance, and instructions that it gets from its corporate masters. Beyond these reporting relationships, the management team is also influenced by a range of corporate functions that may control human resource policies,

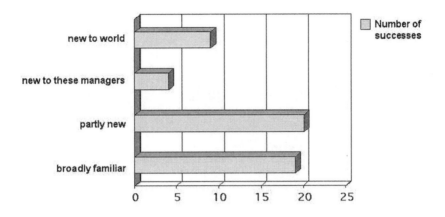

Figure 5.5 Levels of business unit learning

accounting policies, IT choices, and other factors. In the case of Mars, an ice-cream business would have relationships with support functions such as HR, the European research and development function, and the country-based sales and marketing organizations. Each of these functions has established ways of working that may or may not suit the new ice-cream business.

The question that is being asked at this point in the Value Advantage Equation is about the impact of these influences. Do the managers higher up in the hierarchy and their supporting functions understand the new business well enough to give it good guidance and advice, or do they need to learn which parts of their normal influences are appropriate to this new entity and which parts are poisonous? Do the shared resources, such as sales or manufacturing, understand the new business well enough to be a help rather than a hindrance?

Few managers attempt to assess the costs of learning at both the operating level and the corporate level. None, in our experience, puts these costs into the financial analysis. Figure 5.6 overleaf captures these two dimensions of learning. The learning needed at the operating level of the new business is shown on the vertical axis. The learning needed

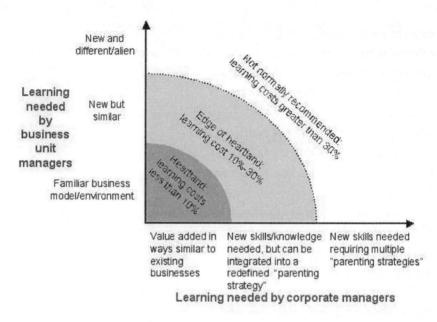

Figure 5.6 The learning challenge

by the corporate managers is shown on the horizontal axis. The more learning required, the greater will be the learning costs.

The difficulty with learning costs is to judge how big they are. The judgment on the vertical axis is about the degree to which the business model of the new business and the types of relationships managers need to have with customers, suppliers, employees, unions, regulators, and other stakeholders are similar to managers' previous experience. What is more, the accumulated experiences of managers generally get built into a company culture, a set of beliefs and behaviors that are often taken for granted by the people involved. This culture pervades the way of doing business, the way of dealing with outside relationships as well as with one another in the company. If the business model or the relationships, or the required beliefs, behaviors, and organizational structures and processes, are different for the new business, the learning costs will be high. If the business model, relationships, and cultural requirements are familiar, the learning costs will be low.

Unfortunately we do not have a clear calibration for what "high" and "low" mean. We have seen managers with inappropriate experience make huge mistakes, resulting in the complete failure of an otherwise promising new business. When WHSmith, a stationery and newsagent company, entered the do-it-yourself (DIY) sector, managers were transferred from the newsagent business into the DIY business. The newsagent business was a mature, dominant retailing format where good performance was easy and improvements were about store ambience, systems enhancements, and product selection. The DIY business was growing fast. Success depended on opening new sites faster than competitors and aggressive branding and pricing in order to get a market leadership position that would give volume advantages. Not surprisingly, the managers from the newsagent business were slow to change, spent too much energy on tinkering with the format, and missed the opportunity to get a leadership position. Do-It-All, the business they were managing, never made acceptable profits and was eventually given away after incurring a string of heavy losses.

If the management team is from the industry, particularly if it is part of an acquisition, the learning costs at the operating level may be zero. More normally they are somewhat negative (at least 5% impact on value) and frequently significantly negative (30% or more impact on value).

In the case of the eye-care and ice-cream examples, it is tempting to think that the learning costs would be low. The health and beauty managers are already experienced retailers, and managers in Mars or Cadbury are experienced in consumer snacks. However, in both examples managers will discover things they need to learn. For example, when Mars entered the business, it launched test products at the time of the two hottest summers in Europe for more than 70 years. Without data going back 30 years and without experience of how to read the market, Mars managers were unsure how much of the market increase was due to their new product offerings versus the summer heat. As a result, they overestimated the volumes they would get and consequently built a factory that was significantly too big. This error alone had a negative impact on the value of their new business that was at least 10% and probably exceeded 30%. Since it is difficult to predict this kind of learning cost, we believe it is wise to presume a somewhat negative learning cost (i.e., 10%), unless the management team has worked for a few years in an identical product/market area.

The judgment on the horizontal axis is also difficult. How far will the parent managers, functional heads and shared resource leaders need to modify their normal behavior and policies in order to give the new business good guidance and influence? If the business can be managed in an identical manner to the other businesses in the portfolio, then learning costs will be low. If the new business requires the parent to learn new behaviors that are compatible to its existing habits and instincts, the learning costs will be significant but manageable. If the new business needs to be managed in a different way from the existing businesses, requiring less compatible behaviors and organizational approaches, the learning costs are likely to be high: over 30%.

For Mars, one of the normal rules of thumb when entering a new category was to build a factory larger than was immediately needed. In the past, this had proved beneficial for two reasons. First, the large empty factory provided the best kind of incentive to the sales team to work hard. As one of the Mars brothers is reputed to have said:

> Build a factory larger than you need and it will cause the sales force to work twice as hard to fill it.

The second benefit comes from economies of scale and market share. The greater the volume relative to competitors, the more competitive the operation will be.

Unfortunately, this corporate influence was instrumental in encouraging the European managers to build a large ice-cream factory. But, partly because of the misleading market data and partly because the sales forces did not feel responsible for the factory—since each sales force reported to a separate country and sold confectionery and ice cream and some other products as well—the factory turned out to be much too large. The influence of the parent company had been negative.

Mars's human resource policies were probably also negative. The ice-cream job was allocated a grade that made sense within the company's broader grading system. However, it made it hard to recruit a manager with the political weight, market knowledge, and strategic skills needed to lead the ice-cream business effectively. Again, the habits of the parent company had a negative influence on the success of the business.

In our experience, stories like these are the norm rather than the exception. When Shell entered the aluminum business, its habits encouraged the aluminum management team to pursue a vertical integration strategy. This had proved a successful strategy in oil, and hence there was some, often unspoken, pressure to try it in aluminum. The result was bad. Shell discovered something that most managers in the industry already knew: that vertical integration does not create value in aluminum.

When Xerox tried to translate its remarkable R&D efforts into a new office-automation business, comprising the Star workstation and the Ethernet, a wordprocessor and a laser printer, the inclination of corporate managers was to require the same product review and involvement in decision making they were used to in the copier business. They had difficulty understanding a business model that required rapid innovation cycles, indirect sales, lower margins, and third-party software. When they hired an outside team and gave them free rein, this team alienated the rest of the company. Xerox ended up abandoning the new business and concentrating on the Japanese challenge in its copier business.

The Mars, Shell, and Xerox examples are common. In our database of successes, which was biased toward situations unfamiliar to the parent company, we found few successes where the parent company managers had lots to learn (Figure 5.7 overleaf).

So how can managers predict whether the impact of the parent company is going to be significantly negative? There are four factors to consider:

❏ *The similarity of the business model of the new business to that of the core businesses.* If the model is similar, the parent influence is less likely to be negative.

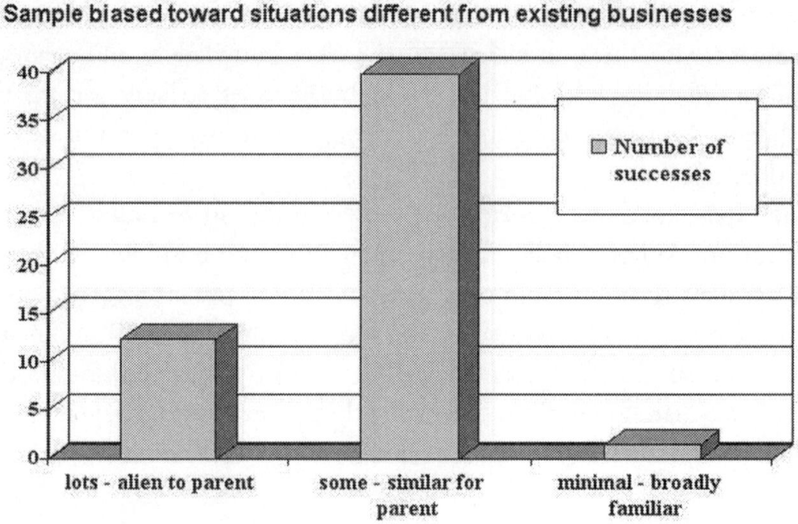

Sample biased toward situations different from existing businesses

Figure 5.7 Levels of parental learning

❏ *The similarity of the needs of the new business to that of the core businesses.* If the new business requires similar cultural beliefs and behaviors and needs similar kinds of support from its parent, the influence is less likely to be negative.

❏ *The commitment and experience of the relevant line managers.* If the line managers to whom the business reports are committed to the new business and have had experience in this new industry, there is less chance of a negative influence.

❏ *The demands of other commitments.* If the line managers are highly committed to this new business and have few other commitments, there is less chance of negative influence.

The managerial temptation is to be positive: to conclude that the parent company influence will be neutral or positive. Our experience suggests that managers should presume that the parent company influence will be a negative 10%, unless there are strong reasons to suppose otherwise. The reason for taking this negative starting point is that, where new businesses are concerned, we have seen more examples of negative influence than positive.

While we recognize the difficulty of putting precise numbers on the overall cost of learning the new business, the biggest danger is to ignore this term of the equation altogether: to assume that managers will be effective in the new area and that the learning costs will be zero. A safer alternative is to assume that the learning costs will be significant (10% at the operating level and 10% at the parent company level), unless there are strong reasons to suggest that they should be smaller or greater.

 HOW ATTRACTIVE IS THE PROFIT POOL?

Insight 3: Managers focus too much attention on the potential of the marketplace they are thinking of entering. Strategy analysis tells us that, in normal situations, a company will earn above-average returns only when it has competitive advantage. Hence analysis of markets should focus on identifying extreme situations that are either so good that even a competitor with disadvantages can earn a good return, or so bad that even an advantaged player may earn less than the cost of capital.

The attractiveness of the profit pool is the second Traffic Light. The profit pool question is about whether the market is a "rare game" (green), a golden opportunity that is likely to give good returns to most competitors who invest today, or a "dog" (red), a rotten market that is either too small, too uncertain, or too competitive, leading to low returns for most players to the point where even the market leader will have a hard time. All other situations, markets that are neither dogs nor rare games, are "possibles" (yellow). If the company has some advantage and executes well, it should make good money.

To help managers identify dogs, possibles, and rare games, we have defined five criteria that need to be assessed (see also Box 5.5 overleaf):

Box 5.5 The potential of the profit pool

Business model potential for high margins
- Value perceived by customers relative to cost of production
- Break-even volume as percentage of market
- Revenue model

Industry structure potential for high margins
- Power of customers
- Power of suppliers
- Competitive rivalry
- Threat from new entrants
- Threat from substitutes
- Growth

Opportunity for us to be a leader in this market

Cost of trying relative to size of profit pool
- Taking account of time to commercialization

Business model vulnerability
- Number of enablers
- Sensitivity to key variables

- ❏ Business model potential for high margins.
- ❏ Industry structure potential for high margins.
- ❏ Opportunity for us to be a leader in this market.
- ❏ Cost of trying relative to size of the profit pool.
- ❏ Business model vulnerability.

The first three questions address the potential for earning a positive spread over the cost of capital. Is the value being offered so important that the customer is likely to pay significantly more than the costs of providing the service? Is the industry one where big margins will not be competed away or bargained away? Is there an opportunity to become the leader and hence earn margins higher than the average?

The next two questions address two other factors critical to the judgment about the attractiveness of the profit pool. Is the ultimate prize—the value of the business once it succeeds—worth the risk, the cash that will need to be put at risk in order to enter the market? How much is the risk under our control: is the profit in the pool vulnerable to the whims of other players, volatility in key variables, or movements in the cycle?

Thus, rare games are markets where the profit potential is so good that almost any competitor entering the business at the right time is likely to make a positive return on its investment. In rare games, the business model gives room for high margins, the industry structure will allow high margins to be earned, and there is an opportunity for the company to become the leader. In addition, the company can enter the market without a big cash exposure and the risks are mainly ones under its control. In other words, all the sub-points are favorable.

The market for internet service providers in the UK in the late 1990s is an example of a rare game. The business model suggested that high margins were possible. The value delivered was significant. Yet the cost of servicing each incremental customer was very small. The volume needed to break even was small compared to the size of the market. The revenue model, which depended on discounts from the telecoms companies and advertising on the portal, made it possible to capture a share of the value being created. In addition, the industry structure was favorable. Customers had little bargaining power. The telecoms providers were more interested in expanding capacity than exploiting their bargaining power. There were no obvious substitutes. The only negative factors were the ease of entry and hence competition between suppliers. Because of the market growth rates and the revenue model, which allowed companies to offer a free service, rivalry was muted. Another positive factor was the availability of the leadership slot, common in new markets. Even the cost of entering the market was small compared to the potential profit pool. The only negative factor was uncertainty about future regulation.

In this rare game situation, many new businesses started up, all of them earning reasonable returns. The leader turned out to be Freeserve, launched by Dixons, a retailer of electrical products. Within three years Freeserve was valued at over £2 billion.

In contrast, dogs are businesses where a weak business model, an unattractive industry structure, and a lack of opportunity for leadership combine with high levels of vulnerability and high risks relative to reward.

The full-service airline business in the US has been a dog market for a number of years. While the business model is not inherently unattractive, the industry structure is bad. The main problem is the substitute: low-cost airlines. Full-service airlines have had to price down to compete with the low-cost companies. In addition, the high fixed costs of the industry have encouraged the full-service companies to compete vigorously with each other as well. When this is combined with the difficulty any new airline would have in becoming the industry leader and the high costs of getting into the industry compared to the size of the profit pool, it is not surprising that no new full-service airlines have been launched in the last 20 years.

In summary, the five elements of the profit pool criteria (business model, industry structure, leadership opportunity, risk/reward ratio, and vulnerability) are not particularly special or unique. The clever part is the insight that managers only need to make a green, yellow, or red assessment. Moreover, since 80–90% of markets are yellow, meaning that they offer reasonable returns for competitors with advantage, managers only need to identify the few outliers. The five elements help managers identify these outliers.

WHAT IS THE POTENTIAL OF THE BUSINESS MODEL FOR HIGH MARGINS?

The business model has the potential for high margins when three conditions exist. First, the value provided to the customer needs to be high relative to the variable (or per-unit) cost of production. A pill sold by a pharmaceutical company is a classic example. The manufacturing cost of the pill may be a few cents, but the value to the customer of better health may be in the thousands of dollars. Similarly, a microprocessor chip made by Intel is relatively inexpensive to manufacture compared with the valuable function it performs in a PC. In both cases, the value is high relative to the cost. The eye-care business is also one where the value to the customer is high relative to the cost of providing the care. The ice-cream business is more balanced. The value is greater than the cost, but not hugely so. This makes high margins harder to earn.

The second factor affecting the potential for high margins is the break-even volume. In investment-intensive businesses, such as steel, where the cost of capacity can amount to billions of dollars, a company may need a large market share to pay for the capital investment. Other businesses such as retailing are less capital intensive, but have high levels of fixed operational costs once a given service level and geographic coverage have been set. These businesses often also require a big share of the market to reach break even.

A pharmaceutical business will require sales of hundreds of millions of dollars to pay back its research costs. A chip manufacturer requires even higher volumes to achieve payback on a new silicon fabrication plant. An eye-care retailer needs to attract a significant share of local trade in order to break even. In ice cream, however, capital intensity is modest, and the break even is low. A small factory may need to operate at above 70% capacity to make good returns, but the factory will only serve a small proportion of the market. Generally, the larger the up-front fixed costs in plant, in service infrastructure, or in developing the product, the bigger the percentage of the market needed to break even.

The third factor is the potential for transforming high customer value into high margins. Businesses selling a physical product are generally able to price their product to reflect the perceived value, depending of course on the intensity of competition (dealt with further below). In certain instances, social considerations and regulation may place constraints on value-based pricing for products like pharmaceuticals or utilities. When the product carries content, like software or music on a CD, value-based pricing can also be difficult. Unless good safeguards can be found, copying or pirating makes it hard to maintain high prices. Equally, businesses selling a service often find it hard to capture the value they create unless they have a business model based on usage or on a subscription. If neither is feasible, as in many types of internet services, advertising may be the only way to derive revenue from the value provided to customers. The revenue model obviously has a critical feedback effect on volume, and therefore on break even.

These three factors affect the size of the available margin and hence the potential profitability. The most unfavorable factor dominates the assessment. In ice cream, the most unfavorable factor is the value-to-cost ratio. The conclusion for ice cream is, therefore, that the business model potential for high margins is average: neither very good nor very bad. In eye care the most unfavorable factor is the market share required in most locations to justify a retail unit. Again, the conclusion is average: eye care does not offer opportunities for exceptional margins.

WHAT IS THE POTENTIAL OF THE INDUSTRY STRUCTURE FOR HIGH MARGINS?

The economics of the business model tells us the potential for profit, but it is the structure of the industry that determines what profit is actually earned. Michael Porter's five forces model is the ideal tool for assessing the structure (Figure 5.8). This model identifies five forces—customer bargaining power, supplier bargaining power, threat of new entrants, threat from substitutes, and competitive rivalry—as being the determinants of actual profitability. In other words, the companies competing in an industry sector, such as pharmaceuticals, eye care, or ice cream, can only earn the profits that their customers, suppliers, rivals, potential entrants, and substitutes allow.

Powerful customers can have a negative impact on profitability. They normally bargain down the price in order to capture as much margin as possible for themselves. Automotive companies are well known as very effective bargainers for low parts prices. Powerful suppliers can also have a negative impact. They also bargain on prices: they push their prices up to suck margin into their business and away from their customers. Intel and Microsoft have been able to exact high prices from PC manufacturers, contributing to the low profits earned by PC companies.

A third force is the intensity of rivalry between competitors. Competitors can be so intent on winning share from each other or competing for leadership that they cut prices, leaving little margin. Home electronics suppliers, such as Matsushita and Philips, have been notorious examples of this behavior. For decades, they have tried to gain superior global market share and dominate industry standards by launching products at attractive prices. The result has been low profitability for most competitors.

The fourth force comes from companies outside the industry. They may enter the market if margins look attractive. This threat from possible new entrants causes existing competitors to keep margins down in order to discourage other companies from coming into the market. This is common in some high-tech industries, such as semiconductors, where prices are frequently kept low to discourage new capacity.

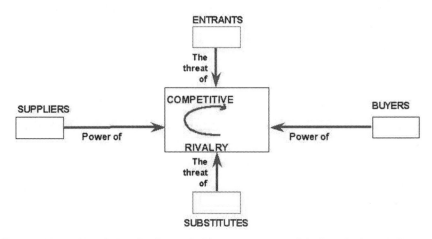

For each force judge whether the force is likely to cause margins in the industry to be below normal levels, at normal levels, or above normal levels

Figure 5.8 Five forces analysis

The fifth force comes from substitute products. Companies often keep their prices down in order to discourage customers from choosing substitute products. Local telecom companies in the US have reduced prices to fend off new entrants and substitute products, like voice over internet.

Any of these five forces can be the cause of low profitability. Companies only earn the full profit potential of their business models when customers and suppliers do not bargain on price, entrants are no threat to prices, there are no price-based substitutes, and competition is muted.

These favorable conditions exist in eye care and pharmaceuticals, but not in ice cream or auto manufacturing. In ice cream in Europe there are few problems with customers, suppliers, new entrants, or substitutes. But the competitors, Unilever and Nestlé, are unlikely to take a new entrant lying down. Rivalry, which is normally not intense, would be likely to increase if a new company entered the business. This would reduce margins for all competitors. In other words, Mars or Cadbury would be likely to earn less than average margins because of competitor reactions. In eye care, a new entrant is likely to earn average margins because the five forces are reasonably favorable.

When assessing a new business the growth rate of the market is normally considered to be vital. Managers place a value on growth simply because growth in revenues and profits is one of the main reasons for exploring new businesses. A marketplace that is growing fast is, therefore, a prize in its own right.

From the perspective of profit pool potential, however, growth is good only so far as it helps raise profitability. It is not valuable in its own right. Growth often affects profitability because it lessens negative forces in Porter's five forces model. Growth makes the customers less demanding because in high-growth markets customers are more interested in the reliability of supply than in the last cent or two of price. Suppliers are less likely to be greedy for margin if they see steady growth. Competitors are more concerned with expanding than fighting for share. Any new entrants that come into the business will be less disruptive because they will be less likely to create volume declines for the existing players. Hence high growth—above 10% volume growth—is normally associated with high profitability.

But growth can be bad news when an industry becomes overhyped. High-growth markets can attract too many competitors. Since most companies are looking for growth, every growth market will be a potential new business opportunity for a number of companies. Frequently, these markets are oversupplied with competitors as each tries to establish a foothold in what they expect to be a promising future. The cellular telephone industry was an example of this in the 1990s, as was the business of fiberoptic communications. The results are high growth and low profits as the threat of new entrants increases and industry rivalry becomes high.

Both eye care and ice cream are growing markets, but neither is growing so fast that it is undersupplied or has become attractive to a large number of new entrants. For these two examples the growth factor is neutral.

WHAT IS OUR OPPORTUNITY TO BE A LEADER?

The potential for the company to achieve a leadership position is important to long-term profitability. Leaders earn greater margins than followers. Leaders are in a position to influence the rules of the game, set standards of performance, and reap scale economies.

In *Profit from the Core*, Chris Zook and James Allen provide some data assembled by their consulting company, Bain & Co. Based on a sample of 185 companies in 33 industries, they conclude that there is a linear relationship between return on capital and leadership. Strong leaders earn 25%, weak leaders 22%, companies at parity earn 14%, strong followers 9%, and weak followers 4%. In the long term leadership is important. Followers have inefficient economics and are more vulnerable to changes in the business that are imposed or readily embraced by large players.

Unfortunately, the path to leadership is sometimes blocked off. The market may have an established leader or a number of large competitors that are unlikely to be up for sale.

If the industry is new to the world or highly fragmented, the leadership position will be open and the opportunity becomes more attractive. Industries requiring high up-front investments in technology, capacity, or infrastructure provide more of an assurance of potential leadership to the first or most-endowed mover than industries where the cost of entry remains low for second or third movers. When the first mover is able to set an industry standard, which will then be used by others, a leadership position is almost assured.

More mature or highly fragmented industries may offer the opportunity of seizing leadership in two ways. One is to buy several existing competitors and consolidate the industry. Another is to upset the status quo with a new business model, technology, or marketing approach. Blockbuster was successful with the latter strategy in the US video rental business and Wal-Mart in the variety retailing business.

In the European ice-cream business the opportunity for leadership is blocked. In Europe, ice cream is dominated by Unilever, with Nestlé a distant number two. However successful Mars and Cadbury might be, they could never hope to wrest leadership from Unilever. In eye care there are dominant competitors, but a new entrant from the health and beauty business might expect some of the eye-care competitors to come up for sale, providing an opportunity to become the leader in the longer term.

WHAT IS THE COST OF TRYING RELATIVE TO THE SIZE OF THE PROFIT POOL?

Entering a new business requires investment. Until the business has established itself, this investment is at risk. The assessment we are suggesting, therefore, is a ratio of the size of this investment at risk (cost of trying) to the size of the profit pool in this new market.

Frequently the amount of money that has to be put at risk is large. This is especially true for new-to-the-world businesses that require many years of technical development and test marketing before the business case can be proven. An example is the domestic combined heat and power project at BG Group. The objective was to create a small gas generator that can be sold to households to provide heat and electricity. After more than 10 years of research the product is still not on the market. Another example is the emergence of electronic detonators for explosives. First developed in the late 1980s, the technology has taken more than 10 years to become commercial.

The assessment that managers have to make is whether the market is large relative to the cost of proving that the business can be profitable for the company. If the total investment needed before profitability has been proven is $10 million, the market would need to be at least $100 million to be attractive. This ten-to-one rule of thumb is based on some simple calculations. If we assume the company gets 20% of the final market and earns a 10% margin, there will be a margin of $2 million per annum available to pay for the start-up costs. It will, therefore, take five years to pay back the start-up costs of $10 million—hence our rule of thumb that the market needs to be at least 10 times the risk investment. Any market size less than 10 times the risk investment is a potential dog. A really attractive market is 50 times the size of the risk investment (i.e., the start-up costs can be recovered from one year's profit assuming a 20% share). If the share ambitions are much lower than 20%, then the size-to-investment ratio needs to be much larger.

For the ice-cream and eye-care decisions, both markets are more than 50 times the risk investment needed to prove the opportunity.

HOW VULNERABLE IS THE BUSINESS MODEL?

Some business models depend on the cooperation of partners or other stakeholders for their success. For example, when Apple launches a new computer platform, its success is dependent on gaining the support of software companies to produce applications that will run on its platform. When Intel launches a new microprocessor, it is dependent on the decisions of a few computer manufacturers. With a large share of the market, Intel's business model is secure. But any new entrant is vulnerable to decisions taken by a few players.

The same is true of businesses in regulated industries where changes in regulation may protect or expose incumbent suppliers.

Often the regulatory framework is quite stable and does not make the business model vulnerable. But in industries like telecoms or health care, uncertainties about regulation can create significant vulnerability.

A third cause of vulnerability comes from joint venture partners. Business models that depend on the commitment of joint venture partners or even suppliers of some key ingredients can be vulnerable to changes in the strategies of these companies.

A further source of vulnerability can come from competitors, who may react in unforeseen ways that limit the capability of a new entrant. Competitors in the electronics industry, for example, have defended their positions by locking in customers through the use of standards and cross-business or multicountry deals, which make market access difficult for a newcomer.

Finally, business models can be vulnerable to movements in critical variables—exchange rates, commodity prices, or prices of substitute products.

The telecoms industry provides an example of high vulnerability. A telecoms operator intending to roll out a new 3G network will depend not only on regulation to permit the construction of the network but also on investments made by suppliers of handheld devices and providers of services. Failure to get support from these bodies will leave the telecoms company without a market for its network.

Both the eye-care and ice-cream businesses appear, on first analysis, to have low vulnerability. They do not depend on partners, suppliers, or regulation, and they are not overly exposed to movements in raw material prices or exchange rates. Deeper analysis, however, would expose a key vulnerability for any new entrant in the European ice-cream business. Unilever and Nestlé own some freezer compartments in retail outlets and will be likely to try to prevent any new entrant from placing its products in these compartments. In a worst-case scenario, this could prevent Mars and Cadbury from distributing their products through some retailers.

CALIBRATION

We have not tried to calibrate each of these variables in the profit pool potential or work them into some equation. The reason is that the judgment required—dog (red), possible (yellow), rare game (green)—does not demand accurate calibration.

A dog market is one where:

❑ the economics of the business model are poor, meaning that the value to the customer is only slightly greater than the cost of production and the break-even volume demands at least a 50% market share; or

❑ the industry structure, even with the benefits of growth, is such that few if any competitors will cover their cost of capital; or

❑ the cost of proving the idea is more than one tenth of the market size; or

❑ the business model is dependent on partners, stakeholders, or variables that are uncertain and could be disastrously negative.

These markets should be avoided regardless of the outcome of the other parts of the Traffic Lights.

A rare-game market is one where all the criteria are favorable, where:

❑ the value to the customer is more than twice the variable costs of production and the break-even point requires a market share of less than 5%; and

❑ the five forces are all favorable and growth is greater than 10%; and

❑ there is an opportunity to become the market leader; and

❑ the market size is more than 50 times the investment needed to test the opportunity; and

❑ the business model is not vulnerable to any major uncertainties.

In these markets, companies can contemplate investing even if they do not have a clear advantage and even if the impact on the existing businesses is slightly negative.

Managers have found it relatively easy to use this tool. Around 90% of markets turn out to be yellow. Hence the analysis is normally focused on making judgments at the boundaries. A few markets will be borderline rare games and a few will be borderline dogs. Rather than agonize over which side of the border to put a market, it is often better to acknowledge that it is a borderline case and move on to the next part of the Traffic Lights.

For both of the two case examples—European ice cream and eye care—the assessment is yellow. The business models have average potential for high margins. The five forces are worrying in European ice cream, but unlikely to warrant a red light: Unilever and Nestlé will compete hard but are unlikely to destroy pricing in the industry. Neither market offers easy access to market leadership. Neither is small relative to the cost of entry. Neither is unusually vulnerable. On balance, the European ice-cream market appears to have a less attractive profit pool than eye care, but both fall in the middle, yellow category.

One final point: A thorough analysis of all the factors under profit pool potential requires a great deal of data. This is rarely available. Our advice is to start by assuming that the profit pool is "yellow." Then scan down the five elements to see if any appears to suggest that a "red" or "green" assessment might be more appropriate. If a red or green assessment seems possible, more detailed analysis will be necessary. In European ice cream the only factors that might signal an assessment other than yellow are the competitive rivalry element in the five forces and the fact that leadership is blocked off. Closer analysis of these two factors would then be necessary.

 ## DO WE HAVE STRONG LEADERS AND EFFECTIVE SPONSORS?

Insight 4: Managers do not give sufficient attention to the issue of who is going to run a new business and, particularly, who the new business is going to report to.

The third Traffic Light is about people. Our research, evidence from the venture capital industry, and pure common sense all point to the importance of people. In our successful cases we were struck by the unique people involved, the often chancy way in which they had come together, and the special experiences that influenced their thinking. In the venture capital and private equity industry a well-worn phrase is that there are only three factors for success: management, management, and management. And common sense tells us not to enter a team in a sporting competition and expect to win unless we have some exceptional players when compared to the opposition. People are important.

Yet new business projects are frequently launched, with the help of managers in a business development function and supported by consultants, on the presumption that the operating management team can be recruited later. If the activity is familiar and the company has a pool of capable managers ready to step up to the challenge, this approach is reasonable. However, if the activity is less familiar, involving a different business model, it will be hard to find the necessary management talent.

The questions that need to be addressed under this Traffic Light are (see Box 5.6 overleaf):

❑ Do the leaders of the new business (the unit head and his or her team) have the passionate commitment, personal insights, entrepreneurial flexibility, execution skills, and influence with the parent that will enable them to overcome the inevitable setbacks, skepticism, and roadblocks, and win in the marketplace?
❑ Does the new business have a sponsor who will provide a compatible home for it in the portfolio, exercise effective oversight, protect it from negative influences, and support it through setbacks?

HOW GOOD ARE THE UNIT LEADERS?

We need to make judgments about some important qualities in the leaders of any new business. First, we need to assess passion and

Box 5.6 Leadership/sponsorship quality

Relative quality of MD/leadership team of the unit
– Commitment
– Personal insights
– Entrepreneurial flexibility
– Execution skills
– Influence with the parent

Status of sponsor within main parent
– Significant line manager
  • Channel resources to the new business, especially during setbacks
  • Persuade other businesses and services to give help
  • Protect the business from overenthusiastic functions
– Compatible home and effective oversight

commitment. Do the leaders of this new business feel passionate about it? Are they going to struggle hard when the going gets tough? Are they going to be able to remain positive when faced with setbacks?

Second, we need to understand the leaders' personal insights. Do the leaders have personal insights about this business based on experiences they have had in other jobs or in the early pursuit of this project? Managers who have personally serviced the first few clients, designed the first few products, assembled and delivered the first orders have often learnt some important lessons and developed advantages over those who have only ever seen the business from the top down.

This combination of commitment and personal insight is necessary when managers are faced with setbacks, skepticism, and roadblocks. The personal belief that "I know there is a pony in here somewhere" will provide the motivation needed. As one of the two founders of Homeserve, a home plumbing and support business that sells annual insurance, said:

We would never have succeeded without Richard [his partner]. He remained convinced that we would succeed, even when all the data was telling us that we were failing.

This faith was based on some personal insights that the two ex-Procter & Gamble managers had developed in their early attempts to get into the plumbing business. They had learnt the following:

❏ Finding an honest plumber is difficult, especially in an emergency.
❏ Customers are concerned about overcharging, even though they are prepared to pay a premium for a good job done in a hurry.
❏ It ought to be possible to provide a plumbing service like the cover you get for your boiler: an annual insurance with guaranteed service levels.
❏ Direct mail is an excellent marketing tool because it is possible to pinpoint the household that is likely to be a customer.

The judgment about personal insights is not all about experience. In fact, long years of experience in a sector can create locked-in mindsets.[3] A management team that has not been programmed by history may be much better able to read the signs about impending changes than the incumbents.

The third quality is entrepreneurial flexibility. One certainty is that the original business plan will need to change and the market and competitor landscape will develop in unexpected ways. As Barry Gibbons, ex-CEO of Burger King, explained: "Your business plan contains the one and only scenario that is guaranteed not to happen."[4] In the face of this reality, the team in charge of the new business needs to have the entrepreneurial skills and courage to adjust its plans when circumstances change.

The fourth quality is execution skills. New businesses involve setting up new operations, systems, and organizations. We need to be confident that the management team has the skills to execute these business-building tasks. This is partly a matter of functional expertise and partly about execution orientation.

The final quality is influence in the parent company. For some new businesses, such as the ice-cream market example, links with the core businesses are critical for success. The new business is likely to depend on other businesses to sell or manufacture or market its product. But even for new businesses with minimal links to the core businesses, as would be the case in the eye-care example, influence within the parent company is necessary to get funding and gain the freedom to break the corporate rules.

The overall assessment of the unit's management team, therefore, is about some specifics, such as insights and influence, but it is also about the overall quality of the management team compared to others. If the different management teams in the industry were put up for auction, would our team sell for a significantly higher or lower price than that of the lead competitor?

If the team is led by top-quality managers, with some track record of taking advantage of new developments and reacting swiftly to new events, some experience or insight relevant to this business, and some passion for success, we can grade unit leadership as green. Sir Peter Davis, then CEO of Prudential, one of the UK's leading insurance companies, hired Mike Harris to run Egg, an internet banking venture. Mike Harris had previously started up First Direct, the UK's first telephone banking operation. He had been involved in converting First Direct to an internet bank as the technology changed. He had also had other successful new business experiences. He and the team he gathered around him were head and shoulders above the management teams of the other internet banks that were starting at that time.

When Royal Bank of Scotland invested in Direct Line, Britain's first direct insurance company, the team led by Peter Wood consisted of two managers with especially strong IT skills, as we saw in Chapter 3. The combination of the entrepreneurial skills of Peter Wood and the IT skills of his colleagues Mike Flaherty and Roy Haveland, all of whom had worked together and innovated together for their previous employer, Alexander Howden, were far superior to those of other direct insurance companies set up around that time. As IT capabilities developed and changes happened in the marketplace, the Direct Line team was quickest to embrace the opportunities and adjust its business model. In fact, the main rival to Direct Line turned out to be Churchill, a company set up by one of the original Direct Line team.

Stories of personal insight, entrepreneurial drive, unique skills, and leadership courage are common in texts on innovation and new businesses. Gary Hamel tells the tale of IBM's internet success in a remarkable *Harvard Business Review* article.[5] He focuses on two characters: David Grossman, "a typical self-absorbed programmer and mid level IBMer stationed at Cornell University's Theory Center, a nondescript building hidden away in the south east corner of the engineering quad," and John Patrick, "a career IBMer and life long gadget freak, who had been head of marketing for the hugely successful ThinkPad laptop and was working in corporate strategy scouting for his next big project." By chance the two link up and become the spark that "built a bonfire under IBM's rather broad behind."

More normally, however, the team chosen to set up a new business has no claim to be the most capable and entrepreneurial in the marketplace. Frequently it consists of a technical person who has been working in the parent company's research function, a commercial person with analytical skills who has been involved in assessing the viability of the project, and a CEO recruited from outside. The chances of this combination being the winning team is low. Hence we suggest that managers start by presuming that this part of the leadership/sponsorship Traffic Light will be a reddish yellow unless there is strong evidence to suggest otherwise.

The only exception to this negative presumption is when the new business is new to all competitors. When Dixons launched Freeserve, a UK internet service provider, the business was new to all competitors. Dixons had no reason to believe that its managers were clearly the best in the industry, but equally it had no reason to suppose that they were inferior. When the business is new to all competitors the starting presumption should be one of neutrality and a yellow score awarded unless there is clear evidence either way.

In our sample of successes, over two-thirds involved management teams who, with hindsight, were unusually strong. In other words, over two-thirds of the successes would have scored a green light for leadership/sponsorship. The venture capital mantra of "management, management, and management" appears to be borne out by the data.

HOW EFFECTIVE ARE THE SPONSORS?

Sponsors are important because they can make up for qualities that are lacking in the management team of the new business, because they have authority over the new business, and because they can help the new business get the positives from and avoid the negatives in the broader parent company. The sponsor should have the following qualities:

❑ He or she should be a manager in the main reporting line with some significant businesses reporting to him or her. The CEO of the parent company or the head of a division or a region is a good sponsor. The head of business development, the head of a corporate venturing unit, or the head of research would be a less good sponsor.
❑ The sponsor needs power to be effective at three critical tasks: channeling resources to the new business, especially during times when resources are scarce; persuading other businesses, corporate functions, or shared resources to give help to the new business; and protecting the business from inappropriate influences from corporate functions or other parts of the organization. A sponsor with significant power in the hierarchy and with significant discretion over resources is ideal. He or she can channel resources to the new business when the official supply dries up. He or she can provide hidden subsidies to the new business when financial performance is weak. Most importantly, he or she can support the new business when doubters, skeptics, and setbacks undermine the organization's commitment. Without a strong sponsor or the likelihood of one, it is often unwise to embark on a new business.
❑ In addition to having control of some resources and having power and influence in the structure, the sponsor should also provide effective oversight and an understanding home for the new business.

❑ The sponsor needs some personal knowledge of the new business or the time and inclination to learn fast.

❑ He or she must be able to spend the time to challenge and coach the business and share in some of the critical decisions that need to be taken along the way.

❑ The sponsor should be influential in the development of the new business. The more the sponsor has the ability, motivation, and real understanding to exert that positive influence, the higher the chances of success. That is why a CEO, or a line manager, is only a good sponsor when the new business is an important part of that manager's strategy.

Companies often set up business development divisions and corporate venturing units to try to create good sponsors. The presumption is that a manager in charge of a portfolio of new businesses will have the time to learn about them and understand the development issues they face. In contrast, a corporate CEO or division head will often have limited time and will be tempted to treat the new business in the same way that he or she treats other businesses. Unfortunately, although the head of a new businesses division may have more time to learn and more understanding of the particular challenges involved in the development stages, he or she usually lacks power in the broader organization (see Chapter 8 for more discussion of corporate venturing units).

A compromise position is to have the new business report to a line manager within the power structure and then provide extra support from a business development function. This has been IBM's solution in its Emerging Businesses program. An arrangement such as this would score yellow. It would only be possible to get a green light for the sponsorship part of this Traffic Light if the sponsor is a line manager with the necessary power in the organization and the appropriate skills.

In our sample of successes, 90% (where we had information) reported to the CEO or a main division head. In just under a quarter of these, the CEO was the initiator of the original plan. Having a strong sponsor in the parent company appears to be as important a factor as having a strong management team at the business level.

Alza was a successful US west coast drug-delivery company. It helped major pharmaceutical companies develop powerful delivery mechanisms for the compounds they had discovered. However, like most drug-delivery companies, Alza was ambitious to become a pharmaceutical company in its own right. One reason was that the margins are much bigger. Despite a number of attempts in the 1970s and 1980s, Alza failed to make the transition. The business of acquiring compounds and taking them to market just seemed too different to its core business of adding delivery technology to other people's compounds.

Then, in the mid-1990s, Alza hired Ernest Mario as its chairman. Mario had been head of Glaxo Wellcome and had led Glaxo through its fastest growth years. Within five years, Mario helped Alza do what it had failed to do in the previous fifteen. For Mario, pharmaceuticals was more core than drug delivery. He found it easy to sponsor and guide the initiatives needed to help Alza make the transition. A few years later, Alza's success was spotted by Johnson & Johnson, who paid a high price to acquire what Mario had created. Unfortunately, now that Alza has achieved its ambition, the original drug-delivery business is getting too little investment and management attention.

Another example of the power of appropriate sponsors is Rexam. When Rolf Borjesson left PLM, a Swedish canning company, to head up Rexam, he inherited a disparate portfolio of specialty paper and plastic packaging businesses and an array of other activities. As he sorted through his options he became more and more convinced that the best plan for Rexam was to become a focused packaging company. At an opportune moment, he bought his previous company, PLM, and followed with other acquisitions in the canning and glass packaging industries, becoming one of the best-performing stocks on the London exchange during the difficult 2000–2003 period. These moves into cans and glass were a huge leap for Rexam, but a small step for Rolf Borjesson. In fact, he understood the canning and glass industries rather better than the specialty packaging businesses he had inherited. It was not difficult for him to be an effective sponsor of these new businesses in Rexam's portfolio.

SCORING AND OVERLAPS WITH OTHER PARTS OF THE TRAFFIC LIGHTS

The leader/sponsor Traffic Light has some overlap with the value advantage Traffic Light. The insights of the leaders or the sponsors may be part of the unique contribution. Also the knowledge that leaders and sponsors have of the new business will affect the learning costs. Hence there is a danger of double counting.

Experience suggests that where double counting does occur it is more likely to be a benefit than a disadvantage. Because the people issues are easy to underestimate when assessing value advantage, the tendency is to give more weight to tangible factors like patents or brands. There is, therefore, a benefit in giving extra emphasis to people issues under the leader/sponsor Traffic Light.

An aggregate score for the leader/sponsor Traffic Light depends on the sum of the leadership and sponsorship assessments. The leadership element should be given greater weighting. However, a strong sponsor can make up for some leadership weaknesses and vice versa. The Traffic Light should not be scored as green without strong leadership and strong sponsorship. It should be red if the leaders are clearly weaker than the competition or if the sponsor has little influence in the parent company or a mindset molded by a different business model. In all other situations the assessment will be yellow.

In the eye-care and ice-cream examples the leadership/sponsorship score would depend on the individuals involved at the time. At Mars and Cadbury there were few, if any, managers with experience in ice cream in Europe and none with personal insights. This would have signaled a potential red light. The health and beauty company considering eye care is likely to be in a similar position unless it recruits a quality manager from the industry or buys a high-quality smaller competitor.

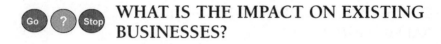 WHAT IS THE IMPACT ON EXISTING BUSINESSES?

The fourth Traffic Light is about the impact the new business will have on existing businesses. The impact might be significantly positive as a result of customer or cost synergies (green), significantly negative as a result of conflicts of interest and/or distraction of key managers (red), or somewhere in between (yellow). There are two dimensions to consider: synergies and distraction risks (see Box 5.7).

Box 5.7 Impact on existing businesses

Size of positive or negative synergies

Risk of distraction costs
- Operating level
- Sponsor level
- Scarce shared resources

HOW BIG ARE THE SYNERGIES?

Synergies can be positive or negative. When commercial banks entered insurance, the benefit for the core business came from greater use of the existing branch networks. By selling additional products and services through these branches, the fixed cost was spread across a larger volume of business. On the other hand, when Grand Metropolitan owned a gaming business alongside its food brands, such as Green Giant, there were negative synergies. The bad reputation of the gaming industry undermined Grand Metropolitan's overall reputation in the US. The solution was to sell the gaming business.

In some situations synergies can be so important to the existing businesses that they become the dominant logic for the new activity. Irish Life, Ireland's largest life insurance and pensions company, merged with Ireland's largest building society (savings and loans) for the benefits it brought to the insurance business. It provided the insurance business with an additional channel of distribution, the branch network of the building society.

When Centrica, a gas and electricity utility, set up the credit card Goldfish, the main logic was the loyalty benefits for the core business. Competitors were introducing loyalty programs that could threaten the core utility activities. Goldfish was Centrica's response. It turned out to be so successful that it quickly developed into a broader financial services business. After a few years the threat from competitors diminished, undermining the loyalty logic for Goldfish. Without the synergy, Centrica decided to sell Goldfish to Lloyds TSB, one of Britain's leading financial services companies.

When medical diagnostic imaging moved beyond classical X-ray into CT scanners and magnetic resonance, all the major X-ray suppliers like Siemens, Philips, GEC/Marconi, and GE developed into the new business. They needed to offer magnetic resonance products to be a credible supplier to hospital X-ray departments.

The synergy criterion is about the benefits for existing businesses. In many cases there are no positive or negative synergies for existing businesses. More than 75% of our database of success stories had no significant synergy benefits for existing businesses. Moreover, it is also comparatively rare for the synergies to be significantly negative. In other words, this criterion is often neutral.

However, in those few situations where synergies are significant, they can be a critical element in the Traffic Lights evaluation. In 11 cases from our database synergies were significant. In five of these, strengthening existing businesses was the prime initial reason for developing the new business.

In the eye-care and ice-cream examples this criterion would probably be neutral. It could be argued that there would be benefits to existing businesses from having the brands more widely used in the marketplace. It could also be argued that a larger company with more businesses offers better career prospects and can, therefore, attract better managers. However, both of these possible positive synergies are likely to be small and can be challenged. The extra exposure of the brands could dilute the image of existing businesses. The greater spread of businesses could make the company appear less coherent to prospective managers. Hence a neutral score is likely to be the most easy to defend.

WHAT ARE THE DISTRACTION RISKS?

Insight 5: Managers often underestimate the loss of performance in the core businesses that occurs when attention shifts to new businesses and some of the most energetic managers are allocated to new business projects.

Distraction risks, our way of capturing the risk of lower performance in existing businesses, depend on two factors:

❏ The degree to which the challenges in the existing businesses demand scarce management and financial resources.
❏ The degree to which the new business will compete for these scarce management or financial resources.

The greater is either or both of these factors, the greater is the scope for loss of performance in existing businesses. The distraction may not result in an actual reduction in performance. The loss may be between actual performance and potential.

However, we have also observed that when managers start investing in new businesses, they often underestimate both the opportunities for growth in their existing businesses and the threats these businesses face from competition.

In order to understand the risks of distraction, managers need first to understand in what areas their existing businesses most need attention. To help managers, we have developed a checklist of questions (see Box 5.8) that identify those areas where existing businesses most need attention. Armed with this analysis, it is easier to judge whether a particular new business is likely to distract from the attention that the core needs.

Box 5.8 Attention tests for existing businesses

❏ *Maturity test*—are existing businesses fully mature (low growth, high levels of saturation, low rates of innovation, and commoditized products)? If not, attention will be needed to keep abreast of developments.

❏ *Dominance test*—are existing businesses dominant in their respective markets (market share twice that of the second player)? If not, attention will be needed to defend the existing position and win share from competitors.

❏ *Profitability test*—are existing businesses generating margins that are better than competitors', given their market and position? If not, attention will be needed to restore profits to their rightful level.

❏ *Threat test*—is the horizon calm (no complaining customers, no new entrants, no new distribution channels, no disruptive innovations)? If not, attention will be needed to find the best response to these threats.

❏ *Consolidation test*—is the industry fully consolidated (three or four major players)? If not, attention will be needed to assess merger partners and prepare for integration.

❏ *Internationalization test*—has the business reached its limits of internationalization (a major player in every major market)? If not, attention will be needed to explore different countries, find entry routes, and drive market share.

❏ *Extension test*—are extensions into adjacent channels, segments, products, or value-chain positions blocked off? If not, attention will be needed to explore these extensions.

Assessing the risk of distraction from a specific new business proposal involves thinking about how the new business will compete for operating managers, for sponsor-level managers, and for scarce resources. At the operating level it is necessary to assess whether the new business will be staffed by any managers from the core. If so, which managers, how critical are they to the areas where the existing businesses need attention, and how easy are they to replace? Often new businesses draw on some of the most innovative and energetic managers in the core, resulting in less innovation and energy focused on the challenges in the core. The head of one business development team explained:

> We always end up talking about the same five or six managers. These managers are important to the core business and are the ones most likely to be able to make a success of our new projects.

Not surprisingly, the struggle over resources in this company was won by the core business and, while we were doing the research, the new businesses team was disbanded.

At McDonald's, Partner Brands such as Chipotle and Pret A Manger might be viewed as providing low distraction risk at the operating level. However, it depends on how these brands are managed. At Chipotle 50% of the top team consisted of managers transferred from the hamburger business. At Pret A Manger the percentage was lower, but not insignificant. Moreover, both of these brands had been acquired to see if it were possible to inject McDonald's skills to help them improve and grow. Hence it was intended that they would take up the time of some managers in the core. Given the attention needed in the core business and given the plans for brands like Chipotle, the distraction part of the "impact on existing businesses" light would have been red.

The second source of distraction is competition for resources at the sponsor level in the parent company. If the person to whom the new business is reporting has other pressing priorities in the core business or could be usefully deployed on priorities in the core business, there is a significant risk of distraction. In a large company like McDonald's, this might seem a low risk. There are large numbers of managers. However, the top teams even at companies like McDonald's or in divisions such as McDonald's South America are often small. If one of these managers is spending significant time on new businesses, it will be at the expense of investing that time in the core business.

At McDonald's the Partner Brands were formed into a division. This was partly to give them more attention and partly to avoid distracting too many managers. However, over five or six years, this division had three or four different heads. Either the head was needed for a more important job in the core business or he proved to have skills that would be better used in another part of the business. In other words, McDonald's found that its Partner Brands were competing for management talent at the sponsor level in the organization.

The third source of distraction risk involves considering how the new business will compete for critical shared resources, like experts in industrial design or miniaturization or software. When a high priority is placed on succeeding in a new business, these experts are drawn away from projects in the core business. If these skills are critical to an area where the core needs attention, the distraction risks are high. However, even if the skills are not part of a current priority, if they are critical to long-term success the core can suffer imperceptibly over time.

Between 1999 and 2005, Mercedes fell from number 3 (out of 38) in the JD Power reliability ranking to number 28 (out of 37) and in 2004, profits from the Mercedes car marques fell 60% to levels not seen since the late 1990s. The reason reported by the *Financial Times* was "the seconding of many of its engineers to work on Chrysler's problems in Detroit."[6] This is a good example of the long-term impact of a new business acquisition made seven years earlier.

We were surprised how frequently the distraction cost issue was raised. Simon Yun-Farmbrough, then head of planning at Prudential, first alerted us to it. He pointed out that the success of Egg had distracted managers in Prudential from making changes in the core UK insurance business. This business was suffering from the rise of direct-to-consumer business models. Egg was Prudential's direct-to-consumer response. However, the initial reason for launching Egg was to help revitalize the UK insurance business. As Egg became more successful and more independent from the UK division, it distracted attention from the issues in the UK and began to make less direct contribution to the cultural changes needed in the UK.

McDonald's was another situation where our attention was drawn to the issue of distraction risks. McDonald's was so concerned about the need to give attention to the core business at the same time as developing new businesses that it set up two executive committees— one for the core business and one for new businesses. This dual structure was a mechanism designed to help managers invest in new businesses without distracting from the core. More recently, the issue is still on the agenda. The Partner Brands have been placed in McDonald's Ventures, and Mats Lederhausen has been asked to decide whether any of them can be significant without distracting from the core.

At Intel distraction risks were also on the agenda. Intel defined two priorities: Job 1, running the core business, and Job 2, investing in new businesses. It was clear to managers that Job 1 was more important, but work should be done on Job 2 so long as it did not risk performance at Job 1.

What surprised us was that, despite this broad awareness of distraction costs, managers did not appear to take them into account when assessing individual projects. The assumption was that the managers in the new businesses should fight as hard as possible for resources. However, although this contest would have a cost, the bigger concern was about the impact on the new businesses rather than on the existing businesses. Our argument is that the cost to the existing businesses can sometimes be many multiples of the benefits from the new business, even if it succeeds. Hence sponsors of new businesses, and even the managers pushing individual proposals, need to make an objective assessment of the likely distraction costs as part of the proposal to proceed.

This objective assessment is best done by defining the main areas where the existing businesses need attention, and then assessing the potential for distraction at the operating level, the sponsor level, and any levels where scarce resources are shared.

In the eye-care example, distraction risks would be likely to be low unless the new eye-care unit draws many managers from the existing health and beauty business or unless the health and beauty unit has important challenges that will require the full attention of its senior management team. In the ice-cream example, distraction risks might be higher. Within Mars, for example, the ice-cream business would need to draw on research, marketing, and manufacturing skills. It would also take up significant time of a senior sponsor, probably the CEO of Europe. Although the risks of distraction are higher in the ice-

146

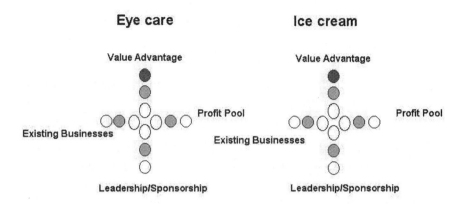

Figure 5.9 Eye care and ice cream summaries

cream example, they are still probably in the yellow rather than the red. With the exception of the CEO's time, the ice-cream venture is unlikely to be drawing on any hard-to-replace resources.

Go ? Stop THE TRAFFIC LIGHTS IN SUMMARY

The Traffic Lights may seem a little daunting. There are four major judgments that need to be made and each depends on a number of sub-judgments. In our experience, however, the Traffic Lights are relatively easy to use. Frequently it takes less than one hour to talk through the four Traffic Lights and to arrive at a preliminary conclusion. Parts of this preliminary conclusion may be easy to challenge, but frequently the overall judgment—red, yellow, or green—is not in disagreement. If it is, more work is needed and sometimes this can take days or weeks to complete. However, it is rarely wasted work. If the judgment is improved, a better-quality decision will result.

The two cases we have been analyzing—ice cream and eye care—can now be summarized (see Figure 5.9). In both cases the answer is to reject the proposal as presented. It does not make strategic sense for a health and beauty retailer such as Boots in the UK or an upscale fashion and beauty retailer such as Neiman Marcus in the US to enter the eye-care business. Nor does it make strategic sense for Mars or

Cadbury to enter the ice-cream business in Europe. In both cases the probability of earning above-average returns is too low.

In reality, Boots did enter the eye-care business in the UK using the Boots Opticians brand. The early results were encouraging. The brand did help generate traffic. However, in part due to being small and in part due to learning costs, the new business found it hard to make significant profits. Then a new competitor, with more aggressive pricing and a franchising model, entered the business making it less attractive for all competitors. Boots's position as one of the weaker competitors is now at risk. In the US, Neiman Marcus probably never even considered entering the eye-care business. As a comparison, it did enter the gourmet food business at one point, but abandoned it after a few years for predictable reasons.

Mars chose to enter the ice-cream business in Europe, while Cadbury did not. With hindsight, Cadbury's strategy of licensing its valuable brands to an ice-cream company has proved to be more value creating. Over more than a decade, Mars has found it difficult to make a profit from its ice-cream sales. Long term, it may have to invest considerably more effort in the ice-cream sector to gain a sustainable position in Europe, and is unlikely to earn a return that justifies the investment. Meanwhile, Cadbury has been earning good royalties for the use of its brands, an earnings stream that has not required the company to invest significant additional capital.

Decision making for new businesses is often focused around a detailed financial analysis and implementation plan. As a result, critical evaluation of the strategic rationale can receive insufficient attention. This is what we believe happened in the Boots and Mars examples. If these companies had used a screening tool such as the Traffic Lights, their strategic evaluation would have caused them to reject the project before doing detailed financial analysis or implementation planning. It would also have helped them develop better proposals to exploit the advantages and resources they had.

The Traffic Lights are a set of questions that managers need to answer that in aggregate form a strategic business case. They are designed to be used early in the life of a project. They can be used as a sanity check for a financial business plan, but they can also be used before managers have developed enough information to compile a business plan. This positioning of the Traffic Lights is important. They can be used very early on before much information is available to assess the potential; they can be used after some exploration and experimentation have been done and more information is available; or they can be used alongside a full business case analysis after detailed research has been carried out on a new project.

The Traffic Lights do not focus on execution issues. They do not, for example, assess whether suitable partners can be found or whether the technology will work. These are important issues, but it is hard to make judgments about them at the idea or even business plan stages. The Traffic Lights presume that operational issues can be surmounted. They focus on the soundness of the strategy rather than the ability to execute. The execution issues are addressed in Chapter 9, when we introduce the Confidence Check.

The Traffic Lights do not provide clear go/no go decisions for every situation. However, they frequently give a no go answer in situations where managers are inclined to "give it a try." As a result, the Traffic Lights screen out a large percentage of new business projects that would subsequently fail, saving managers both time and money.

There should be very little in the Traffic Lights with which experienced strategists or academics disagree. The intention has not been to create some dramatic new theory. The intention has been to pull together the fundamentals of good strategic thinking in a way that will help managers arrive at better judgments. The insights are not major theoretical breakthroughs. However, they are important advances in our thinking: they were insights to us.

Despite offering no new theory, the creation of the Traffic Lights has advanced our thinking about diversification. For readers who like to position ideas against current theory, the next chapter reviews the literature on diversification and positions the Traffic Lights within this stream of thinking.

CHAPTER 6

DIVERSIFICATION

D iversification has come to mean something bad. It is a word that is associated with "overdiversification," "conglomerate," and investments unconnected with existing businesses. When asked whether a new business project is a diversification, managers will frequently respond in the negative: "This is not a diversification, it builds on our relationships with ... and it exploits our skills at ..."

Yet given the way we have defined new businesses—new business model and separate organizational unit—all new businesses involve some form of diversification: they all take the company into some new markets and involve some new management skills. Hence, for those readers who like to place ideas in context, it makes sense to look back at the literature on diversification and position the New Businesses Traffic Lights against other theories about what sorts of diversification make sense.

The concept of diversification—entering new businesses—was first discussed in the 1960s. Since then there have been two parallel tracks of thinking about the issue. One track has focused on the vertical reporting relationship in an organization and has explored different views about why it would make sense for companies to have a spread of businesses and what sort of skills the corporate-level managers need to have in order to justify entry into new businesses. We will call this the General Management School. The second track has focused on the lateral relationships in organizations, the relationships between businesses. This track of thinking has explored different views about the sorts of connections, overlaps, and relationships that need to exist between businesses to justify entering a new area. We will call this the

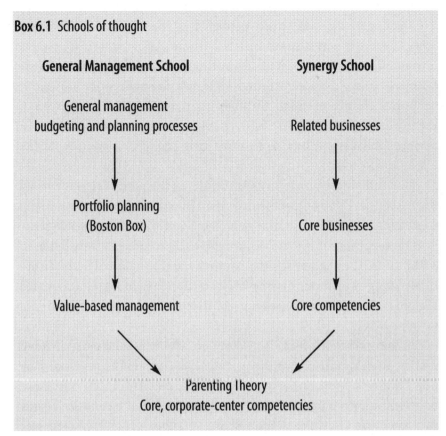

Box 6.1 Schools of thought

General Management School   Synergy School

General management budgeting and planning processes → Portfolio planning (Boston Box) → Value-based management

Related businesses → Core businesses → Core competencies

Parenting Theory
Core, corporate-center competencies

Synergy School. Frequently the different tracks become intertwined, but it is worth distinguishing between them for purposes of greater understanding (Box 6.1).

GENERAL MANAGEMENT SCHOOL

In the 1960s many companies, such as ITT in the US and Slater Walker in the UK, diversified widely. The logic at the time was "general management skills." These companies believed that they had developed an understanding of how to make money in business, and skills at planning, budgeting, performance monitoring, and control that enabled them to buy almost any underperforming business and tune it up.

Their thinking was given credence by the rise of the business schools and the belief that management was a profession that could be learned. Good managers had, it was thought, the skills to manage any business. Initially, therefore, the logic for diversification was one of performance improvement through good management. Managers in the parent company knew how to improve the performance of an acquired business or how to help set up a greenfields business so that it would succeed.

This thinking became hard to refute as the conglomerates of the time, such as ITT, outperformed most other companies. As a result, many companies followed the same logic and started diversifying.

The recession of the 1970s brought this diversification trend to an abrupt stop. Companies ran out of money, and were faced with the task of deciding which businesses to keep and which to close or sell. Helping them was a consulting company called Boston Consulting Group (BCG).

Building on work BCG had done on why companies with leading market shares make the highest profits, its consultants developed the now famous Boston Box (Figure 6.1). This, the first of the consultant's matrices, asked companies to plot their portfolio of businesses against two axes: their relative market share and the market's growth rate. Based on these two inputs, the matrix categorized each business as cash cow, dog, question mark, or star. Companies were advised to keep their cash cows, because these provided the funds to fuel growth, keep the stars, because these provided today's growth opportunities, and invest in a few question marks and new businesses with star potential, which would provide tomorrow's growth. Dogs and doubtful question marks could be sold or closed.

The logic for being in multiple businesses was still based on general management skills: any business was acceptable. What the Boston Box added was a financial logic and a growth logic. Companies can provide a service to shareholders by putting together a portfolio of different businesses that produce a balanced, stable performance record. When choosing which businesses to include in the portfolio, companies should try to maintain a balance: some cash cows to fund expansion,

Market share

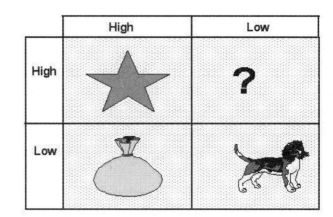

Figure 6.1 The growth share matrix

some stars to deliver today's performance, and some investments in "businesses of the future" to deliver tomorrow's performance. The growth challenge for managers was thought to be about identifying businesses of the future and maintaining a reasonable portfolio balance.

Excited by the rigorous analysis supporting the Boston Box, many companies applied it not only to cull their existing portfolio but also to define target companies to acquire or target markets to enter. Companies with high growth prospects looked for cash cows to help fund their growth. Companies with low growth prospects looked for high-growth businesses that could be propelled into a leadership position.

By the mid-1980s, however, disillusionment had started setting in. Researchers were noting that the best performers in most industries were companies like Coca-Cola, McDonald's, or Boeing, which were not diversified: companies that stuck to one business.[1] At the same time, managers in diversified companies were finding it hard to manage their wide spread of businesses. Diversified companies were underperforming focused companies. Some were even choosing to spin off businesses and break up their portfolios. In addition, the finance theorists were arguing that shareholders could spread risk more easily than companies. It made no sense, they argued, for companies to diversify in order to produce a portfolio with a stable performance. Shareholders could do it more cost effectively themselves.

By the early 1990s, with the collapse of the last committed conglomerates such as Hanson, the General Management School of thinking had become completely discredited and the Synergy School had become dominant. Nevertheless, with tools like value-based management, the idea that corporate-level managers could develop skills that are appropriate to a wide range of businesses was still alive.

THE SYNERGY SCHOOL

Like the General Management School, the Synergy School has deep roots. The idea was that some businesses are sufficiently similar or have sufficient connections that they can be or need to be managed by one company. The concept was discussed in the 1960s by Igor Ansoff, one of the earliest business strategists.[2] He invented the product/market matrix, suggesting that managers should avoid diversifying into businesses that involve both new products and new markets (see Figure 6.2). He also invented the term synergy as applied to business.

In the early 1970s, Richard Rumelt published a study of diversification giving factual support to Ansoff's ideas.[3] He noted that over 50% of companies had diversified into multiple businesses. However, when he correlated performance against type of diversification, he found that the "related diversifiers" performed best. The implication was that companies should diversify into businesses that are related in product, market, or skill terms. The idea of relatedness caught on. Those companies that were not diversifying based on a belief in general management skills were actively looking for related businesses.

The process of defining related businesses begged the question "related to what?" The answer was "related to our core businesses." But this required companies to define their core businesses. Hence this school sparked a process of defining core businesses in order to be able to identify related businesses.

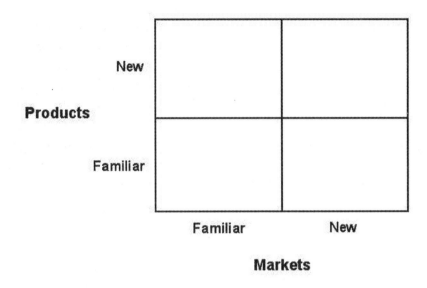

Figure 6.2 The product/market matrix

The development of the resource-based view of strategy in the 1980s gave a further boost to the Synergy School. This argued that success in any industry goes to the company that has the most appropriate resources in terms of location, relationships, assets, technology, skills, and other factors. Since commonly available resources, such as skills that can be hired easily from the marketplace, do not distinguish one company from another, it is the unique resources a company possesses that drive its success or failure.

When the resource-based view was applied to the issue of diversification, Gary Hamel and CK Prahalad came up with the idea of core competencies.[4] Successful diversified companies, they argued, are companies that possess an operating competence important to the success of all of their businesses. The competence might be a certain kind of marketing, such as P&G's skill at mass-market consumer goods. It might be a technology, such as 3M's knowledge of thin film coatings. Any competence that is important to the success of a number of different businesses could, Hamel reasoned, provide the logic for diversification. To decide which new businesses to enter, managers should identify their core competencies and spot businesses where these competencies add value.

The popularity of the core competencies idea was in part due to the fact that it provided a potential answer both to the question of what is core and to the question of what is related. It seemed compelling at the time.

PARENTING THEORY

Work by Michael Goold, Andrew Campbell, and Marcus Alexander in the early 1990s attempted to bring the two schools together into one theory of diversification.[5] Parenting Theory stated that general management skills, such as planning and control, could not provide the logic for diversification decisions because, by definition, the skills are generally available. This undermined part of the logic for the General Management School.

However, special and not generally available skills do exist at the corporate levels of some companies. For example, financing mines in awkward places at awkward times in the cycle and with awkward political risks is a skill possessed by the mining company Rio Tinto. This helped it diversify into a range of mining industries. The skill of orchestrating a cadre of product managers across an international network helped Unilever diversify into more and more countries and expand its portfolio of fast-moving consumer products. Companies with unique corporate-level skills and other resources, such as brands or relationships or patents, can, Goold and colleagues suggested, diversify into new businesses where these skills or resources will add value. Parenting Theory acknowledges the importance of corporate-level skills. However, rather than focusing on the general management skills at the corporate center, Parenting Theory focuses on the unique skills that one corporate center has compared to others. It is these unique skills that justify one parent owning a business rather than another.

Parenting Theory also challenged the basic ideas in the Synergy School. Parenting Theory stated that lateral relatedness between businesses was not in itself enough to justify diversification. There were two challenges to the relatedness thesis. First, synergy potential is not a sufficient reason on its own. Synergy, in the form of alliances and coordinated working, can be achieved between independent companies. Coca-Cola can have a joint marketing campaign with McDonald's without owning McDonald's. Hence relatedness only offers a logic for diversification if the synergy opportunity requires joint ownership.

If the synergy benefits can be achieved without joint ownership, an alliance or licensing deal or trading relationship is all that is needed. Joint ownership is only required for synergies that cannot be achieved through arm's-length arrangements. For example, if one company believes that it can improve the performance of another company by imposing its strategy on the other, joint ownership is normally needed. Also, if one company believes that there is potential to cross-sell products with another company, but the other company does not, joint ownership is required to release the potential. Only some kinds of synergy require joint ownership. Therefore, only some kinds of synergy justify diversification.

The second challenge to the Synergy School was that, even when there is a synergy logic that requires joint ownership, it may not be sufficient to justify joint ownership. For example, in the aluminum industry, most companies in smelting have tried to get into fabrication and other downstream businesses. Not only are these businesses less capital intensive, offering higher returns on assets, but they can pull volume through the fixed-asset smelting business.

In practice, almost all the attempts failed. The reason for the failure was not the lack of synergies from pulling through extra volumes, but the different management skills required in the downstream businesses. The upstream parent proved to be "incompetent" at managing the downstream businesses, which lost money or underperformed. The implication is that lateral synergies can only justify diversification if ownership is necessary *and* if the management approach needed in the new business is one that the parent managers understand. This normally means that the management approach that is best for the new business needs to be similar to the approach applied in the existing businesses.

Putting together these thoughts about top-down skills and lateral synergies, Parenting Theory defines three conditions that need to exist to justify entering a new business.

❏ First, the business must be underexploiting its potential in some way: there must be an opportunity to improve it either through top-down management guidance or through synergies.
❏ Second, the parent company must have the appropriate top-down skills or synergy capability so that the improvements can be achieved.
❏ Third, parent-company managers must understand the management approach needed in the new business well enough to be able to adjust normal corporate policies and rules of thumb so that the new business is not inadvertently damaged.

Parenting Theory focuses on the role of the parent managers. It is these managers who will deliver the top-down guidance, orchestrate the necessary synergies, or damage the new business with inappropriate guidance, people decisions, or policies. The alignment between the General Management School and the Synergy School is achieved by recognizing that there are top-down reasons and synergistic reasons for entering new businesses. Parent managers play a vital role in both. Whereas the Synergy School focuses on core operating competencies and the General Management School focuses on corporate-level skills, Parenting Theory combines the two in focusing on the unique skills of parent managers: the core, corporate center competencies (see Box 6.1).

Like both schools, Parenting Theory is a competitive theory. Companies should be aiming for a "parenting advantage": their core competencies at the corporate level should be superior to those of rival parent companies.

ASHRIDGE PORTFOLIO DISPLAY

Parenting Theory is summarised in the Ashridge Portfolio Display (Figure 6.3).[6] The axes of the display capture both the potential for parent managers to add value to a business and the risk that they will inadvertently harm the business. Top-down guidance or synergy management is part of the value-added axis. This is where Parenting Theory has brought together the ideas from both the General Management School and the Synergy School. The other axis, the risk of value destruction, is largely overlooked by both schools. One of the contributions of Parenting Theory is to give attention to this value-destruction axis.

Businesses that fall in the top right of the matrix are ones where the parent company can add a lot of value and there is little risk of value destruction. For Unilever, these would be fast-moving consumer goods businesses in new geographies but in product categories where Unilever already has other businesses. For Exxon, these would be oil exploration, refining, or distribution businesses in geographies where Exxon can link to existing assets. These "heartland" businesses are the company's core businesses.

"Edge-of-heartland" businesses are ones where either there is less opportunity for the company to contribute value or more risk of value destruction. They are businesses where the parent managers will need to learn some new skills in order to succeed. For example, when Mars entered Russia after the collapse of the Communist bloc, it was entering a marketplace of which it had little previous knowledge. The edge-of-heartland section of the matrix is the equivalent to the new product/same market or new market/same product sections of Ansoff's product/market matrix.

"Value traps" are businesses where there is an opportunity to add value, yet the management approach needed to make the business a success is so different from the experience of parent managers that there is a big risk of value destruction. Aluminum fabrication businesses, for example, were value traps for aluminum smelting companies.

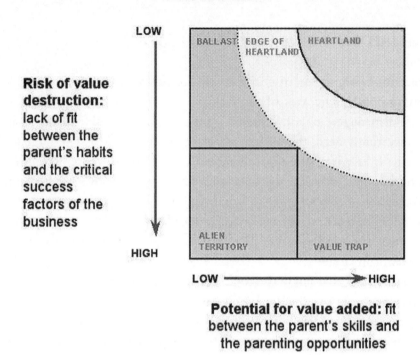

Figure 6.3 The Ashridge Portfolio Display

When Unilever acquired Elizabeth Arden, an up-market cosmetics company, it was venturing into a value trap. While the product development, manufacturing, distribution, and research activities of Elizabeth Arden were all familiar to Unilever, the pricing and marketing of the products to up-market customers was less familiar. In the early years of ownership, Elizabeth Arden's performance improved significantly as Unilever's skills in areas such as research and product development influenced Elizabeth Arden managers. However, over a decade, the mismatch between the management approach for a mass-market company like Unilever and that needed for an up-market company like Elizabeth Arden caused problems.

After more than 10 years of ownership, Unilever sold Elizabeth Arden in a private equity deal. Within a couple of years, the managers of Elizabeth Arden had changed many of the policies from the previous era, significantly accelerated growth, and improved profits. Despite being able to add value to Elizabeth Arden in the early years,

Unilever's investment was not a success. The skills of managing up-market brands were sufficiently alien to most Unilever managers that they inadvertently gave some wrong guidance and imposed some wrong policies.

"Alien territory" in the Ashridge Portfolio Display includes businesses where the company has nothing to contribute and the management skills needed are unfamiliar. For Unilever, aluminum smelting would be in alien territory, as would fast-moving consumer goods for an aluminum company.

"Ballast" refers to those businesses parent managers know well, but are able to add little to. Normally these are businesses that have been in the company for a long time. The managers at the parent level probably spent most of their early years in these businesses and ran them before rising to the corporate level. The corporate guidance and policies are aligned to these businesses, but the businesses are already well managed: there is little opportunity to add value. The margarine businesses in Unilever might be ballast, as might US oil exploration for Exxon.

The Ashridge Portfolio Display gives guidance about the sorts of businesses a company should consider entering. First, it should enter businesses in its heartland: businesses where it has a lot to add and where it understands the management challenges. Second, if there are no heartland opportunities, the company should consider edge-of-heartland opportunities: businesses where the ability to add value is less certain or the knowledge of the challenges facing managers less complete. Third, the company should avoid businesses where it can contribute little or where its understanding of the management challenges is weak.

Does the Ashridge Portfolio Display, published in 1994, say more than Ansoff's product/market matrix, published in 1965? Yes and no. Both matrices suggest that managers should stick to businesses they understand and diversify into new businesses cautiously. Ideally they should build on knowledge they already have and avoid businesses where everything needs to be learnt afresh. The difference is that the Ashridge Portfolio Display emphasizes different dimensions of knowledge. Parenting Theory focuses on the skills of parent managers and on the management approach that these managers find most natural, while the Ansoff matrix focuses on knowledge about the markets or the products.

Clearly, the products and markets that form the current core businesses will have influenced the skills of the parent managers and the management approach that they find most natural. In other words, there is a link between Ansoff's thinking and the Ashridge thinking. But the focus of the latter is the management approach that the parent managers find most natural and how appropriate it is for the new business. Some products or markets may seem similar using the Ansoff matrix, for example aluminum fabrication for an aluminum smelting company or up-market perfume for Unilever, yet require a rather different management approach and involve some different management skills.

The Ashridge Portfolio Display also focuses on added value. Given that there will be some learning costs in any new business, it is important that the parent company brings some contribution to the new area. Without some value added, the parent company will find it hard to earn back its start-up costs, acquisition premium, or learning costs. Ansoff's matrix presumes that management will be able to add value to businesses in similar product or market areas. This is not necessarily the case.

The final point to make with regard to the Ashridge Portfolio Display is the link between the display and the research project that led to this book. The research was aimed at understanding how some companies successfully entered businesses that are not in their heartland or edge of heartland. How did Mannesman, a German engineering company, become a major mobile phone operator? How did Dixons, an electrical goods retailer, become the leading internet service provider in the UK? How did GE, a manufacturing company, become one of the strongest global players in financial services? How did DSM, a mining company, transform itself into a competitor in the life sciences industry? As a result, our database of successes is skewed to situations in the edge of heartland or outside. Most of the new thinking contained in this book is therefore about how companies diversify into areas that are not obvious.

LINKING PARENTING THEORY AND THE TRAFFIC LIGHTS

The Traffic Lights, we believe, have taken the thinking about diversification decisions a step further forward. They build on Parenting Theory but, informed by our research, they add some important new elements and give additional focus on some others (see Box 6.2).

First, Parenting Theory has a lot of links with the value advantage section of the Traffic Lights. The "valuable contribution" element is similar to Parenting Theory's added-value concept. What does the company bring to this new business? However, the thought in the Traffic Lights is more inclusive than the added-value concept in Parenting Theory. Whereas Parenting Theory gives special attention to the contribution of the parent levels, the Traffic Lights just demand that there is some significant contribution. For example, when Boots entered the wellbeing services business, one of the contributions was spare space at some of its drugstore sites. This kind of contribution is not easy to label as parenting added value. By using the looser term "valuable contribution" and recognizing that this contribution can come from operating levels or parenting levels, the Traffic Lights have an advantage over Parenting Theory.

"Tradability" is an element particular to the Traffic Lights. This is a significant addition to previous thinking. Since the reason for entering a new business is to create additional value, the Traffic Lights point out that a new business is only needed if the value cannot be created through a less risky approach: a sale, a license, an alliance, or a joint venture. Parenting Theory does not include an equivalent concept.

When taken together, the "contribution" and "tradability" variables often arrive at an answer that is similar to the "added value of the parent" variable. This is because many types of contribution, such as the spare space in Boots's drugstores, can be traded for value. In other words, a contribution is frequently discounted because it can be turned into value without entering a new business. Contributions that are hard to trade are often skills or knowledge, particularly corporate-level skills

Box 6.2 Traffic Lights and Parenting Theory

Elements of Traffic Lights	Parenting Theory coverage
❏ Value advantage	❏ Addressed directly, but
– Unique contribution	– focused on parent level
– Tradability	– not included
– Contribution of rivals	– included
– Learning costs	– focused on parent level
❏ Profit pool potential	❏ Not included
❏ Leaders/sponsors	❏ Focus is on sponsor more than leader
❏ Impact on existing businesses	❏ Does not include distraction risks

and knowledge. As a result, sources of parent added value are often among the strongest reasons for entering a new business.

The "contribution of competitors" is taken into account in all theories that acknowledge the competitive nature of business. Parenting Theory, like the Traffic Lights, explicitly recognizes the importance of rivals: the value added by the parent needs to be greater than that of competitors.

The "cost of learning the new business" is another element where the Traffic Lights offer a more complete picture than Parenting Theory. The Traffic Lights include the cost of the learning that will need to be done by the managers leading the new business unit, as well as the cost of the learning that will be required by parent managers. Parenting Theory only explicitly addresses the latter. Parenting Theory presumes that business-level managers will know their business well enough. If the new business is an acquisition, this may be the case. However, if the new business is a greenfields operation, the managers in charge may have little experience in the new area.

Second, the Traffic Lights include a section on the profit pool potential. This section is not part of Parenting Theory, in the same way that it is not part of Ansoff's matrix or core competence thinking. These theories are all focused on the fit issue: does this new business fit with the company? Clearly, however, fit is not the only issue. As every manager knows, there is also the question of how attractive the new market is. In fact, for most managers this is a more important question than the fit one.

As we explained in Chapter 5, most markets offer the opportunity to earn a good return, at least for good competitors. However, some markets do not, and these "dogs" need to be avoided. Also, some markets are so attractive that they offer good returns even for weaker players. These "rare games" may provide the opportunity for a diversification that would not be considered for other reasons.

Third, the leadership/sponsorship section is unique to the Traffic Lights, but it is connected both to the concept of value destruction that is central to Parenting Theory and to the concept of competition.

Unless the leaders and sponsors of the new unit are strong individuals who are trusted by the rest of the organization, the new unit is liable to be subjected to the rules and policies applied to the other businesses. Hence value destruction by parent managers, a frequent danger when developing a new business model, is best kept in check by having strong leaders and sponsors who can fight off the well-meant, but deadly, influences.

Strong leaders and sponsors are also essential for winning in the marketplace. Without them, a new business has little chance of taking advantage of changes in the market or weaknesses in competitors. Strong leaders and sponsors could be thought of as part of the contribution or added value that the company brings to a new business. However, leaders and sponsors are treated as a separate term in the Traffic Lights because the research exposed how critical they are to success.

Fourth, "impact on existing businesses" is another term that is partly unique to the Traffic Lights. The Parenting Theory concept of added value includes positive and negative synergies, but it does not include distraction risks. The research that led to the Traffic Lights has highlighted this element, suggesting that special attention should be given to the impact of distraction risks.

In summary, the Traffic Lights include some ideas that are not part of Parenting Theory, such as tradability, profit pool potential, and distraction risks. They also give some added focus to issues such as unit leadership and operating-level contributions. As a result, the Traffic Lights give more clarity to the edge-of-heartland section within Parenting Theory and point at two types of diversification that would be overlooked by Parenting Theory: saplings and rare games.

SAPLINGS AND RARE GAMES

In our database of 50 successes, a number of the successes could not be classified as either heartland or edge of heartland. In fact, the database was put together in order to understand these "outside-heartland" successes.

Saplings are a type of new business opportunity. Saplings are activities that are already part of the company, but are not heartland or edge-of-heartland activities. In fact, they are often not thought of as separate businesses. They exist for two prime reasons. They were created in support of some core business or they were acquired along with some core activity and never sold. For example, Hewlett-Packard started making its own computers in the 1960s because it was finding it hard to get a reliable supply of minicomputers to support systems using its test equipment. In the 1970s, the unit started selling minicomputers for use with other technical systems not involving its instruments. The management of the unit frequently tried to persuade the parent company to allow it to enter the broader computer business for general-purpose commercial applications. However, HP was reluctant to take on IBM and other large mainframe companies. Then in the early 1980s, as IBM was dismantling its research into RISC technology, HP decided to acquire IBM's research team and enter the general-purpose computer business. Over the following 20 years, the computer business grew 25-fold and became the dominant part of HP.

Another example is from the drug industry. Boots, a British retailer of drugs, also owned a pharmaceutical business. This pharmaceutical business primarily produced prescription drugs, but it also manufactured a few over-the-counter products for sore throats and minor ailments. When Boots sold its pharmaceutical business, it retained these over-the-counter products and decided to set them up as a separate, globally focused consumer products business. The products had never been given much marketing support by their pharmaceutical parent and Boots was able to build a substantial business in over-the-counter consumer products.

These are two examples of how an activity that exists for one reason can sometimes be turned into a significant new business, even though it is not in heartland or edge-of-heartland territory. Other examples include GE's financial services business and GrandMet's drinks business.

Just being an existing activity is not enough. The special quality of a sapling is that it has a very strong management team. Often the management team of this activity has been trying to raise the status of the activity within the portfolio, but has been turned down or ignored. This was true in both Hewlett-Packard and Boots. The sapling analogy is appropriate here. Think of a young tree that has been cut back two or three times but is still growing vigorously.

The Traffic Lights explain why saplings make sense. Saplings will normally get a yellow light for value advantage even though they are not heartland or edge-of-heartland businesses. This is primarily because they will have low learning costs. Because the activity has been part of the portfolio for a few years, the learning has already happened. Saplings will get a yellow light for profit pool potential, as do most businesses. Saplings get a green light for leadership/sponsorship because they happen to have unusually strong management teams. Finally, saplings get a yellow or green light for impact on existing businesses because they normally exist originally to support the current businesses.

Based on our database, the sapling category is important. It accounts for about 15% of our sample (see Figure 6.4 overleaf). The implication is that companies seeking new businesses should look around their existing activities to see if any of these are potential saplings. They do not have to look very hard. Because saplings have

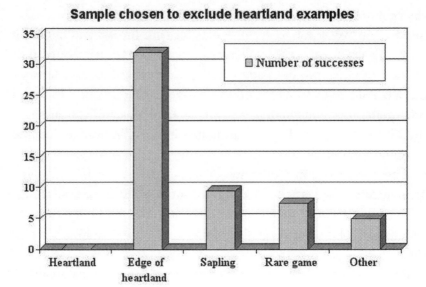

Sample chosen to exclude heartland examples

Figure 6.4 Parenting logic

strong and pushy management teams, they are likely to be noisily communicating their ambitions already.

The problem with saplings is that, as they grow, they will not sit easily with the existing businesses. If they do, they are more edge of heartland than sapling. More normally, they either take over the nest, cuckoo-style, or they are subsequently sold. In the case of Hewlett-Packard, computers took over the nest and turned the company into a very different organization both in portfolio and cultural terms. At Boots, the drug-retailing business is so dominant that the consumer products business, Boots Healthcare International, will almost certainly be sold at some point. At GrandMet the drinks business became the dominant division and provided the logic for the merger with Guinness. Subsequently all the other businesses have been sold. At GE financial services has become the biggest generator of profits and is likely to be demerged at some point.

Rare games are the second type of new business opportunity that falls outside heartland and edge of heartland. Rare games are those few business opportunities that will reward almost anyone who invests at the right time: bulk chemicals in the early 1970s, personal computers in the early 1980s, telecommunications in the early 1990s.

Rare games exist when demand outstrips supply for a significant number of years and when the main advantage comes from investing early. Companies who invest early have written down assets by the time others enter the market. This enables them to earn a decent return on their investment, even when supply catches up with demand.

Rare games get a yellow light for value advantage because the advantage of early investment balances the disadvantages of learning costs. Moreover, they are normally "new-to-the-world" opportunities, such as internet service provision, where no company has any obvious value advantage. They get a green light for profit pool potential. They get a yellow light for leadership/sponsorship, so long as the company can find quality managers to lead the effort. Finally, they get a reddish yellow light for impact on existing businesses, because they are normally unrelated to existing businesses and require different managers.

In our sample, around 15% of the successes are rare games at least in part. Hence, even though rare games account for probably less than 5% of the opportunities, they are an important category for a company looking to diversify.

DISRUPTIVE TECHNOLOGIES

A category of new businesses that has been much discussed in the last five years is the so-called disruptive technologies. This term was coined by Clayton Christensen and means that either the product technology or the business model is difficult for existing competitors to copy. Christensen argues that many of the most significant new businesses are successful because they benefit from disruptive technologies.

In this section we will compare the Traffic Lights criteria with Christensen's disruptive technologies criteria to show that the Traffic Lights are more comprehensive. Those readers unfamiliar with Christensen's work or uninvolved in technology-led industries may want to skip to the end of the chapter.

Christensen identified two types of disruptive innovations:

❏ Low-end disruptions that start with a technology better able to serve the bottom end of the market. Over time as this new technology develops, it gradually becomes competitive in more and more up-market segments.

❏ New-market disruptions that start with a technology or business model that can serve the "non-consumers," potential customers who are excluded from the market because current products do not meet their needs or are too expensive. As the technology develops, it also becomes more and more competitive and gradually wins share from the mainstream.

In his latest book, Christensen argues that disruptive innovations are the best way to develop significant new businesses. Companies looking to create a significant new business should focus on looking for and then organizing to support disruptive innovations.

Christensen suggests that low-end disruptive opportunities arise because companies pursue product improvement and innovation, often outstripping the needs and desires of many customers. Customers at the low end thus become overserved, and are often unprofitable as a result. Innovation at the low end, providing simpler and cheaper products, can be very attractive to newcomers. If the innovation is sufficiently low cost it can be highly profitable. Incumbents have no immediate incentive to retaliate since price retaliation could undermine more profitable segments and their least profitable customers are being targeted; indeed, losing these customers is often beneficial in the short term. Thus margins remain high for the traditional incumbents.

The real threat to incumbents is that the technology used by the newcomer improves. Over time it becomes competitive in more and more segments. Steel mini-mills are a classic example, entering in the late 1960s via reinforcing bars (poor quality, low cost, highly unprofitable products for major integrated steelmakers), only to innovate upward through the product range, product by product, until they now dominate the industry.

In addition to new-market disruptions, Christensen also distinguishes between sustaining innovations and disruptive innovations. Sustaining innovations are those that can be incorporated as part of a company's existing business model. Incumbents nearly always succeed against newcomers if the innovation is sustaining and nearly always fail if the innovation is disruptive. Hence, companies wanting to enter new businesses should look for disruptive innovations.

In summary, he identifies three types of innovation:

- ❏ *Sustaining innovation*, which can be incremental or breakthrough performance improvement in attributes valued by the industry's most demanding customers, targeted at the most profitable customers most likely to pay for improvement, and improves profit margins by exploiting existing processes and cost structures, making better use of current advantage.
- ❏ *Low-end disruption*, which provides good enough performance at a lower price, targeted at lower-end, overserved, often unprofitable segments with a new operating or financial business model that is profitable on low price.
- ❏ *New-market disruption*, which provides lower performance in traditional attributes but higher in new attributes (e.g., simplicity and convenience), is targeted at non-consumption (typically customers without the money or skills), and with a business model that makes money at lower unit prices and volumes.

Christensen's advice to companies to look for disruptive innovation opportunities is good counsel. These opportunities can produce remarkable performance as the disruptive innovation gradually wins out against the incumbent players. However, disruptive innovation opportunities account for less than 10% of our success stories. Christensen would argue that this is because managers have only recently understood the enormous potential of focusing on disruptive opportunities. In the future, he would predict that a higher percentage of successful new businesses will come from following a disruptive innovation strategy. As a result, we thought it would be useful to compare his advice with our Traffic Lights concept.

CHRISTENSEN'S CRITERIA

Christensen poses a number of tests to help identify disruptive opportunities. For a new-market disruption:

❑ Is there a large population who have not had the money, equipment or skill to do this for themselves, so have gone without or paid someone else to do it?
❑ To use the product, do customers need to go to an inconvenient central location (i.e. involve high search costs)?

For a low-end disruption:

❑ Are there customers at the low end who would be happy to purchase a less good (good enough) performance at a lower price?
❑ Can we find a profitable business model at discount prices?

In addition, to help managers decide whether an innovation is sustaining or disruptive:

❑ Is the innovation sustaining to at least one significant incumbent, so giving them an immediate incentive to retaliate?

DISRUPTIVE TECHNOLOGIES AND VALUE ADVANTAGE

Christensen points out that any company in possession of a disruptive technology has a huge advantage compared to the incumbents using the old technology: the unique contribution is likely to be large relative to the other terms in the Value Advantage Equation. However, he overlooks most of the negative items in the equation. He does not distinguish between innovations, such as patents that can be "traded," and those, such as new business model ideas, that require the owner to enter the new business. Also, he does not explicitly recognize the dangers of other companies entering the business with the same technology, but with other advantages to bring to the market. Finally, he does not address the learning cost issue. One of the reasons disruptive innovations cause incumbents to lose out to new entrants is the learning costs. The incumbents need to unlearn the rules that apply to their current business before they can fully learn the rules that apply to the new business.

DISRUPTIVE TECHNOLOGIES AND THE PROFIT POOL

Christensen's criteria are not easily compared with our Traffic Lights. On the issue of profit pool potential, disruptive innovations are likely to have attractive business models, although this may be less evident at the early stages of the new technology. As the technology improves, the business model becomes more and more attractive. Hence when dealing with disruptive technologies, it is important to look ahead at the business model that may be possible once the technology has developed. Disruptive technologies are also likely to be high-growth opportunities and to present the potential for leadership.

In addition to a focus on disruptive innovations, Christensen also argues for managers to be "impatient for profit" and "patient for growth." This suggests that he, like us, favors opportunities where the cost of proving the potential is small relative to the ultimate market.

Christensen does not address directly the five forces criterion. In our experience, this is a common oversight. Managers are drawn by the size of the opportunity and forget that promising opportunities often attract many competitors in a race that makes it hard for any to earn a decent return. The telecommunications business in both mobile phones and fiberoptics is an example.

Christensen also does not explicitly focus on vulnerabilities. Some new technologies are particularly vulnerable to developments by partners or complementers. Also, improvements in existing technologies often occur in a way that undermines the profitability of the new technology.

Christensen's disruptive technologies are therefore likely to score well on profit pool potential unless they involve technologies that are made available to many competitors or are particularly vulnerable. In fact, if it is possible for a company without the new technology to enter the new area, it is likely to be unattractive from a five forces perspective. This suggests that most disruptive opportunities would score either green, because a few competitors have hard-to-copy technologies, or red, because the technology is available and likely to attract many competitors.

DISRUPTIVE TECHNOLOGIES AND LEADERS/SPONSORS

Christensen does not given enough attention to the role of leaders or sponsors of the new business. His focus is on the disruptive innovation and he presumes that appropriate leadership will accompany the innovation. Often this is not the case. There are many examples of an innovation being developed in a particular company or country only to be exploited by a different company or country. This is because the innovator did not have the leadership skills to develop the business.

Christensen gives more attention to the sponsor issue. He recognizes the danger of inappropriate sponsorship and recommends that disruptive innovations should be set up in separate divisions reporting at the same level as the businesses with which they are competing. Again, however, he presumes that the manager to whom the new business reports can be an appropriate sponsor. While he provides ample evidence of parent companies whose influence on a new disruptive technology is negative, he presumes that the solution is for them to understand the importance of disruptive technologies. Our experience suggests that the causes of negative parenting are often much deeper and harder to overcome than Christensen suggests. Given that these managers will almost certainly have grown up in the rival business, it is unlikely that they will be good sponsors.

DISRUPTIVE TECHNOLOGIES AND THE IMPACT ON THE CORE

Christensen acknowledges the negative synergies implied by disruptive technologies, pointing out that these are often one of the reasons for incumbents failing. He correctly argues that incumbents should ignore these negative synergies because they will happen anyway. If the incumbent does not cannibalize its own business, some competitor will gain market share.

Christensen, however, overlooks the distraction risks. By launching and supporting a rival business model, the company may be hastening the collapse of its existing businesses in a way that would not happen if it focused on the incumbent business model. Certainly a paranoid pursuit of every new innovation, in case it proves to be a disruptive technology, is likely to lead to underperformance when compared to a company that sticks to its core business.

In analyzing our case studies of success, only three seem to fit the disruptive model: IBM with its PC, Dixons and Freeserve, and the Royal Bank of Scotland and Direct Line. The rest relate to a variety of other insights, for example a sustaining innovation, the acquisition of assets at an attractive price, or opportunities from discontinuous change such as new market regulation or other political events.

Although car insurance business Direct Line clearly has been a highly successful disruptive business model, it does not entirely fit the Christensen template. It was not targeted at the low end of the market. It exploited better information about risk and the realization that the least risky, and so most profitable, customers were cross-subsidizing poorer risks. Wood and his colleagues at Direct Line thus focused only on this segment, using a low-cost operational model. Incumbents had every reason to retaliate, and eventually did so. Direct Line's phenomenal profitability was badly damaged for a period, but it had created a sufficiently strong position to ride the storm and come through to be the UK's biggest and most profitable car insurer.

As well as the three examples that broadly fit the disruptive innovation model, three have been the direct consequence of disruptive innovations in adjacent markets. UK retailer Dixons has ridden the PC disruption with PC World, and the mobile telephony disruption with The Link. However, the new retailing concepts were sustaining innovations for Dixons. Acer, a Taiwanese computer manufacturer, made the transition from games modules to major computer company through early moves in PC clone manufacture. Although the PC was a disruptive innovation for IBM, it was a sustaining innovation for Acer.

In conclusion, Christensen's concept of disruptive innovations is useful and suggests some additional questions that managers should ask when assessing the attractiveness of the business model and the size of the unique contribution. However, identifying a disruptive innovation is neither necessary nor sufficient for those seeking significant new businesses. Once a disruptive opportunity has been identified, managers still need to put it through the Traffic Lights to decide if they should launch a new business. More important, there are many ways of successfully developing new businesses that do not involve disruptive innovations.

A MORE COMPLETE THEORY

In this chapter we have compared the Traffic Lights with previous theories about diversification. We have focused in particular on Parenting Theory, not only because it has become the dominant theory of corporate-level strategy but also because it influenced our research. We were focused on companies who had succeeded in or were ambitious to break the rules of Parenting Theory. We wanted to find out if it needed some embellishment.

Our conclusion is that it does. The Traffic Lights point to a number of variables that are not given sufficient attention in Parenting Theory or in any of its predecessors. As a result, the Traffic Lights point to two additional logics for entering new businesses: saplings and rare games (see Figure 6.5). This shows where saplings and rare games would normally be plotted on the Ashridge Portfolio Display. The dotted circles are meant to signal that only a few of the businesses positioned in these parts of the display will be saplings or rare games. In practice, for an Intel or McDonald's there may be no saplings or rare games.

As a further test of the proposition that the Traffic Lights offer a more complete theory, we have compared the Traffic Lights with

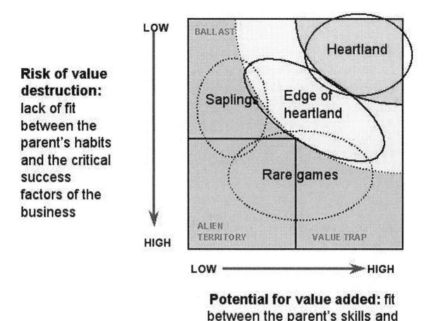

Risk of value destruction: lack of fit between the parent's habits and the critical success factors of the business

Potential for value added: fit between the parent's skills and the parenting opportunities

Figure 6.5 Four strategies for new businesses

Christensen's disruptive technology ideas. Again, we were able to demonstrate that the Traffic Lights offer a fuller explanation of the wide range of new business successes. A management team considering new businesses will find more that pass the Traffic Lights than pass Christensen's disruptive innovation criteria.

CHAPTER 7

SEARCHING FOR NEW BUSINESSES

All companies face the question of what they should do to increase the chances of successfully creating new businesses. Managers want to know what organizational units and process to set up. They also want to know what activities should be part of preparing the ground and what activities will be needed once a promising new business has been spotted. This latter question, what to do once a promising new business opportunity has passed the Traffic Lights, will be addressed in Chapter 9. In this chapter we deal with the first issue: what a company should do to increase the chances of finding a significant new business opportunity.

This question is complicated by the fact that we are focusing on a particular kind of situation: companies, like Intel and McDonald's, that want to find some new business to solve the problem of a slowdown in the growth of their core. In other words, we are trying to help companies that want to look outside their current core. In the previous chapter we have referred to the current core as the heartland, and the focus of this chapter is to advise companies what they need to do to increase their chances of finding edge-of-heartland, sapling, or rare-game opportunities.

Some authors argue that all companies should be investing a small amount every year in new businesses. In this way they will have a healthy "third horizon": projects that may have a significant impact on the company in five or ten years' time.[1] Other authors argue that companies should not distinguish between innovation in their existing businesses and new business creation. By having a healthy innovation process they will create both new products and new businesses.[2] Other authors are more aggressive. They argue that every company needs to create a process for developing new businesses that is managed in parallel with the process for running existing businesses.[3] Still others assert that every company has a natural flow of initiatives driven by the exploratory behavior of managers at all levels and that the only requirement is to manage this flow effectively.[4] Others propose that companies should focus on disruptive technology developments, particularly those that are undermining the core businesses.[5] Finally, some argue that companies should stick to their core businesses and support only those new business opportunities that are natural adjacencies.[6] Our view is both different from and an amalgam of these ideas.

One of the difficulties of thinking clearly about new businesses is that it is easy to become confused between efforts to develop new products for existing businesses, efforts to add businesses in the existing heartland, and efforts to find edge-of-heartland opportunities, saplings, or rare games. Investments in a central research function, for example at Unilever or Intel, are often thought of as an appropriate way of developing new businesses. However, most of the work of these research functions will be and should be devoted to technologies and products for the existing businesses and the existing heartland. So how much should be invested in more speculative research that might lead to new businesses outside the existing heartland? A similar question can be asked of the new product development function, the corporate venturing unit (if one exists), and the efforts of the strategic planning team. The most obvious answer is that more should be invested in exploring outside the heartland the more urgent the need. If growth in the core is slowing fast, the company should pump up its investment in research, new products, new ventures, and strategic analysis outside the heartland. Nevertheless, our research has led us to be wary of this seemingly obvious answer.

THE NATURAL FLOW OF NEW IDEAS

Every company has a natural flow of new ideas for new products, new markets, and new businesses. This flow is dependent on the environment the company is in and the business model of the parent company.

The environment has an important impact. In the late 1990s, the internet boom and the entrepreneurial bubble that it unleashed gave rise to a period when many new businesses were being developed. Almost every company was inundated with proposals. For example, when we were doing research on the impact of the internet on corporate centers, one question we asked was how the corporate center handled the flow of potential new businesses, joint ventures, and alliances. A senior executive at AstraZeneca, a pharmaceutical company, responded mischievously: "We have set up machine guns in the lobby!" In order to deter the flow, managers were turning away every proposal that did not have some privileged route of access.

Another example was tobacco company BAT. To respond to the internal and external pressures, BAT set up two units. Imagine was set up to work with managers or external agents to refine and develop new ideas. Evolution was set up as an investment unit, to provide funds for new ideas that seemed promising. While, with hindsight, BAT probably overreacted and AstraZeneca kept its feet more firmly on the ground, both companies experienced a huge increase in the natural flow of new business ideas.

Some industries, at certain points in time, have a higher rate of flow than others. Industries faced with disruptive technologies, as most were during the internet boom, have a higher flow. Industries undergoing other major changes, such as changes in legislation (utilities), fragmentation (financial services), or the collapse of a dominant competitor (computers in 1990s), also have a higher flow. Industries that have been stable for many years, where few of the sources of advantage are changing (mass-market consumables, mining), have a lower flow of new business ideas.

The second factor affecting the natural flow is the business model of the corporate parent company (and/or of divisions within the parent company). Some companies, such as Philips or Canon, invest heavily

180

in research as part of the strategy for their core businesses. Inevitably, even if the research is focused tightly on the needs of existing businesses, it will spawn new technologies and new product ideas that can be developed into new businesses.

Other companies, such as 3M, have businesses built on innovation as a source of competitive advantage. All of 3M's businesses seek to be the technology leader in their markets and to earn superior margins as a result. This encourages managers throughout the organization to search for technical or innovative solutions. Inevitably, these companies will also have a higher flow of new business ideas.

Other companies actively seek new businesses. Virgin is famous for its openness to new ideas and entrepreneurial behavior. As a result, the central team at Virgin receives tens of new business ideas every day. When Richard Branson, the founder, flies on a long-haul flight, people come up to him on the aeroplane with ideas for new businesses. "After a transatlantic flight, he will come back with five to ten business proposals," commented Virgin's head of strategy.

Virgin is therefore more like a venture capital company than a normal corporation. Richard Branson has demonstrated that he is prepared to consider any interesting new business proposal. As a result, he attracts a larger number of proposals than most companies would be interested in. Virgin is not in an environment that is particularly vibrant. The reason it has such a high flow is because the business model of the parent company is more about spotting and launching new businesses than administering its existing businesses.

In Chapter 1 we described the growth efforts at Intel and McDonald's. Without analyzing their situations in detail, we might speculate that Intel's natural flow of new business ideas is richer than McDonald's. This would not be because they have significantly different corporate business models: both companies are heavily committed to their existing businesses, and were exploring new businesses in an attempt to find growth. Intel's flow would be likely to be greater because Intel's environment has more new business activity. Nevertheless, Mats Lederhausen of McDonald's pointed out that there are many new ideas even at McDonald's:

We have plenty of people out there with ideas. What we do not have are managers skilled at helping to accelerate these ideas. My team's main role is to act in support of the businesses to help them make more out of the ideas they already have.

Robert Burgelman, a professor at Stanford Business School, has devoted much of his research to understanding this natural flow of new ideas.[7] He recognizes that there are two sources: the top-down strategic planning process and the bottom-up, autonomous initiative process. The top-down process identifies changes in the environment, proposes new solutions, and is stimulated by ideas from investment bankers and alliance partners. The bottom-up process stems from marketplace and technical initiatives taken by managers in response to customer requests, partner initiatives, and perceived opportunities. Often these bottom-up projects start out as "skunk works," below the radar of top-down plans. However, if successful, they get written into the plans retrospectively. Burgelman argues that the bottom-up process is as natural a managerial activity as top-down planning: it should be recognized as a normal part of corporate development. We agree.

SHOULD COMPANIES TRY TO INCREASE THEIR NATURAL FLOW?

Managers often conclude that they are not getting enough new ideas. They look at companies like Virgin or 3M and envy their higher flow rate. Since they can do little about the environment, they try to solve the problem by changing the corporate business model to encourage more ideas.

Typically this will involve setting up a corporate venturing unit or business development function. It will involve analyzing trends in the industry to generate more ideas. It may involve increasing investment in research or new product development. It may involve a series of workshops to generate ideas and stimulate the thinking of managers at all levels in the organization. These workshops or brainstorming sessions are often supported by corporation-wide innovation training. It may involve setting up a small M&A team to look at acquisition targets. It may involve creating multiple sources of finance for new ideas in order to encourage more internal entrepreneurs to come forward.[8] These are the sorts of things that both Intel and McDonald's did in the 1990s to increase their chances of finding new businesses. Unfortunately, trying to pump up the flow of new ideas does not seem to work. More new ideas are generated and processed, but the flow of successful, significant new business initiatives does not seem to increase.

Managers should use the New Businesses Traffic Lights to screen ideas that are part of the current flow and invest only in those that get sufficient green lights. Sometimes this will lead to a large number of potential new investments. If so, the company needs to be more selective until it has a list of projects that matches its managerial capacity. Sometimes there will be few or no investment opportunities. When this occurs, managers should focus on maximizing the performance of their existing businesses (see Chapter 4) rather than launching initiatives to pump up the flow of ideas. Certainly, managers should remove blocks in their existing cultures or processes, and they may need to increase the innovative activity within their core businesses. But they should not view a lack of good opportunities as a failure that needs to be corrected. In our experience it is the norm rather than the exception for many companies.

We recognize that there are pressures on managers to grow and that these pressures often demand some investment in new businesses. The environment may be bursting with new proposals, managers' existing businesses may be being undermined by new technologies or other changes, or their current businesses and their current corporate business model, though sound, may not be producing enough growth. Rather than viewing these pressures as a call to arms, managers should treat them as pitfalls to be handled cautiously. By auditing their natural flow of ideas, managers can assess whether there are plenty of opportunities or only a few. By clinging to the New Businesses Traffic Lights, managers can resist the temptation to roll the dice when the chances of success are low. By having a bias in favor of focusing on the core, managers can ensure they do not prematurely lose faith in or focus on their core businesses.

Of the 50 or so examples in our database of successes, none started out as an initiative stimulated by a desire to "get more ideas into the hopper." They all occurred through the natural flow processes. They either emerged from below as a result of initiatives taken by managers near the marketplace or they were part of top-down strategizing. Some also came as unexpected and unplanned opportunities brought to the company from outside. In other words, the successes came from the natural processes, not from forced processes.

Johnson Matthey's move into manufacturing controlled substances is an example. Johnson Matthey, an expert in platinum, had worked with Bristol Myers Squibb to pioneer the use of platinum in anti-cancer treatments. The platinum for these treatments was manufactured in a plant in West Deptford, New Jersey.

Looking for growth opportunities, the company considered other opportunities to supply the pharmaceutical industry. After some careful analysis, management decided to apply for a license from the Drug Enforcement Agency to manufacture controlled substances. The company's experience of managing a secure facility and producing small volumes using difficult catalysis proved decisive. Today, Johnson Matthey is the number three supplier of analgesics in the US.

Nevertheless, managers argue: "But we want to be more like 3M and Virgin. If we had a corporate-level business model that championed new businesses and attracted internal and external entrepreneurs, we would be able to have a continuous flow of new businesses like them." And this is true. The problem is the size of change that is needed. In order for a McDonald's or an Intel to operate a corporate-level business model like 3M or Virgin, these companies would have to change too many things. They would have to change most of their top managers, certainly including their CEO. They would have to change many of their most cherished management processes. They would have to change their portfolio of businesses, or at least signal widely that the management team in charge of their core business has no privileges over the teams of lesser businesses. They would have to change many of their board members. They would need to change many shareholders.

Interestingly, this objective—to become more like 3M or Virgin— is the advice given by a large percentage of the current literature.[9] Companies are encouraged to develop new corporate processes and make other changes in order to be more attractive to new business ideas. Not surprisingly the success rate is low, if not non-existent. Even some of the strongest proponents of this kind of change admit that no companies have yet succeeded in doing what is necessary. The reason is that companies are organisms with well-entrenched habits and processes. Improvements are possible, but dramatic change is not, at least not without dramatic change in personnel. Moreover, even if dramatic change were possible, it might not be appropriate. Would Intel run its microprocessor business as well if its corporate team operated more like the corporate team at 3M or Virgin? The answer is no. The likely cost in loss of performance in the core business would be a multiple of any gains made in new businesses.

By pouring cold water on efforts to generate a richer flow of new business ideas, we are not trying to discourage companies from innovation or entrepreneurial activity. We are trying to discourage them from investing a lot of energy in forcing the pace.

Gary Hamel and his colleagues at Strategos argue that companies should focus their innovation efforts on regenerating core businesses. Once their core businesses are effectively using innovation to improve performance, there will be a knock-on effect for new businesses: some of the ideas will form part of the natural flow of new business ideas. We have not seen this happen, but it makes sense. Innovation in existing businesses is aimed at something managers understand, where their instincts about what makes sense are likely to be sound. In these circumstances, managers have a feel for how much to spend and when ideas are becoming foolish. New business ideas that emerge from this process are likely to be sensible.

However, when the innovation effort is focused on areas where managers have little understanding, their ability to know how much to invest in the search effort or when ideas are losing touch with reality is curtailed. As a result, little of value comes out.

For example, in an attempt to stimulate growth, the Prudential identified the ageing population as an interesting trend. Clearly this trend was having an impact on its core insurance businesses. But the question managers asked was whether the Prudential could exploit this trend outside the insurance industry. To pursue this idea, it hired a major consulting company to help look at the opportunities. Obvious ideas like care homes were considered, along with less obvious ideas like housing or holidays in warmer climates like Spain. Unsurprisingly, nothing emerged that looked attractive to the Prudential, and the effort was closed down after quite a bit of money had been spent. We believe that companies can avoid these kinds of wasteful exercises by relaxing into the natural flow of ideas that will emerge anyway.

WHY FORCING THE PACE OF IDEA GENERATION DOES NOT WORK

When we suggest to managers that they should "relax into the flow," we get odd looks. Are we smoking something? Surely, managers argue, it is possible and sensible to increase the number of new business ideas that are being considered: to fill the hopper with ideas? It seems such an obvious thing to do, and it is more managerially attractive than waiting for something to turn up. Yet we are arguing that it is "make work": work that makes managers feel good, but fails to add anything useful.

Our argument is simple. It concerns people. Successful new businesses depend on the leadership of rather unusual managers (our leader/sponsor Traffic Light). These managers normally have an insight into some aspect of the market or business model that enables them to see opportunity where others do not. But not only do they have the insight, they also have the entrepreneurial initiative to get the new business going.

When managers with the entrepreneurial courage have important insights, they are only too keen to tell other managers about the opportunity and to start lobbying for support from their organization. They will try to influence the top-down strategy process or create a bottom-up skunk works. In other words, when the natural flow of things brings together special insight and entrepreneurial talent, you are not going to have to look very hard to find it. It will not be necessary to set up search parties to turn over every stone. It is more likely that the manager with the idea will beat your door down whether you are looking or not. At Johnson Matthey, Forrest Sheffey, the CEO of the pharmaceutical materials division, championed the move into controlled substances based on his intimate knowledge of the sector.

If instead of waiting for the natural flow to produce ideas managers try to force the pace, plenty of ideas can be generated. In a recent discussion, one consultant proudly explained that the idea-generation process he had been leading, involving innovation workshops, sector surveys, and incentives, had produced 387 ideas for new businesses for the client. The problem is that 99% of these ideas will be lacking a key ingredient: an entrepreneurial manager willing to lead the new business who has a significant insight about the market or the business model and sufficient status and support within the parent company. When properly screened, the client will end up with the same number of promising projects as would have been identified if the work had just focused on the ideas that were available before the consulting project was launched. What is more, with 387 ideas the temptation is to ensure that 5% or 10% pass the screening.[10] This means the client will end up with more projects and more investment but no more successes.

"But this contradicts the normal behavior within a business," some managers argue. "If you are losing market share, one of the tried-and-tested ways of responding is to pump up your new product development process. Why would this not work at the portfolio level?" The answer links back to the people argument. In an existing business, managers understand the market, technical risks, and their own skills well enough to be wise at selecting new products with a good chance of success. When screening new businesses involving some unfamiliar markets, technologies, and business models, managers are less able to distinguish the good ideas from the bad ones. They are therefore easily tempted into pursuing ideas that will not pass the Traffic Lights.

WHAT IMPROVEMENTS CAN BE MADE TO THE NATURAL FLOW?

The message of this chapter so far has been that managers should not try to pump up the natural flow of ideas. The argument is that it achieves nothing in the short term. But is there not something a company can do over the longer term? The answer is yes, although not as much as many authors suggest. The next two sections look at the top-down and bottom-up processes and describe the type of action we believe most managers should take.

IMPROVING TOP-DOWN PROCESSES

While we believe in discouraging managers from trying to force the pace of idea generation, we are not trying to discourage them from analyzing their situation and thinking hard about their corporate strategy. The most important work that top managers can do is to produce a vision of how they are going to develop their portfolio of businesses and articulate why this vision is likely to create value for all stakeholders.

Top-down, corporate-level strategy involves a number of steps. First, managers will assess the industries in which they are currently competing. This work ought to have been done in the business-level plans, but it often needs extending. Particular attention needs to be given to the periphery of the industry, where disruptive innovations may be evident or where new business opportunities may be emerging (see Box 7.1).

The overall objective of the analysis is to make sure that managers have thoroughly explored the developments around their existing businesses.

Second, managers will allocate each business to one of four categories—develop, improve, maintain, or harvest—based on the business's longer-term potential in its industry. Though simplistic, this is a good starting point for achieving focus. It also stimulates challenging debate with business managers.

Third, managers will develop a list of corporate-level skills and resources. These will then be used to screen other industries to see

188

Box 7.1 Analyzing the periphery

Strategy work usually focuses on the main competitors and the core of the market. New business models, however, often emerge from the edges of existing businesses and may go unnoticed unless special attention is given to analyzing the periphery. There are three steps.

1 First, managers should record all the competitors and business models that are in some way connected to the current business. These may be competitors up or down the value chain, in different channels, in adjacent segments, in substitute technologies, and so on. Particular attention should be given to new competitors and small but successful competitors.

2 Second, some of these competitors should be analyzed in more detail—reverse engineered to understand the economics of their business models. Choosing which ones to analyze is an art. The objective is to focus on those competitors from which the company has most to learn.

3 The final step is to extract the messages from these analyses. The messages may be about potential disruptive technologies or business models. They may be about new market segments and new customer expectations. They may be about innovations in any aspect of the business. It is important that this assessment is not done solely by the senior managers of the existing businesses. Their commitment to the existing business model may make them blind to changes that are happening in their industries. The team extracting the messages should be broadly based and include managers from the periphery, whose visceral understanding of the trends may be better than that of managers at the center.

where else these skills could be deployed (see Box 7.2). These other industries or markets should include those adjacent to the ones in which the company is already competing. However, the analysis should not be limited to adjacent industries. The industries chosen will depend on the corporate-level skill.

The final step is to decide which parenting opportunities and which parenting propositions the corporate level currently is or could become good at. This is done by deciding which parenting opportunities offer the biggest value increment and which best match the

Box 7.2 Defining corporate-level skills

The skills and resources at the parent company level are an important input to corporate-level strategy.[11] There are four steps involved.

1   Managers should identify where the existing businesses need most help from parent managers. By identifying the main tasks of each business and predicting which of these tasks managers will find hardest to complete well, parent managers can identify the opportunities to help (parenting opportunities).

2   Managers should record the mistakes that are typically made by managers in the industries the company is in. The analysis should include mistakes the company has made and mistakes made by competitors. Mistakes include things like investing too much at the top of the cycle, unnecessarily creating a price war, underinvesting in IT or technology, and so on. Having developed a list of mistakes, managers should then examine each and assess whether the parent has been good at helping businesses avoid these mistakes or whether it has been complicit in the mistakes.

3   Managers should record the different ways in which corporate functions and line managers are currently trying to help and influence the businesses. These "parenting propositions" will be based on the views of the current managers at the corporate level.

4   Managers should record the habits, biases, and normal instincts of the parent managers as a group. It is useful to ask questions about how the parent normally behaves and why. What is their usual reaction to a threatening competitor? How do they typically deal with underperformance? How do they decide what is a suitable growth rate?

These four questions provide data for a strengths and weaknesses analysis of the corporate levels.

skills of corporate-level managers. The objective is to build around some corporate-level skills where the company has or can reasonably expect to be able to create an advantage over competing parent companies.

Finally, managers can develop a corporate-level strategy that defines which existing businesses and which new businesses best fit with corporate-level skills. The strategy also defines how the corporate-level plans will help existing businesses and new businesses maximize their performance.

Whitbread's work on corporate strategy in 2002 is a good example of effective top-down strategizing. The company has a diverse portfolio of restaurant and leisure brands, mainly in the UK. Some of these brands—Marriott Hotels, Pizza Hut, and TGI Friday's—are managed in collaboration with their US brand owners. Others, such as Beefeater (steak houses), Travel Inn (low-cost hotels), David Lloyd Leisure (tennis clubs), and Brewer's Fayre (pub restaurants), are UK-focused brands.

Whitbread's top-down review examined each brand and its market sector. Travel Inn was allocated to the "develop" category and Beefeater to the "improve" category. Travel Inn was growing fast in the UK and had clear opportunities to grow overseas. Beefeater was the UK's leading steak restaurant, but was underperforming. The priority was to ensure the brand was earning its cost of capital.

In addition, the work involved surveying 30 other market sectors. Changes in the way consumers used their leisure time, such as the increasing link between eating-out occasions and a leisure activity, were creating new opportunities.

The 30 market sectors were put through a brief screen and quickly reduced to two that appeared to offer promise for Whitbread.

Whitbread defined its corporate-level skills as developing leisure brands, driving performance, improving brand positioning, and developing a pool of managers good at operating leisure brands. While these skills did not point especially at any sub-sector in the leisure industry, they fit well with the two opportunities identified.

One of these two interesting sectors, an opportunity closely linked to an existing business, was worked up into a business plan. Within nine months of the strategy review, the business proposal had been approved and work had started on the first site.

Another part of the strategy looked at the potential for expanding two existing brands into new geographic markets. For one brand the first step was a joint venture in Spain. For the other brand the way forward was an extension of its franchising concept to other markets.

Whitbread's corporate vision continued to be focused on leisure and restaurant brands. However, in the medium term the plan now included an additional UK leisure brand and an ambition to develop some brands internationally.

We like the Whitbread story because the top-down strategizing resulted in a few crisp decisions, because it took less than a year, because the new business efforts were seen as an integral part of the corporate strategy, and because managers across the group were committed to the initiatives.

Despite the advice of some authors that companies should do less top-down portfolio strategizing and more bottom-up experiments, we believe that crisp, top-down thinking is evident in all but a few of the companies in our success database. Without it, companies easily fall into the trap of investing in a range of new initiatives, none of which has sufficient corporate support to ensure success.

IMPROVING BOTTOM-UP PROCESSES

Since the most important insights about markets and business models normally occur first to managers close to the market or close to operations, it is not surprising that every company has a natural flow of bottom-up ideas and ventures. How can this bottom-up process be effectively facilitated?

At one extreme, there is a danger that the company is so focused and so controlling that it does not tolerate any activity outside its existing businesses. Entrepreneurial managers in these situations take their ideas elsewhere.

At the other extreme, companies can create so much slack and tolerate so many promising new initiatives that every dreamer is funded and managers are distracted from driving the core businesses forward.

Most authors suggest that companies are too focused and controlling. They argue that, until companies change their cultures to give more support to managers ready to take a risk, no new business ideas will emerge. Clearly, some companies are like this. However, our observation is the opposite. We believe that most companies are too tolerant of new ventures and new projects: they support too many improbable initiatives and take too long before cutting the funding to failing projects. Hence our bias is to encourage companies to recognize the existence of the bottom-up process, but to improve with tough love rather than open arms.

We should, however, admit that we have not researched bottom-up processes in detail. Our views are based on experience, on the shadowing work, and on the database of successes. Fortunately, Robert Burgelman has studied the bottom-up processes rather carefully, in particular in his work with Intel. Although we do not agree with all of his recommendations, much of his advice, which we summarize below, is sound.[12]

1 *Promote a "rugged, confrontational/collegial culture."*[13] The company needs a way for bottom-up thinking to challenge top-down thinking. The best solution is a process of debating issues that is vigorous, issue driven, and indifferent of rank. It is also a process where disagreements do not interfere with execution. Intel, according to Burgelman, has both features. "Constructive confrontation" is the Intel name given to robust debating, and "disagree and commit" the label for the execution follow-through once the confrontation is concluded.

2 *Tolerate sponsored initiatives.* Encourage the CEO to explicitly tolerate a few initiatives that do not easily fit into the current corporate strategy, but are sponsored by the divisions reporting to the CEO.

3 *Embrace ambiguity.* Suspend, for new ventures, the drive for certainty that is often part of the budgeting and planning process. This may require more frequent reviews and milestone reporting, but should not result in interference.

4 *Don't separate.* Those involved in bottom-up venturing should not be isolated from the mainstream. Linkages are important to the success of the venture, to the willingness of the parent to keep supporting it, and to the process of developing the corporate strategy.

5 *Bolster the will to terminate.* Bottom-up initiatives are experiments and should be terminated if they are not making progress. Top management needs an explicit termination process.[14]

6 *Ensure sufficient general managers.* New ventures require managers capable of linking new ideas with the marketplace and accessing resources from different parts of the company. Without a sufficient number of managers with generalist skills, ventures have less chance of succeeding.

As opposed to authors like Rosabeth Kanter, Burgelman does not suggest radical changes. He acknowledges that there is a bottom-up process that exists regardless of the context. However, he believes that there are actions managers can take to facilitate the process. We agree with this positioning.

One area where we disagree with Burgelman is his presumption that the bottom-up process will be and should be continuously creating new ventures. We believe that, at certain points in time, the bottom-up process may be generating no new ventures at all. While it is not difficult to resolve the issue by observation, and indeed some companies at some points in time have no bottom-up-generated ventures, Burgelman's view is that this is a signal of failure. In contrast, our view is that a lack of bottom-up ventures may be totally appropriate. It may be caused by a lack of opportunities or the existence of more important tasks, such as driving the existing businesses. So managers worried about the vibrancy of their bottom-up processes need to analyze the situation carefully before they make too many changes.

An example of careful analysis and thoughtful change is IBM's Emerging Business Opportunities (EBO) process.[15] Faced with low growth, a concern that IBM had missed out on some of the emerging opportunities in the computer and internet industry, and a belief that insufficient new ventures were coming through the bottom-up process, CEO Sam Palmisano commissioned a group of managers to suggest a process for boosting IBM's success in new businesses.

The team concluded that there was a problem: IBM's core management processes and complex organization matrix were blocks to the bottom-up development of new businesses. The management processes were focused on profitability rather than value, and the matrix structure required that new businesses win support separately from research, sales, and a business group. After some consideration, the team decided to set up a program to support the bottom-up processes. First, some new businesses emerging in the divisions were selected as EBOs. They were given some protection from the normal resource-allocation process, some additional funding from a corporate resource pool, and a good deal of attention and help from central research and strategy.

Over the first three years the program was considered a success. It gave additional attention and support to some new businesses that might otherwise have made little progress. The program also encouraged some managers to propose businesses as EBOs when under different circumstances they might have focused their energies only on the existing businesses. By 2003, the EBO businesses were generating sales of $10 billion (although reputedly not much profit). Some of these initiatives would clearly have happened in any case, but the program was believed to have given these projects a substantial leg up.

IBM's growth challenge remained, however. The EBOs were adding to growth, but not enough to make a significant difference. In 2003, IBM decided to try to add significantly to its current program of 18 EBOs. This involved graduating some of the existing EBOs and "filling the hopper" with a larger number of new EBOs.

If this expansion happens (which is described in a Harvard Business School case but somewhat contradicted by internal sources), we expect IBM's EBO program to become less successful rather than more. The desire to use the program to "fill the growth gap" is in our view the wrong motivation. The program should be used to help reduce the barriers to the natural flow of new business projects rather than pump up the flow in order to hit a growth ambition. Identifying the right balance of initiatives is hard, even in a company as thoughtful as IBM. This is especially true against the backdrop of the pressures to grow that influence all managers.

BRINGING THE TOP-DOWN AND BOTTOM-UP PROCESSES TOGETHER

With a crisp top-down process and a blockage-free bottom-up process, there is an issue of how to bring them both together. This is another area where our thinking diverges from Burgelman's. He, like other authors, argues that managing both the bottom-up process and the top-down process is very difficult:

> Top management must also help the company exercise both disciplines simultaneously. Companies find it extremely difficult to do so.[16]

Burgelman believes it is difficult to manage the two processes because the bottom-up process is intuitive and entrepreneurial, while most top-down processes are locked into past concepts of the company's corporate strategy.

We think that both of these problems can be overcome. We see the bottom-up process as a healthy entrepreneurial activity that needs to be kept in proportion. The way to do this is to impose on the entrepreneurial managers a clear set of criteria for deciding which bottom-up ideas will be supported and which will be rejected. The Traffic Lights provide the criteria. So long as the Traffic Lights are fully communicated down the line, managers at any level can experiment and launch new initiatives, either as skunk works or with approval from middle managers, knowing whether their ideas are likely to be well received or badly received higher up. The entrepreneurs can control themselves.

Inevitably, some strong-minded managers will push forward ideas that do not pass the Traffic Lights, or will judge some of the lights as green when a more objective analysis would score them yellow or red. When this happens, corporate-level managers should not hesitate to use the Traffic Lights to expose the inappropriate venture. It can then be formally closed down with a clear explanation of why. Other entrepreneurially minded managers will not be discouraged unless they have ideas that will be hard to justify using the Traffic Lights. We see the corporate-level managers playing a critical role of disciplining the entrepreneurial energies lower down.

Burgelman would prefer corporate-level managers to suspend judgment until these bottom-up ventures have had a chance to develop further, because it is hard for them to be sufficiently open-minded given their commitment to the past corporate strategy. For example, it took a change in leadership at Intel, from Moore to Grove, before the strategy officially changed from memories to microprocessors. We recognize this problem. But we think that the Traffic Lights provide the solution.

The Traffic Lights are a generic set of criteria for screening new business ideas. They are not dependent on the past corporate-level strategy of any particular company. Inevitably, managers with different views of where advantage lies and what the organization's skills are will score the lights slightly differently. But they provide a language that top managers can use to communicate with front-line managers and vice versa.

In some companies, such as Whitbread, the top-down strategy development process defines clear paths for future development that make sense when considered against the Traffic Lights. Once these have been selected, managers lower down should be encouraged to channel their entrepreneurial activity along these paths. However, a manager lower down who has an idea that does not fit these paths can still use the Traffic Lights to argue his or her case, and corporate-level managers should give the proposal due consideration. In other words, the Traffic Lights provide a language around which the top-down and bottom-up processes can integrate.

Problems emerge when the top-down process creates confusion lower in the organization. This happens when managers at either level use inappropriate criteria to screen ideas, when top managers are locked into outdated strategies, or when top-down screening judgments are not consistent. Our research and Burgelman's work show that this kind of confusion happens frequently. Burgelman suggests that the solution is achieved by middle managers acting as go-betweens. Middle managers interpret corporate-level strategy for managers lower down, while giving air cover from the inappropriate thoughts of senior managers. At the same time, they interpret new ventures for their bosses, helping them to see how they can be incorporated in a redefined corporate-level strategy. In our view this puts an unreasonable burden on middle managers. Moreover, we do not need to make them into go-betweens. Disciplined use of the Traffic Lights can provide the clarity that solves the problem: managers lower down know how managers higher up are going to evaluate their projects and can use the Traffic Lights to argue for adjustments to the corporate strategy.

Burgelman presumes "bias" among top managers and sees the bottom-up process as an essential antidote. While this is an accurate description of many companies, and Intel in particular, there are enough examples of a better top-down process to demonstrate that proper use of clear criteria helps top managers be wise and clears up confusion lower down.

HOW MUCH SHOULD BE INVESTED IN NEW BUSINESSES?

Our analysis of the top-down and bottom-up processes should help managers decide what to do when they feel the need to create new businesses. But it has still not answered the question: "How much should we invest in new businesses?"

The simple answer is "enough to support all the new business ideas that pass the Traffic Lights, constrained only by managerial capacity." In other words, if no ideas pass the Traffic Lights, managers should make no investments in new businesses and use spare cash to buy back shares or pay larger than usual dividends. If many ideas pass the Traffic Lights, managers should invest in as many as the managerial capacity allows. In a large divisionalized company this could mean investing in 10 or 15 new business projects, assuming two projects led by each of five divisions plus some additional projects led by the corporate center and a large business unit. This is about the number of projects in IBM's original EBO program.

It is also the number of new business projects on which Philips chose to focus in the early 1990s. At a time when painful downsizing targets were imposed on each division, managers decided to identify those new business initiatives that were worth protecting from the cuts. Thus 15 initiatives were singled out for corporate review and support, and were put under the spotlight of the top 100 managers in the company. In total they absorbed at least 10% of R&D spending. They included electronic lighting, flat-panel displays, cellular telephones, medical ultrasound, high-definition television, interactive CD, and car navigation systems. Over the next several years, a number were discontinued or divested. About half ended up as successful additions to the business portfolio of their divisions.

Is there a financial limit on the amount that should be invested in new businesses? In principle, no. For a new independent company, 100% of the capital is invested in "new businesses." For large established companies with growing core businesses, like McDonald's or Intel, the amount is likely to be less than 5% of total capital spend. For a company that is exiting one core business and investing in a new area, the amount invested in the new area may be close to 100%.

Managers, we have found, are not satisfied with our simple answer to how much to invest. First, they believe that there ought to be some minimum ongoing investment "in the future" or "in the third horizon" or "to keep the pipeline full." We hope that by this point in the book we have persuaded you that, although this pipeline thinking is appropriate for new products and for research functions, it is not helpful when companies are looking for new businesses.

The second argument is more difficult to respond to. Managers argue that companies ought to invest more when their core business is slowing down and less when it is growing fast. In addition, when the industry is fragmenting or changing dramatically (as with financial services), managers should be investing more in new business models than when the industry is consolidating (as with consumer products).

It is possible to produce a simple matrix (Figure 7.1 overleaf) based on these two dimensions: the degree of growth of existing businesses

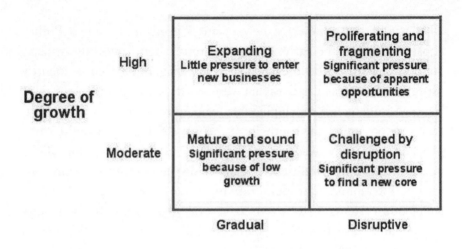

Figure 7.1 Four types of industry environments

(high or moderate) and the nature of change in the industry (gradual or disruptive).

The matrix divides the industry environment into four quadrants: mature and sound, expanding, challenged by disruption, and proliferating and fragmenting. The matrix also highlights the very understandable pressures managers face in each of the four quadrants. Apart from the benign top left quadrant, expanding, where there is continued growth and little challenge from change, each of the other environments puts significant pressure on managers to develop new businesses.

While we recognize the pressures managers are under, we do not believe that they should let these pressures be the primary driver of their strategy for new businesses. Interestingly, our database of successes is spread across all four environments (Figure 7.2). Most were in the bottom left-hand quadrant, mature and sound, perhaps because of our bias toward major companies in mature markets. However, the second-largest group was in the top left quadrant, expanding, and the smallest in the proliferating and fragmenting quadrant. Hence managers may have limited opportunities that pass the Traffic Lights when

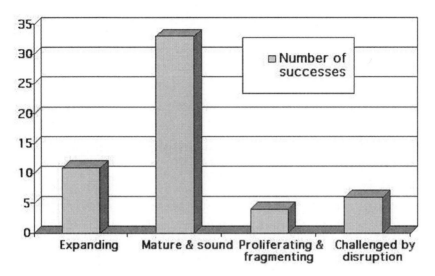

Figure 7.2 Successes by industry environment

their industry is "challenged by disruption" and many opportunities when their company is "expanding." In other words, it is better for managers to build their strategy for new businesses around those opportunities that pass the Traffic Lights rather than around the pressures they are under.

The industry environments matrix is useful in guiding managers to give particular attention to different Traffic Lights at different times.

Intel probably sits in the top left quadrant. Its core business is sound and expanding. Clearly, Intel should be considering opportunities adjacent to its microprocessor business. But managers should give special attention to distraction risks, since any loss of attention on the core microprocessor business will be very expensive. It may be appropriate that the microprocessor business is a "creosote bush."

In the bottom right quadrant, the industry is changing and creating opportunities but existing businesses are under threat. This was probably what managers at McDonald's thought they were facing in the late 1990s. The core hamburger business was being challenged by many new fast-casual formats.

In this situation, the focus for managers should be to understand these potentially disruptive challenges. For example, if the conclusion is that the challenges will disrupt the hamburger business, then McDonald's would need to identify one or two of the new casual formats to invest in. Once the choice has been made, McDonald's should be prepared to milk the core business in order to invest in the new format. Instead of worrying about distraction risks, managers in the bottom right quadrant should be focused on making sure that they choose a new area where they have sufficient advantage and where the profit pool is not a dog.

Based on McDonald's recent actions, it seems management has decided that the threats from fast-casual businesses are not disruptive. They are probably in the bottom left quadrant. As a result, their decision to invest in new businesses only if they can become significant and without any disruption to the core hamburger business seems appropriate.

DSM, now a Dutch life sciences company, has been a good bottom right example, on two occasions. In the 1960s managers decided that coalmining was no longer competitive in the Netherlands. This led them to close the mines and invest in petrochemicals. By 1975, they had completely exited the mining business and successfully entered the chemical industry. In the 1980s, managers concluded that DSM would be unlikely to be a winner in the consolidation of the petrochemical industry. They backed a strategy of developing fine chemicals and biochemicals. This led to some success in the life sciences industry. As soon as these successes became clear, the company began to shed its petrochemical businesses.

In some bottom right situations, none of the new business opportunities pass the Traffic Lights. This happens when there are few, but highly contested opportunities. The existing company does not have advantage or the scramble for survival is making the profit pool into a dog. The only rational choice is to focus on the existing businesses and manage the decline gracefully. However, since managing a public company in decline is an unpopular activity with both managers and shareholders, one strategic option is to sell the company to a management buyout or private equity firm.

The bottom left quadrant is one where managers should be comfortable continuing to drive their core business, using the cash to buy back shares or pay high dividends. These companies often have good low-growth performance. New businesses should not be a priority, but should not be ignored. The Traffic Lights analysis of opportunities will give particular attention to distraction risks and leadership/sponsorship issues. If sufficient lights are green, the company should be happy to invest with confidence.

Anglo American's move into European forest products is an example. The existing businesses, primarily mining, precious metals, and coal, were slow growth and stable. The company considered many directions for expansion, but rejected most of them because it did not have sufficient advantage or sufficient management talent. However, when Tony Trahar became chief executive, he arrived with good knowledge of the paper industry and of the management skills available to expand this business. He therefore sponsored investments in the European paper industry, placing the project in the hands of one of his best managers. Over 10 years this business has become the most successful forest products company in Europe.

Managers often presume that the amount they should invest in new businesses should be determined by the degree to which their core business is under pressure and the degree to which they have a pipeline of new businesses in development. If the core is under threat or growing slowly and the pipeline is empty, the presumption is that they should invest heavily in new ventures, acquisitions, and other initiatives.

Our advice encourages managers to ignore the pressures they are under and focus on the attractiveness of the opportunities that they have in front of them. The nature of the pressures they face should cause them to give more or less emphasis to different parts of the Traffic Lights. However, the amount they invest should be determined only by the number of projects that get sufficient green lights.

HOW TO ENSURE THE RIGHT PROCESSES FOR NEW BUSINESSES

The following three guiding rules will help every company set up the right processes for developing new businesses.

1 MANAGE THE FLOW OF NEW BUSINESS IDEAS

To manage the flow of new business ideas, start with the strategies of the existing businesses, avoid overstimulating the idea flow, yet design a process for capturing and screening ideas.

Time and again, we have found that failure to understand the dynamics of the existing businesses leads managers to underestimate their potential or the challenges they face. This can lead to overestimating the managerial and other resources available to support new businesses and underestimating the distraction costs. Without a thorough analysis of the existing businesses, managers do not have a sound platform from which to approach the screening of new business projects.

The strategy review should not only focus on the current business model and current product–market segments, but also on adjacent business models and on new disruptive competitors. This will give senior managers across the company the insights needed for developing top-down ideas for new businesses. However, just as often the review will conclude that there are sufficient management challenges and sufficient growth opportunities within or around existing businesses.

Excessively stimulating the idea flow has many disadvantages. It encourages managers to launch too many new ventures. It distracts them from the one or two that have real potential. It causes the rest of the organization to give minimal support because of the high failure rate.

At the same time, senior managers need an organized way to capture bottom-up ideas that originate within the company, be it from R&D or from marketing and sales. It is important people know that a process exists to deal with such ideas and that decisions get taken in a timely and rational manner. Some companies have used a venture board to fill that role. Others simply use the top executive group to deal with such decisions.

It is extremely helpful to managers in dealing with both the top-down and bottom-up flow of ideas to be able to refer to a generally accepted and clearly communicated strategic framework. People mostly look to the CEO to spell out the company strategy in terms that will help them understand which ideas might be welcome and why certain initiatives are supported while others are rejected.

2 DILIGENTLY USE THE NEW BUSINESSES TRAFFIC LIGHTS

Whether a company invests in new-ideas workshops or limits itself to looking at opportunities that emerge, the Traffic Lights can help ensure that foolish ideas do not get through the screening process. In fact, if the Traffic Lights are widely communicated as a tool for assessing the "strategic business case," managers at all levels will feel empowered both to propose ideas that fit and reject ideas that will not pass the Traffic Lights.

Every tool can be used inappropriately. Managers who are determined to get their ideas approved can consciously or unconsciously bias their thinking. Hence the Traffic Lights need to be applied as part of a decision process that includes some skeptics and some managers less committed to developing new businesses. The tool itself is not enough. The company also needs a governance process that is objective and strong enough to turn down the pet projects of the CEO, the CFO, or the head of the largest division.

3 EFFECTIVELY PARENT EACH NEW BUSINESS INITIATIVE

Once a new business idea passes the Traffic Lights, managers need to pay considerable attention to parenting it appropriately. Multidivisional companies will often have a number of these initiatives ongoing, and will need a process for assigning a good sponsor, putting them at the right place in the organization, orchestrating the right amount of support, and reviewing progress effectively. The EBO program at IBM and the new projects program at Philips are examples.

The toughest decision is faced when progress deviates from the original plan in some major way. This will occur several times in the course of developing a new business. The choice between repositioning the initiative, altering its objectives, increasing the commitment of resources, or pulling the plug often involves agonizing judgments. We say more about how to address this issue and how to parent new businesses in Chapter 9.

CHAPTER 8

IS THERE A ROLE FOR CORPORATE VENTURING?

In earlier chapters of this book we have argued against corporate venturing units. We have given evidence that corporate venturing units do not help companies develop significant new businesses and we have explained why. In this chapter, we want to ask the question: "Are there any uses for venturing techniques inside large companies?" In answer, we will define five types of venturing unit that can add significant value if used in the right circumstances—five different venturing business models. None of these five, however, will help a company develop significant new legs.

It is worth starting with some history. In 2002, companies were questioning the wisdom of their investments in corporate venturing units for the third time in 40 years. These incubators, corporate venture units, and new business development units were set up predominantly in the late 1990s as vehicles for companies to achieve a variety of objectives: to explore new business opportunities created by the internet; to speed growth; to exploit internal resources; and to tap into the entrepreneurial boom that was exploding all around them (Figure 8.1).

Many concluded that these investments were part of a managerial madness connected to the internet bubble. Like Compaq, Vodafone, and Royal Sun Alliance, they closed down their corporate venture unit and resolved to avoid such foolishness in future. Some, like Diageo, Ericsson, and Alcatel, continued in a cautious manner uncertain whether the current bust would be as temporary as the previous boom. A few, however, such as Intel, Johnson & Johnson, and Nokia,

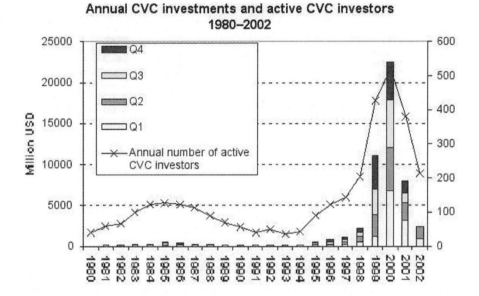

Figure 8.1 Investment levels for corporate venture capital, 1980–2002

continued undeterred. They had a logic for their corporate venturing that was still sound, and they remained committed. Finally, some companies stepped up their commitment and a few, most notably Unilever, established new vehicles to stimulate and invest in new ventures. McDonald's set up a venture unit in 2003, but in a rather different format from Unilever. While Unilever was using venturing to explore new consumer trends, McDonald's set up McDonald's Ventures as a way of containing its remaining new business investments.

The reason for this confusing picture is that corporate venture units encompass five different objectives each requiring a different business model.[1] *Harvest venturing* involves setting up a unit to turn spare internal resources into cash. *Ecosystem venturing* involves investing in companies that are complementary to existing businesses. They may be suppliers or customers, or, as at Intel, companies making complementary products or software. The objective is to benefit existing businesses by creating a more vibrant environment for these businesses to operate in. *Innovation venturing* involves using venturing techniques to stimulate entrepreneurial activity within an existing function of an

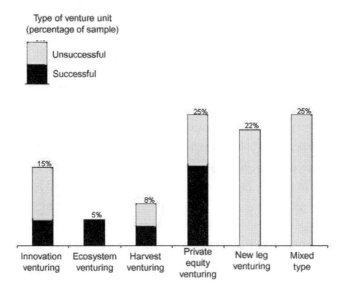

Figure 8.2 Success at different types of venture units

existing business. *Private equity venturing* involves setting up a unit to compete in the private equity and venture capital industry. *New leg venturing* involves setting up a unit to develop internal or external projects and businesses with a view to generating significant new revenue streams (i.e., new legs) for the corporation. The first three of these business models appear to be commercially sound when the appropriate circumstances exist. Private equity venturing appears to have been viable in the past, but is unlikely to be appropriate in the future except for a very few companies. New leg venturing appears to be fundamentally flawed regardless of the circumstances (see Figure 8.2).

The reasons for failures, both in the last three years and in the previous two corporate venturing booms (early 1970s and mid-1980s), are the same:

❑ Some companies chose commercially sound business models but were caught out by the boom and bust in valuations. They invested too much at the top of the cycle. These companies should not abandon their efforts now. Instead, they should develop processes to curb enthusiasm and limit investment budgets when valuations are booming.

❏ Some companies chose new leg venturing and reaped the consequences, incurring huge losses. These companies need to understand why their efforts failed, so that they can avoid making the same mistakes in the future. They also need to recognize that some forms of corporate venturing may still be appropriate for them.

❏ The vast majority of companies, however, had unsatisfactory results because they failed to understand that different venturing objectives require different business models. As a result, they set up corporate venture units with broad remits and multiple objectives. Without focus and an appropriate business model these units floundered, often losing credibility with the rest of the organization before a viable model could be developed. These companies need to reflect on their experience, decide whether any of the viable business models is appropriate, and define a venturing strategy for the future that is built on firmer foundations.

In this chapter we will describe the five types and identify the key managerial challenges associated with each (see Box 8.1 on pages 228–9). In doing this, we build explicitly on a number of earlier studies of corporate venturing units.[2]

HARVEST VENTURING

The objective of turning excess corporate resources into cash is one that does not always need to involve the techniques associated with corporate venturing. For example, the corporate property function is frequently involved in sub-letting spare office space and selling spare land or developing it for sale. While the corporate property department usually is a separate unit, it does not normally use venturing techniques to stimulate or process projects.

However, for some corporate resources, such as technology, managerial skills, brands, and even fixed assets, a venturing approach can be used alongside or in place of the licensing or selling of these assets. We would describe any unit that is set up to "harvest" spare resources as a harvesting unit whether it employed venturing techniques or not. For example, BG Property was set up to exploit the large land holdings of the BG Group, holdings that had been inherited from a time when the company, then British Gas, was government owned. Venturing techniques were a minor part of a broader harvesting business model that was primarily driven by the need to prepare land for sale. Harvesting is, therefore, a concept that is much bigger than harvest venturing. However, in this chapter we are interested in units that employ venturing techniques as an important, if not prime, part of their business model.

Lucent New Ventures Group is a good example. It was set up in 1997 to commercialize intellectual property and technology that was not immediately supported by a business unit. Bell Labs, the research arm of Lucent, is famous for its innovations, patents, and technology. Lucent NVG's objective was to create value by exploiting these underused assets. Over four years, the unit evaluated over 300 opportunities, started 35 ventures, and drew in $350 million of external venture capital.

Tom Uhlman, who was in charge of Lucent NVG, attributed the success to having financial return, rather than some strategic goal, as the primary objective. Could Lucent NVG have succeeded if it was linked more tightly to the parent company? Uhlman asserted:

> No! We certainly would have failed to get outside investor interest, and probably would have made some lousy decisions.

However, by 2001, the market for new ventures was weak, and Lucent Corporation was so short of money that the New Ventures Group was sold to a UK private equity firm, Coller Capital.[3]

BT Brightstar was set up in 1999 and had similar ambitions: to harvest value from the 14,000 patents and 2,500 unique inventions arising at BT's R&D establishment at Adastral Park and to effect cultural change in what was still a rather traditional organization. BT Brightstar operated a rigorous stage-gate process for progressing ventures and enjoyed some early success. By 2001, 330 ideas had been presented, with 4 transactions concluded, and revenues of £30 million generated. As the dot-com bust took hold, BT Brightstar found the harvest venturing model increasingly difficult to execute, primarily because it was relying on external venture capital funding for its spin-outs, and the market for such investments had dried up. In January 2003, BT sold a 60% stake in Brightstar, also to Coller Capital, as its only means of gaining funding for its pipeline of start-up ventures.

A harvest venturing unit is an appropriate vehicle under three circumstances:

1 Management must believe that the company has some resources—intellectual property, brands, assets, and so on—that are not being fully exploited.
2 New businesses need to be created around these resources in order to exploit their full value. For example, a technical development may not have any obvious value until its commercial potential has been demonstrated. Unless a new business is needed, venturing techniques are not necessary. The company can sell or license the resource.
3 The third condition is that the resources are not needed either by the existing businesses or as new growth platforms. If they are needed for a non-harvesting purpose, one of the other venturing business models may be more suitable.

In both BT and Lucent, these conditions existed in the late 1990s. Managers were convinced that the research laboratories contained valuable technologies. The technologies were not needed by the existing businesses. And the booming venture capital industry was hungry for new businesses that contained promising technology. These companies needed to set up harvest venturing units in order to exploit this opportunity. As it turned out, both units found that the window of opportunity—the period of venture industry hunger—was quite short-lived, and their new business proposals had few other markets. The subsequent buyout and rationalization of both units by Coller Capital was therefore an appropriate response to the new market conditions.

Lucent and BT are examples of good practice in harvest venturing. But our research suggests that harvest venturing units, even when set up in the right conditions, are frequently unsuccessful.

There is one main reason for them often underperforming: they frequently attempt to turn spare resources into significant new revenue streams, a mistake we refer to as the *new legs pitfall*. The unit may be set up for harvesting reasons, but is given or develops the additional objective of delivering new growth opportunities for the parent company. The new legs pitfall is understandable. It is common to launch a unit with a brief, such as "have a look in our laboratory and see if you can use venturing methods to turn some of our technology into commercial ventures. If you spot some new businesses that will give us additional growth or add to our portfolio, so much the better." It is also understandable from the perspective of the managers in the unit. Even if they are not explicitly asked to look for new growth opportunities, they are likely to want to. If they find a major new growth platform, they will be contributing much more to the success of their company.

The problem is that new leg venturing, as we shall outline later, is not a viable business model. By adding a new leg ambition, managers in the unit set themselves up for failure and can pollute the effectiveness of their harvest venturing model. In one company, the desire to find new growth platforms caused managers in the unit to align themselves with projects with "new leg" potential in the hope of building their career as the businesses grew. Much less attention was given to finding an exit. When the parent company's growth ambitions abated in 2001, the exit window had closed, leaving the unit with no successes and heavy costs.

Harvest venturing has other pitfalls. Managers in the unit often find themselves working on poor-quality ideas because the assets they are trying to exploit are not as promising as originally expected. Existing businesses or functions hold on to their best assets and only offer less promising properties to the venture unit. Another problem arises when managers stay with projects too long in the hope of capturing more value. Forgetting that their primary objective is to turn existing assets into cash, they start to treat their portfolio of initiatives as an

213

investment in new ventures. Normally lacking the skills to make the right decision about exit timing, these managers often overinvest in their projects and get caught holding the baby when setbacks occur.

These pitfalls make it necessary for harvest venturing teams to stick closely to their business model (see Box 8.1). A harvest venturing unit should be cash driven, turning its new ventures into cash as quickly as possible. The unit should be funded only for its operating budget and should be measured on cash returns against total funds spent. New ventures that could become part of the parent company's portfolio should be "sold" back to the parent. Assets that the harvesting unit is working on should be transferred to the unit or there should be a clear agency agreement between the division that owns these assets and the harvesting unit.

Some units appeared to avoid these pitfalls, while others learn through a process of trial and error. Lucent NVG, for example, sold back to its parent three of its ventures, avoiding the new legs pitfall. BT Brightstar focused its initial efforts on liberating ideas and technologies in the R&D organization, but then in 2001 it changed its focus toward generating a cash return on its ventures. This included refocusing its efforts on technologies that were closer to commercial readiness. Philips's corporate venturing unit in Amsterdam, which has had mixed success in spinning off ventures, learnt the importance of getting control over assets. Rene Savelsberg, the head of the unit, explained that he made business divisions sign "divorce documents" that ceded control of assets before he would begin work.

The importance of clarity about the business model is underlined by the acquisition of Lucent NVG and BT Brightstar by Coller Capital. Neither unit was primarily cash driven, and in our view underperformed as a result. Because Coller has no interest in building new technologies or new businesses for their own sake, we expect its managers to be more disciplined in executing the harvesting business model.

ECOSYSTEM VENTURING

Some companies depend on the vibrancy of a community of connected businesses for their success. The community may be suppliers, agents, distributors, franchisees, technology entrepreneurs, or makers of complementary products. Often this community does not need support from the company other than through normal trading relationships. However, sometimes the vibrancy of the community can be multiplied to the company's benefit by careful ecosystem venturing: by acting as a venture capital support to entrepreneurs in the community.

Consider the case of Intel Capital. Its development has tracked that of the microprocessor industry. In the early days, and until 1995, most Intel Capital investments were made in suppliers, often to guarantee availability of components. As the industry matured and venture capital became available for small businesses, Intel turned its attention to investing in healthy fellow travelers, in order to promote the use of Intel technology and to act as a window on new technologies.[4] This period coincided with the rapid expansion of the internet, and these investments helped to reduce the risks that would be associated with backing the wrong horse.

By 2001, Intel Capital had over $3 billion under management and was viewed by Intel managers as having contributed significantly to the success of the company as well as delivering a healthy return on invested capital. Despite the unsavory market conditions in the following three years, Intel Capital continued making investments.

Another example is Johnson and Johnson Development Corporation (JJDC), which was founded in 1973 as a stand-alone unit to make strategic investments in the healthcare sector. JJDC makes minority investments in a broad range of start-up companies, in areas of technological interest to the parent company Johnson & Johnson. Very occasionally, these investments lead to acquisitions. But in the vast majority of cases, the value lies in helping to establish new technology areas that the company believes in, and in providing the existing businesses with a window on new technologies. Like Intel, JJDC is one of the few clear-cut success stories in corporate venturing—it has been around for 30 years, and it delivers returns comparable to a top-second-tier venture capital firm.

Ecosystem venturing is appropriate when an existing business depends on the vibrancy of a community of complementary businesses and the entrepreneurs in the community do not have sufficient support from existing suppliers of venture capital. This normally occurs because of the area's newness. The company may be able to see the potential, at least in terms of the benefits for existing businesses. But the venture capital industry may not yet have focused on this area. One additional condition is that the company doing the ecosystem venturing needs to be a strong player in its business.

If the community is already well supported, the company with an ecosystem venturing unit will struggle to gain benefits in its existing businesses. Moreover, it will have to compete for the attention of entrepreneurs with existing suppliers of capital. For example, Intel Capital moved its focus away from suppliers and onto software companies as the support for and strength of suppliers improved.

If the investing company is not a strong player in its industry, not only will the returns to its existing business be smaller than those available to strong players, but also the success rate of the investments is likely to be lower. A new venture that is building on something the market leader is doing is likely to be more successful than one that is building on the activities of an also-ran. As a result, ecosystem venturing is a strategy used more frequently by industry leaders, such as Intel, Microsoft, and Johnson & Johnson, than by smaller players.

The major pitfall to ecosystem venturing is the *loss of focus temptation*, where the unit managers invest in a wider deal stream and seek greater autonomy than that which justified the creation of the unit. This temptation is understandable. Many interesting prospects cross the manager's desk and, once a hot investment prospect has been identified, it is easy to get caught up in "doing the deal" rather than analyzing the benefits for an existing business. But focus is absolutely central to making this form of corporate venturing work, because it is only in a narrow range of technologies that the company has something to offer over and above the independent venture capital firm. As

216

a partner in Siemens's highly successful Mustang Ventures unit explained:

> The hardest part of my job, the saddest moments, are when we find a great company to invest in, but we cannot find the alignment to our business units, so we have to drop it.

To avoid the loss of focus temptation, the venture unit needs to have clear objectives, in terms of both the sectors in which it is investing and the relative balance between financial and strategic returns (see Box 8.1). Financial returns are necessary because the venture unit has to justify its existence to skeptical colleagues, but it is the benefits for existing businesses that are the unit's real *raison d'être*.

One way of reinforcing focus is through performance measures. If the unit is assessed on its impact on existing businesses, using a ratio such as "value of benefits for existing businesses divided by invested capital," managers are encouraged to focus on the impact benefits and discouraged from staying with an investment through the second, third, and fourth rounds of financing.

Another way of promoting focus is to give existing businesses a significant level of influence over the unit. The agreement of existing businesses can be sought before any investment is put forward for approval, as at Intel and JJDC. Managers from existing businesses can be appointed to the boards of each new venture, as at Shell's Internet Works (an ecosystem venturing unit that closed in 2002). Managers from current businesses can be used to help with due diligence, as at JJDC. Managers from the ecosystem venturing unit can be located in each division, as at Intel Capital.

A form of ecosystem venturing comes under the banner of "a window on new technology" or "a better understanding of market developments." The logic of getting this information by investing in start-up businesses can be questionable. It may be cheaper and less risky to get the information by monitoring companies and market trends. But where the logic is justified, the unit should follow an ecosystem venturing business model. It should have tight links to the businesses or functions for which it is generating information, and its performance should be measured in ways that encourage focus. Many units with a "window on technology" objective fail to stick to the ecosystem venturing business model and mutate into *de facto* private equity or new leg venturing.

INNOVATION VENTURING

The methods of the venture capital industry—rewarding people for value created, investing in many projects to overcome uncertainty, stage-gate targets to help with assessing progress, particular care in the formation of the management team, and so on—can be appropriate ways of executing some of the functional activities of existing businesses. Although these methods need to be separated from normal functional management, they can still be part of the execution of a broader, more traditional business model. Innovation venturing is the name we have given to a wide range of uses that managers have found for venturing-like processes as part of existing functions.[5]

Shell's Gamechanger program is one example. Originally established in 1996, Gamechanger was set up to increase innovation in the technical function of Shell's exploration business. The idea was to take 10% of the technical budget and spend it in a venturing way. Ideas were identified and screened. Initial finance was provided for promising ideas, and additional finance was available on a structured basis if ideas progressed through further screening hurdles. In the following four years this new approach to innovation was taken up by the technical functions of other divisions in Shell, and is viewed as having produced a step change in some areas.

That is not to say that everything has gone well. A number of high-profile "step-out" projects sponsored by a corporate-level Gamechanger and operating more like new leg venturing failed to generate support. But where Gamechanger projects have been in support of the core businesses, there have been notable successes. By mid-2002, 400 ideas had been screened by Gamechanger, with 32 new technologies commercialized and 3 new businesses established. Gamechanger appears to provide a "purpose" and an "outcome" for the sort of hunch-based research that scientists demand, but that hard-pressed business sponsors are loath to underwrite.

A different kind of example comes from Lloyds TSB. The company was concerned that its strategic planning and budgeting processes, with a focus on economic value, were discouraging the development of long-term growth opportunities. Rather than change these processes and risk undermining a well-developed performance culture, Lloyds TSB decided to try to solve the problem with a central venturing unit. This unit, Lloyds TSB Strategic Ventures led by Michael Pearson, is doing something in a venturing way that might normally be part of the strategy function. Not surprisingly, it reports to Group Strategy and Planning. Its role is to identify opportunities within existing divisions or involving more than one division that are not getting enough attention, and then, using a venturing methodology, "help" the divisions develop these opportunities. For some projects the unit provides only funds and advice. For others the unit takes operating control. Initial results are promising.

A third example is Nokia's New Growth Business (NGB) unit, which was established in 2001 to find and develop new businesses for Nokia. It carries out large-scale systematic idea generation (for example a venture challenge process during 2002 yielded several hundred new ideas), using a combination of technology-push and market-pull techniques. Most ideas come from within the company. And it has a small group of senior executives running the operation, who are free to invest in and develop any new projects that they believe have long-term strategic benefits for Nokia. So far, NGB has invested in over 10 ventures, ranging in size from 7 to 60 people. Two ventures are now in an acceleration phase with their first products coming out.

Innovation venturing is appropriate when an existing function is underperforming against its potential because there is insufficient energy directed toward commercially oriented innovation and creativity. Disruptive technologies, for example, are often best handled through innovation venturing.[6] There must also be some belief that the entrepreneurial energy is latent inside the company and can be fostered by stimulating "intrapreneurs" or by tapping into external entrepreneurs.

The belief is that, by providing the right conditions, internal or external managers with entrepreneurial instincts will take more risks and invest more energy in developing new technologies or new ways of working. This involves an acceptance of entrepreneurial behavior, financial support for entrepreneurial projects, and rewards for successes.

In some cases the psychological value this delivers to entrepreneurs—allowing them to pursue their instincts or hobbies and attributing status to this activity—means that they are prepared to work, on average, for less total reward. Like farmers, who choose a career that produces a meager return on capital because of its life-style benefits, entrepreneurially minded managers may be prepared to work for less if they are allowed to develop their own projects with a promise of significant rewards if the project succeeds.

The key pitfall to innovation venturing is to view the unit as a way of addressing a general concern about lack of entrepreneurial spirit in the company, rather than addressing a specific opportunity to improve the effectiveness of a specific function. We call this the *culture change pitfall*. During the late 1990s there were countless examples of companies making this mistake, in industries as diverse as investment banking, media, consumer goods, and information technology, typically under the banner of embracing the free-market principles of Silicon Valley and creating an internal market for ideas, people, and capital.[7]

To avoid this pitfall, the innovation venturing unit should report to and be governed by the function it is part of—the R&D function in the case of Shell's Gamechanger, the strategy function at Lloyds TSB, and Nokia Venture Organization. It should be managed by a small, senior-level team with its own operating budget (see Box 8.1). Of course, the unit also needs sufficient separation so that the team running it can make its own investment and development decisions and avoid the gravitational pull of the existing function. For innovation venturing to work, it has to balance on a knife edge—if it is too far from the core function, it is likely to succumb to the culture change pitfall, and if it is too close to the core function, it will struggle to carve out a distinctive role.

Obviously, we are not suggesting that managers should abandon attempts to make cultures more innovative. Rather, we believe that venture units are not the best tool for such culture change initiatives. Because it is hard to make venture units successful without close adherence to one of the three viable business models, the lack of financial success can undermine the culture change effort. Instead of using venture units to promote culture change, managers are better advised to focus on training or changes to planning systems or incentives.

PRIVATE EQUITY VENTURING

Some companies set up venture units to work with and compete with the venture capital industry. The goal is financial: there is no requirement that the unit will assist existing businesses or find a new growth platform to add to the portfolio. The company is doing little more than diversifying into the private equity industry.

GE Equity is one example of private equity venturing. Set up in 1995, GE Equity grew in five years from a zero base to a fund of $4 billion invested in 300 companies and a staff of over 200, with offices in Asia, Europe, and Latin America.[8]

Another example is Nokia Venture Partners (NVP), which was established in 1998 as a stand-alone unit in California, and subsequently with offices in London, Helsinki, and Israel. NVP makes significant minority investments in start-ups in the wireless internet space, and in all respects it operates as a venture capital firm (e.g., in terms of fund structures, sequenced investments, and carried interest for partners). Its success is measured purely in financial returns, rather than in terms of any particular benefits to Nokia Corporation. Its biggest success to date was the IPO of Paypal, in 2002. As one of the partners explained, "We do not do strategic investments [for Nokia] but the reason we exist is strategic for Nokia."

Private equity venturing is appropriate under rather limited circumstances. On the surface, it might make sense for a company to get into the private equity business if it had something significant to contribute. For example, research has been done that suggests that new ventures supported by corporate investments on average do better than ones that are not.[9] The investment of a major corporation appears to lend credibility to the new venture. This in turn helps the venture acquire customers, suppliers, and finance. On this logic, almost any large company with a good corporate brand could justify getting into private equity venturing. But this surface logic is flawed.

In order to justify entering the private equity industry by setting up a private equity venturing unit, a company needs to believe that it has unique access to a flow of deals. In other words, it has better access to good deals than normal, independent, private equity companies. When is this likely? In rather rare circumstances relating to a company's position in a marketplace or a technology. For example, GE Equity started off with a number of advantages that equipped it for success. GE Capital, its parent organization, had been doing deals for a number of years and had access to a promising external deal flow. In addition, GE Equity invested mainly in projects that could benefit from links with existing GE divisions, and attracted these divisions with a policy of co-investing.

The possession of something of value to new businesses, such as a well-regarded corporate reputation or even access to a market, is insufficient reason to enter the private equity business, because the "something of value" can normally be traded either directly with these new businesses or with an independent private equity company. In other words, the corporate parent that has a contribution to make can turn that contribution into value by trading it, without the risks and learning costs involved in getting into the private equity business.

In addition to unique access, managers also need to believe that the deal flow they are tapping into is in the early stages of an upswing. All new venture activity appears to go in cycles. First, some technical advance or change in law or in consumer tastes creates a new opportunity. Then entrepreneurs begin to exploit the opportunity. Soon the new opportunity is heavily overexploited, like a gold seam at the peak of a gold rush. Failures start to increase and greatly outnumber successes as the winners begin to emerge and dominate. Over the next few years the winners gradually squeeze out the weaker companies and new entrants fall to a trickle.

To make money in this cycle of boom and bust, investors must invest early and exit before the shake-out—even if they have invested in winners. The shake-out period is one of low profitability and high growth, not usually one that is comfortable for the corporate investor. Launching in 1996, GE Equity did get into many new markets early in the boom. In fact, the high percentage of successful units (65%) may be as much to do with the benign environment as with GE's unique access. Nearly everyone did well in private equity during these years.

The main pitfall in private equity venturing stems from hubris—the *anyone can do this syndrome*. Managers become attracted because others are making a success of something similar. They then enter the business, misjudging both the timing and the skills that are needed to create a success. Not only do they invest too late in the cycle, often putting together a second-rate team to compete in a booming sector, but they multiply their errors by overpaying for poor projects, losing sight of their unique contribution (if they had one), and holding on to investments for spurious strategic reasons. The examples are too numerous and too embarrassing to list.

The best way of avoiding this pitfall is simply to avoid getting into the private equity business unless the internal logic (the internal contribution and superior access to deals) is so strong that it can be justified without any evidence of external success stories. There are also some key elements to the business model that should be borne in mind (see Box 8.1). First, the unit should be fully separated from the company, with its own closed-end fund with a short investment period chosen in the light of the current private equity cycle, but of not more than five years. Second, it should be staffed with seasoned managers from the private equity industry. Third, the managers should be evaluated and rewarded as they would be in the private equity world—on the basis of return on investment, and through carried interest in their portfolio companies.

GE Equity may have been a victim of the anyone can do this syndrome. Its early timing was immaculate, but management did not have a closed-end fund that required early exit and did not reward staff on carried interest. Moreover, at the height of the boom, managers started investing in general internet opportunities rather than sticking to the deal stream where GE had an advantage. Possibly for these reasons GE Equity failed to cash in its successes before the bust, and by 2003 the unit had stopped making new investments and was considered internally to have been of doubtful value.

NEW LEG VENTURING

The fifth type of corporate venturing unit is more associated with an objective than a particular business model. New leg venturing involves using venturing techniques to identify and invest in new businesses that have the potential to become new legs to the portfolio. It is a remarkably common type: 22% of our examples were categorized at least in part as new leg venturing.

New leg venturing is common because many companies have core businesses that are growing only slowly or declining. In their search for new growth opportunities, managers realize that the pickings adjacent to their existing businesses are limited. They therefore start searching more widely and latch on to corporate venturing as a low-cost way of experimenting and trying out new areas. Moreover, they are encouraged in this by some of the most influential academics and management gurus.[10]

Unfortunately, new leg venturing does not appear to work. None of the units that were wholly or partially categorized as this type was successful. Whether the focus was external, using a business model similar to private equity venturing, or internal, using a business model similar to innovation venturing, no new legs were created and most units have been closed down with large losses. Recognizing the significance of this finding, we went in search of at least one success story—and failed. Our success criterion for new leg venturing units was demanding. We were looking for a unit that had spawned at least one significant (20% of sales or $1 billion in value) addition to the parent company portfolio. BG's Corporate Development Division came close. It screened 24 ideas and launched 11 ventures. Within 18 months one of the ventures—telecoms—seemed about to be a success: it was thought to have a value of $1 billion. However, the telecoms bust caused a reevaluation when the company closed the project with a write-off of £350 million.

The reason for this repeated failure rate is less clear. The logic for using a corporate venturing approach to explore new avenues for growth seems sound, but in practice it appears to be flawed. We have therefore hypothesized five reasons for this type of corporate venturing not working:

1　Managers only feel the need to use a corporate venturing approach if the obvious growth paths in adjacent businesses are blocked, hence the unit is focused on low-probability projects in the first place.
2　Because the new ventures are developed within a separate unit, they attract little attention or commitment from the core of the company.
3　The length of time it takes to develop a successful new division is longer than most business cycles, causing managers to draw back from the effort before enough resource has been committed.[11]
4　If one of the ventures begins to show promise, it starts to compete for funds with the core. Often the result is to short-change the new initiative.
5　Early-stage venturing is a tough environment even for professional, independent venture capital companies. On average, the activity of these venture capital experts probably earns less than its cost of capital, even after including the few big successes. Companies that enter this tough environment without some advantage cannot expect to beat the odds.

As we pointed out in Chapter 2, much of the current literature on innovation and growth encourages managers to set up venturing processes and venturing units. The logic is that these units will stimulate innovation and that they will provide a better support system for the large number of new developments that every company should be sponsoring. Our position in this book has been different. We believe that managers should not play the numbers game. This is because the problem of generating new growth businesses is not solved by multiplying the number of tries. It is solved when insights about how to do something better coincide with entrepreneurially minded managers and a host organization that has the right combination of resources and sponsorship. Each of these elements happens infrequently. Hence, they only come together at the same time extremely rarely. Efforts to force the pace are largely wasted. Rather than trying to stimulate the frequency of each of the ingredients, managers do better to scan the opportunities waiting for a good one to emerge.

Intel, as we have seen, has had one of the more successful experiences at corporate venturing. This is because its unit was designed around a venturing model that made sense. McDonald's has been less successful. For three or four years it had a unit with a venturing remit, although not formally a corporate venturing unit. This unit appeared to be part innovation venturing, helping the core business to be more innovative, and part new leg venturing, looking for major new businesses. The fact that the unit did not survive the 2002–2003 refocus suggests that it was not a huge success.

Instead, in 2003 McDonald's set up McDonald's Ventures. In terms of our venturing models, this is a harvest venturing unit. It contains five businesses that are the remnants of McDonald's venturing and partner brand efforts. The brief to Mats Lederhausen, the unit head, is to identify whether any of these businesses can be built into significant new legs for McDonald's without distracting from the core. For those that cannot achieve this difficult feat—and we might expect that none of them can—Mats is expected to find a suitable exit strategy.

THE ROLE OF CORPORATE VENTURING

This chapter has provided a detailed analysis of five different types of units that coexist under the corporate venturing banner. We began with the straightforward observation that most venture units fail, and in the course of the discussion we highlighted the key pitfalls that lead to failure in each of the five models. In each of the first four models, these pitfalls can be avoided and we gave examples of companies that have been successful. The fifth model, new leg venturing, rarely works. The single biggest cause of failure is that managers simply fail to define which model their venture unit is supposed to be following. As a result, the strategic and/or financial objectives are ambiguous, the structure and staffing decisions are out of alignment, and the unit's managers find themselves being pushed in several directions at once.

One example, from a UK financial services firm, is illustrative of this problem. Its venture unit was established in 1999 to create new businesses, and to establish a process for innovative thinking and renewal across the firm. In the first year, the venture unit manager spent £30 million setting the group up, and generating and developing internal ideas. But without any immediate successes from this effort, and without the skills to develop really big new projects, he switched focus toward ideas from outside the company. The manager toured venture capital companies and investment banks looking for investment opportunities, and he received several hundred business plans. But again, without a clear focus on which ones to invest in, the seed funding was not well spent, with only one significant business taking root. In late 2001 a new chief operating officer took control of the company and started to focus back on the core business. The venture unit attempted to rethink itself as an internal consultancy, but it was closed down and the few remaining activities were folded into the strategic planning group. This venture unit was essentially doomed from the start, because it never figured out its own business model—it migrated from new leg venturing to innovation venturing to ecosystem venturing, all within the space of three years.

Compare this to Nokia Ventures Organization (NVO), which has succeeded in generating some new businesses and some positive finan-

Box 8.1 Key elements of the five venturing models

Venture harvesting

❑ Focus—Generate cash from harvesting spare resources, exclude support to existing businesses and new leg ideas.

❑ Main pitfall—The new legs pitfall: seeking to develop new growth platforms in addition to the harvesting remit.

❑ Source of ideas—Mainly internal, but also external VCs and other companies.

❑ How separate—Clearly separate financial unit; separate ownership of resources of "agent" for primary owner. Report to top management level, often finance. No special governance required, but a board can be a useful way to involve outsiders.

❑ Skills—Mix of managers: some who understand the resources and some who can "sell" or "do deals." Good knowledge of venture capital industry and process of new business creation. Joint venture skills.

❑ Funding—Operating budgets. Some limited investment funds. Project-by-project funding for significant projects.

❑ Performance measures and incentives—Cash performance against "allocated" assets. Large bonuses paid against performance targets. No "carried interest."

Ecosystem venturing

❑ Focus—Take minority stakes in suppliers, customers, and/or complementors to improve prospects of existing businesses. Generate value through commercial links with investee firms.

❑ Main pitfall—The loss of focus temptation: investing too widely and seeking too much autonomy.

❑ Source of ideas—Mainly external. VCs and direct approaches from candidate ventures. Ideas linked to existing businesses.

❑ How separate—Separate financial unit reporting to investment board including top management of existing businesses. Close links to existing businesses through overlapping staff. Each investment should be sponsored by an existing business.

❑ Skill—Small senior-level team of "investors": some with strong credibility in the existing businesses and some with strong credibility in the VC industry. Team must be comfortable collaborating with existing businesses.

❑ Funding—Operating budgets. Investment funds ring-fenced in operating plan but subject to project-by-project sanction.

❑ Performance measures and incentives—Significant cash bonus scheme based on impact on existing businesses and portfolio performance. No "carried interest."

Venturing innovation

❏ Focus—Use venturing techniques as a more effective means of performing (part of) an existing functional activity. Often, but not exclusively, applied to R&D.

❏ Main pitfall—The culture change pitfall: aiming for a broad impact on culture change rather than a narrow focus on improving part of a function.

❏ Source of ideas—Mainly internal, but also external VCs and other companies.

❏ How separate—Separate financial unit not essential. More of a separate process than a unit. Report to investment board led by functional director and external (to function) advisers.

❏ Skills—Small team of "nurturers": some with strong credibility in the existing businesses and some with good knowledge of VC industry and process of new business creation. Joint venture skills.

❏ Funding—Operating budgets. Budget of replaced activity reduced accordingly. Investment funds ring-fenced in operating plan, subject to stage-gate sanction by investment board.

❏ Performance measures and incentives—Performance benchmarked against rest of function. Financial interest given to entrepreneurs not to "nurturers."

Corporate private equity

❏ Focus—Take advantage of a unique deal flow and relevant and non-tradable assets to participate directly in the VC/private equity industry.

❏ Main pitfall—The anyone can do it pitfall: believing that it is easy because others are being successful.

❏ Source of ideas—Mainly external through VC network. Ideas screened against pre-agreed search specification.

❏ How separate—Clearly separate business and financial unit, located in relevant financial center(s). Report as other business units. Governance through investment board with a majority of external directors.

❏ Skills—Primarily VC industry specialists with relevant sector experience: some with in-depth knowledge and network to tap into the host company's non-tradable asset.

❏ Funding—Closed-end fund with defined exit date of five years or less. Unit funded through annual management fee.

❏ Performance measures and incentives—Bonus and share-carry incentives in line with VC industry norms.

cial returns for its parent company. Rather than create a single unit with multiple or changing goals, NVO has created multiple units, each with its own highly specific goals and its own dedicated team of employees. As described earlier, New Growth Businesses is an innovation venturing unit, whose objective is to complement the existing R&D activities of the businesses. Nokia Venture Partners is a private equity venturing unit dedicated to providing a financial return by investing in wireless internet start-ups. In addition, there is the Nokia Early Stage Technology unit, which invests in promising technologies, most of which will end up being spun out of the company—a harvest venturing operation.

The NVO example highlights the key message of this chapter. There is a role for corporate venturing, but it takes many different forms. Companies need to choose which form they want and build a unit to match. Mixed objectives and vague ambitions about building new legs condemn a venturing unit to muddled thinking and failure. Success comes from limiting the ambitions of the unit to something achievable and setting it up with a business model that can deliver.

CHAPTER 9

POSITIONING AND SUPPORTING A NEW BUSINESS

Much of this book has been about selection: which new businesses, if any, should your company invest in? It has also been about how to organize the search for new businesses: whether to set up a corporate venturing unit, whether to launch many or a few experiments, and whether to create a group at the center of the organization whose responsibility is the development of new businesses. We now want to turn to the question of how to make sure a new business is successful: how to grow the new business into a significant division within your company.

Many books on new businesses cover topics ranging from staffing and resourcing to market entry strategies to the different stages of growth. In fact, one good book on growing new ventures has chapters covering selecting, evaluating, and compensating venture management; developing the business plan; and organizing the venture.[1]

Instead of revisiting these topics, we are going to focus on four corporate-level issues that are critical to success:

1 How far should the new business be integrated with or separated from the existing businesses?
2 At what level in the organization should the new business report?
3 What support should be provided to the new business by the layers of management "above" it?
4 How should corporate managers monitor progress, and when should they pull the plug?

We have chosen these four subjects because they are all about the way the parent company looks after the new business and because they are all issues where we believe our research has generated some fresh insights.

INTEGRATE OR SEPARATE?

The received wisdom is that new businesses should be kept separate from the existing businesses so that they receive dedicated attention and can develop ways of working, cultures, and strategies that are appropriate to their customers and competitors.[2] If they are integrated with existing businesses, they are likely to end up with similar strategies and cultures and get less attention and resource whenever the existing businesses hit a bump.

There is much evidence to support this received wisdom. Charles O'Reilly and Michael Tushman looked at 35 "breakthrough" product initiatives.[3] Seven of the initiatives were carried out within the existing functional design. Nine were managed using cross-functional teams within the existing functional structure. Four were set up as project teams outside the existing functional structure. Fifteen were set up as separate business units with their own functional structures. While 90% of the separate business units were successful, none of the cross-functional teams or project teams was. Only four of the nine "existing functional structure" initiatives were successful. Moreover, eight of the initiatives started out with one of the first three structures and then set up a separate business unit. In seven of the eight cases performance improved.

O'Reilly and Tushman propose high degrees of separation, what they call an ambidextrous organization. The businesses are completely separate for operational purposes but integrated at the next layer up; in other words, they have the same parent as the existing businesses. In this way the new businesses are protected from inappropriate influences from sister companies, but can still draw on some of the strengths of the parent company.

Design alternatives

Operational relatedness	Very important	Uncertain	Not important
Unrelated	3 Special business unit	4 Independent business unit	9 Complete spin-off
Partly related	2 New product/ business dept	5 New venture division	8 Contracting
Strongly related	1 Direct integration	5 New ventures department	7 Nurturing and contracting

Strategic importance

Figure 9.1 How to structure new businesses: Burgelman's matrix

Clayton Christensen also argues for separation rather than integration when the new business is different from the existing businesses.[4] He offers two dimensions of fit: fit with processes and fit with values. If the new business requires processes and values different from the existing businesses, it should be set up as a "heavyweight" autonomous unit. If both processes and values fit the existing businesses, the new initiative can be part of the mainstream functional structure.

Robert Burgelman, another academic who has studied these issues, offers a range of structural solutions using some different dimensions to Christensen. Burgelman argues that the structural solution depends on the degree of "operational relatedness" and the importance the new business has for the corporate strategy. He identifies nine different solutions, showing how each can be linked to these two dimensions (see Figure 9.1).[5]

Although each author recognizes that there is a choice of how to organize and that the choice depends on how different the new business is from the existing businesses, the default position is "separate unless there are good reasons not to." We agree with this broad rule of

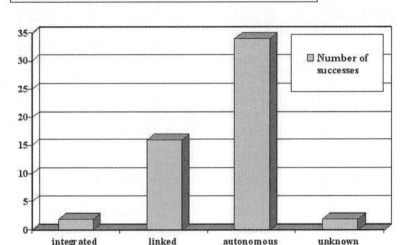

Figure 9.2 Degrees of autonomy of new businesses

thumb, especially because managers are often biased against separation.[6] They are often reluctant to make the commitment necessary for the creation of a new business unit. They believe that the new initiative will be easier to control in the existing structure. They prefer to keep the new initiative less visible, allowing it to be less accountable for success or failure. In our database of successes, over 60% operated as autonomous business units, and most of the rest had some degree of independence (Figure 9.2).

In practice, the decision is often more complicated than Christensen and Burgelman's simple matrices suggest. Other issues will influence the decision. The availability of management talent, the need for clear accountability, the impact on the motivation of the managers involved, and the need to be able to change the structure as the project evolves are all factors that can influence the final organization structure.

Fortunately, Michael Goold and Andrew Campbell have developed a framework for designing organization structures that can be used to address the separate or integrate issue.[7] The framework is built on nine principles of organization design, each of which has been turned into a

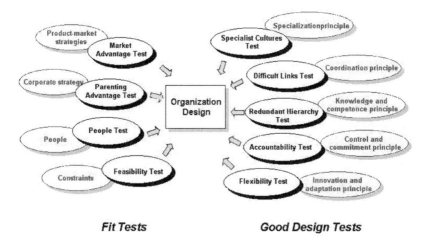

Fit Tests   **Good Design Tests**

Figure 9.3 Nine tests for organization design

test (see Figure 9.3). For example, the principle around product-market strategies is that the organization structure should give sufficient management attention to the priorities in the company's product-market strategies. The market advantage test therefore has two parts to it. The first part is about checking that there is an organization unit dedicated to each market segment that is a priority in the strategy. The second part is about checking whether any sources of competitive advantage or important operating tasks require collaboration across these unit boundaries. Where they do, the test asks whether the organization has processes or mechanisms that ensure sufficient management attention is focused on making the collaboration work well (see Box 9.1 overleaf for an explanation of the tests).

This framework of tests makes it possible to do detailed analysis of the separate or integrate issue. The default position—separate unless there are good reasons not to—can still be the starting point. In fact, the market advantage test suggests that a separate organizational unit is required for any new product-market priority, especially if the new priority involves some different operational initiatives and sources of advantage. Egg, the internet bank set up by Prudential, is a classic example. It was initially established to provide a deposit service to existing customers, suggesting that it should be a separate production

Box 9.1 The nine tests of organization design

Four fit tests

❏ Market advantage test

"Does the design allocate sufficient management attention to the operating priorities and intended sources of advantage in each product-market area?"

❏ Parenting advantage test

"Does the design provide the layers and mechanisms needed to implement the parenting propositions and strategic initiatives?"

❏ People test

"Does the design accommodate and build on the motivations, strengths, and weaknesses of the available people?"

❏ Feasibility test

"Does the design take account of the constraints that may make the proposal unworkable?"

Five good design tests

❏ Specialist cultures test

"Do any specialist cultures—units with cultures that need to be different from sister units and the layer above—have sufficient protection from the influence of the dominant culture?"

❏ Difficult links test

"Do all important 'difficult links'—links between units that will be hard to achieve on a networking basis—have 'coordination solutions' that will ease the difficulty?"

❏ Accountability test

"Does the design make it possible to develop performance measures for each unit that are appropriate to the unit's responsibilities, low cost to implement, and motivating for the managers in the unit?"

❏ Redundant hierarchy test

"Does the design have any levels in the hierarchy or any responsibilities retained by higher levels that are not justified by a knowledge and competence advantage?"

❏ Flexibility test

"Will the design help the development of new strategies and be flexible enough to adapt to future changes?"

unit but draw on the existing salesforces. However, as the ambitions of Egg expanded to include internet banking and credit cards, it developed a different product-market focus, different operating priorities, and different sources of advantage. It needed to become a separate division within the Prudential group.

The value of the nine tests is that they offer a framework. They provide a checklist to see whether a new business should follow the default solution of separation or not. Each of the four fit tests can suggest that a new business should be more rather than less integrated:

❏ The *market advantage test* may suggest more integration if the new business is selling to the same market, using the same product or technology, dependent on some common operating initiative, such as an IT platform, or drawing on a shared source of advantage, such as a shared brand or shared economy of scale.

❏ The *parenting advantage test* may suggest more integration if the new business is part of some overarching corporate- or division-level strategy. For example, if the corporate-level strategy is to provide a full range of products to a certain customer base, a business set up to add a missing product to the range would need to be less separated from the other businesses than one set up to address a different customer base.

❏ The *people test* may suggest more integration if the business unit needs to draw on the skills of particular managers or teams that cannot be fully allocated to the new business.

❏ The *feasibility test* may suggest more integration if some constraint, such as regulation or IT systems, makes separation impractical.

Each of the five good design tests can also suggest that a new business should be more integrated:

❏ The *specialist cultures test* is about achieving sufficient separation. But if this test concludes that the cultures and business models are similar, more integration becomes possible.

❏ The *difficult links test* often suggests more integration. Where links with other units are difficult to resolve on an arm's-length basis (e.g., transfer pricing, shared resources, coordinated strategies), partial or even full integration of the units may be necessary to get the optimum outcome.

❏ The *redundant hierarchy test* may suggest more integration if the next level above the new business needs to draw on managers in the new business to achieve division-wide or corporate-wide initiatives.

❏ The *accountability test* may suggest more integration if the new business's performance is highly dependent on the actions of other units in the organization. In this situation it may be hard to make the managers of the new business fully accountable. It may be better to hold performance reviews and set targets in combination with the units on which the new business is dependent.

❏ The *flexibility test* may suggest more integration in situations where the market or technology across a group of businesses is changing fast. Firm boundaries between units may need to be more flexible to accommodate experiments with selling different product combinations to different market segments.

Mars's move into ice cream in Europe is an interesting example of how to apply these tests. Mars in Europe was a strong player in confectionery, pet foods, and some other foods such as rice. The confectionery division wanted to enter the ice-cream market using technology and product ideas from Mars's US ice-cream business and the division's confectionery brands, such as Mars, Snickers, and Bounty.

The default position—separate unless there are good reasons—applied. The market advantage test suggested that a new unit would be necessary for this new product segment. In addition, the specialist cultures test suggested that separation would be needed because ice cream might need some different strategies. However, some of the fit tests pointed in the opposite direction. The division was integrating some functions, such as manufacturing, across Europe and other functions, such as human resources, across divisions. Major savings were being achieved. Hence the idea of setting up a separate business unit with its own functions ran counter to the division-level strategy (parenting advantage test). In addition, the confectionery division did not have and could not easily locate a manager who would be capable of running a completely separate business focused on the ice-cream market while at the same time linking closely to the existing Mars organization (people test). Mars had found that recruiting managers from outside at a senior level rarely worked.

The good design tests also suggested more integration. The new ice-cream business would be competing with Unilever and Nestlé from a standing start. If it had its own manufacturing, own sales, and own marketing, it would have a cost disadvantage to its competitors. It could only be cost competitive if it leveraged the cost structure of the confectionery business. This created some potential difficult links between the new business and the functions of its parent organization (difficult links test). To get the best cost position, the solution was to integrate the functions so that the manufacturing was done by the confectionery manufacturing function, sales by the confectionery salesforce, and so on. There were some exceptions, such as a dedicated salesforce for seaside resorts.

Once the decision to integrate the functions had been made, the ice-cream business looked more like a new product within the confectionery business than a new business. But should the ice-cream unit be a small project team within central marketing or should it be set up as a separate business unit? The conclusion initially was to establish it as a separate business reporting to the head of confectionery Europe. This would ensure that it received dedicated attention and did not get lost in the priority-setting process within marketing (market advantage test). It also helped create accountability and motivation (accountability test). In addition, it made it possible to attract a more senior manager to lead the unit (people test).

A simple analysis of Mars's ice-cream ambitions in Europe, using either Christensen or Burgelman's matrices, would have reached the conclusion that some middle-ground solution—neither complete separation nor complete integration—would be appropriate. But it is only by using the nine tests of organization design that managers can be confident that they have thought through all the issues and can test fine-grained alternatives to see which is likely to work best.

REPORTING LEVEL

The choice about who a new business should report to is a subset of the organization structure choice and hence can also be analyzed by using the nine tests. In the Mars ice-cream situation, the choice initially was to have the new business report in at the European level rather than the marketing level. Later, Mars created a new businesses division within confectionery Europe. Ice cream, along with three other new businesses, formed part of this division.

The choice of reporting level is between low down, meaning reporting into some function or smaller unit, or high up, meaning reporting into the chief executive. In our database of successes, 63% reported to the CEO and 24% to a major division. None reported to a new businesses division or new ventures group (Figure 9.4 overleaf).

The reason for devoting a separate section to the question of reporting levels is because, as in Mars, this is frequently a tricky decision and because we have some new insights to share.

The advantages of reporting high up—to the chief executive—are substantial:

❏ It ensures that significant attention is focused on the opportunity (market advantage test).
❏ It ensures that the wisdom of the organization is applied to helping this new business, because the CEO is the person most able to call on his or her colleagues to help (parenting advantage test)
❏ It makes it easier to recruit high-quality managers (people test).
❏ It makes it easier to provide protection from intrusive functions or divisions (specialist cultures test).
❏ It can help with difficult collaboration issues between the new business and other businesses in the portfolio, because the chief

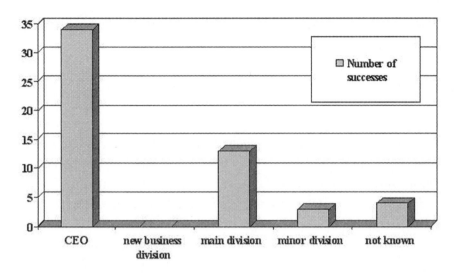

Figure 9.4 Reporting relationships

executive is likely to learn about them and has the power to step in and solve them (difficult links test).

❑ It ensures that there are no unnecessary layers of management between the unit and the chief executive (redundant hierarchy test).
❑ It provides motivating accountability (accountability test).

The main problems with high-up reporting are the following:

❑ The chief executive is usually already overburdened with reporting relationships. As a result, it can be hard for him or her to give sufficient time to the new business (feasibility test).
❑ The arrangement is often rather inflexible, because managers who have reported to the CEO are reluctant to change to a reporting relationship lower down in the organization at a later date (flexibility test).

As a result, although the default position is often high-up reporting, a lower-down reporting relationship can be a better choice.

To help with the choice, we have developed some thoughts that guide managers to the right compromise between high up and low down. These thoughts are additional to rather than a replacement for the nine tests.

WHERE IS THE NEW BUSINESS IMPORTANT TO STRATEGY?

First, the new business should report into a layer in the organization for which the new business is an important part of the strategy at that layer. For example, the ice-cream initiative at Mars Europe should not report into Mars Inc. in the USA. It was not a significant part of Mars Inc.'s corporate strategy. It was a significant part of the strategy of the confectionery division in Europe, hence this was a good level at which to report. The European ice-cream initiative might have been a significant part of the strategy of the broader business in Europe (confectionery, petfoods, and other foods). If it had been, it could have reported in at a level above confectionery. The initiative might also have been a major strategy for Mars's ice-cream business, Dove, in the US. If it was, then the unit could have reported to Dove.

There is no right or wrong level with regard to the strategy question. The rule is purely pragmatic. At which level in the organization is the new business a major part of the strategy? This is the level to which the unit should report. If it is important to more than one level, there is a choice. The Egg initiative at Prudential was important both to the UK division and to the corporate level. Hence this rule would not have pointed to a final choice for Egg.

IS THERE A MANAGER WITH THE RIGHT KNOWLEDGE AND SKILLS?

Second, the new business should report to a manager with the knowledge, skills, and time to be a good parent to the business. This is a restatement of the redundant hierarchy test. The knowledge and skills needed depend on the industry that the new business is in, the skills of the management team running the new business, and the nature of the links between the new business and the existing businesses. The "parent" manager will need to understand the industry in order to be able to give good counsel to managers. Understanding the industry will also help him or her protect the business from inappropriate influences from corporate functions or other divisions. He or she will need to have, or have access to, skills that the management team of the new business is weak in. This might be IT skills or negotiating with regulator skills or financial control skills. Finally, the parent manager will need to be able to smooth the links with other parts of the organization.

In the Mars ice-cream example, there was no ideal parent manager for the unit. The head of Europe did not have particular knowledge of the ice-cream industry and, although he had most of the other skills needed, he had limited time available.

HOW MANY LAYERS BETWEEN INVESTOR AND ENTREPRENEUR?

Third, there should be the minimum of layers between the manager allocating the money and the manager leading the new business: between the investor and the entrepreneur. The reason for this is that the manager allocating the money is the manager who ultimately makes the decision about whether to support this new business or not. In addition, as the business develops, this manager makes important decisions about how much money to allocate to the new venture. This manager or committee (in some companies the tough allocation decisions are made by a committee) needs to be as close to the new business as possible, so that he or she (or they) has as much understanding of the issues as is needed to make wise allocation decisions.

One of the advantages that the venture capital companies have over corporate parents with regard to supporting new businesses is that the venture capitalist has no layers of management. Each partner in the venture capitalist firm will have his or her own portfolio of investments and will make the allocation decisions. The decisions are subject to approval, but the head of the venture is dealing with a principal of the firm not an agent. Moreover, because the partners in the firm do not have many operating responsibilities, they are able to spend as much time as necessary getting close to their investments and understanding the issues. Corporate managers need to try to mimic this way of working as far as possible.

The disadvantage of having intermediate layers of management is significant. One problem is that the intermediate layer becomes risk averse. Since the intermediate layer is neither leading the new business nor taking decisions about how much support to give the new business, the role has few upsides and significant downsides. If the new business does not work out, some of the blame will fall on the intermediate manager. If it does work out, most of the credit will go to those making the tough decisions. This reality normally makes the intermediate manager risk averse.

An additional problem is that the intermediate manager inevitably screens information from the layer above. Sometimes this is intentional, but more often it is merely an inevitable consequence of having the extra layer. Without the extra layer, there is direct dialogue between the manager in charge of the new business and the manager making the investment decisions. This direct dialogue inevitably results in more information flow. Again and again in our research we encountered problems where new businesses were reporting to an intermediate layer.

This does not mean that all new businesses should report into the corporate board. What it does mean is that they should report into a layer in the organization that has the discretion to allocate money to this business without being second-guessed by layers above. For small projects, this may be low down in the structure.

This guiding thought appears to be in contrast to recent work done by Burgelman.[8] Burgelman argues that intermediate layers play a vital role of communication. They help the managers running new businesses understand the corporate-level strategy and they help corporate-level managers decide whether to extend the corporate strategy to incorporate some successful new initiative.

In our view, these apparently divergent positions can be reconciled. Where the intermediate manager has discretion to allocate money to the new venture, it is possible for Burgelman's and our objectives to be achieved. If, however, the intermediate manager is a "middleman" without the power to approve budgets, then we have observed that the damage done through risk aversion and information screening outweighs the benefits of having an intermediary helping the communication flow with corporate levels.

DO REPORTING RELATIONSHIPS ALLOW OBJECTIVITY?

Fourth, the reporting relationships should provide some process of objectivity or governance in order to offset the risk of having the manager allocating the money becoming its champion or major sponsor. As one chief executive explained to us:

> The greatest mistake I have made was getting too close to a manager who was in love with his business. He got me to fall in love with it too.

The cost to the company was many millions of write-offs.

When the manager with discretion to allocate money to the business is not the corporate chief executive, there are normally plenty of checks and balances. The layer or layers above will provide sufficient challenge and objectivity to spot when the sponsoring manager has "fallen in love" with the new business.

When the new business reports to the chief executive, however, the risks increase. In our sample of major successes, while 63% reported to and were encouraged by the corporate chief executive, many of the most expensive new business failures are ones that report to and are protected by the chief executive.

Nevertheless, the problem does not only exist when new businesses report to the chief executive. It can also occur when a new business reports to a powerful member of the top team. If this person is firmly committed to the new venture, it can be hard for the other senior executives to act as an objective safety net.

A solution is not always possible. Without a balance of power in the executive team, strong-willed individuals can ignore the counsel of colleagues and overrule objective guidance. Hence when new businesses report to managers on the corporate executive team, especially the chief executive, the chief finance officer should form a governance board for this new venture consisting of some executives and some non-executives. The role of this board is to provide the extra objectivity that can be so necessary when the new business starts to underperform.

SUPPORT FROM LAYERS ABOVE

New businesses can be new ventures that need a great deal of support, or acquisitions of established companies that need very little support, or something in between. It is important, therefore, that explicit analysis is carried out to define the support required. We call this Parenting Opportunity Analysis (see Box 9.2 overleaf): it is an analysis of the opportunities that exist for parent managers to help the new business.

Our approach to providing support to new businesses is highly tailored: we believe that parent managers need to think about each new business individually and decide both what support is needed and, importantly, what support is not needed. In our view, one of the main reasons for new business failures comes from giving new businesses too much support rather than too little. We are not referring here to money, but to advice and guidance. Parent managers and functional experts are either so eager to help the new business or so determined to control it that they burden it with too much guidance, interference, and support. Finding the right balance is critical.

When Unilever bought Calvin Klein, a luxury perfume and cosmetics business, senior managers were concerned that there would be too much influence on this new business from the Unilever central functions and the Unilever culture. Unilever businesses were mainly mass-market consumer products, in contrast to Calvin Klein's up-market products. As a result, the culture and ways of working at Calvin Klein were rather different. In order to provide some protection to Calvin Klein, Unilever decided to create a gatekeeper. For the first year all contact between Unilever managers and Calvin Klein

Box 9.2 Parenting Opportunity Analysis

1   List the major tasks that managers in the business unit will need to complete in the next period. For a new venture, the period may be six months or a year. For a more established business the period should be two to three years. The tasks will be items such as:
- ❑ get regulatory approval for the new technology
- ❑ put in a new integrated IT system
- ❑ enter the German market and win 5% market share
- ❑ upgrade skills in the supply chain function
- ❑ reduce the cost of manufacture for product X

2   Examine each task (a typical business unit will have five to ten major tasks) and assess whether the management team of the business is likely to do the task excellently, well, averagely, or poorly. For tasks scored averagely or poorly, consider what support could be given to the management team to help it complete the task more effectively.

3   List other areas of support that managers in the parent layers consider the new business will need. Start by listing the thoughts of the line manager to whom the unit reports. Add the thoughts of higher levels of line management. Add to this list other areas of support suggested by corporate functions, such as finance, marketing, planning, research, and so on.

4   Review the full list of areas of support and decide which the company is capable of providing. Then consider this subset and identify the top three to five areas of support in terms of their likely impact on the performance of the new business. The objective is to focus the support on those few areas that will really make a difference. Finally, check that the line manager and supporting functions have the capacity to provide the support needed, and make adjustments either to capacity or to support plans (or even reconsider investing in the new business at all) to ensure that the support plan is reasonable.

managers had to be channeled through one individual. This is a process solution to the issue of what support to provide.

In contrast to our view about tailoring support for new businesses, many authors advise companies to set up a new businesses support team or new ventures incubator to help new ventures find their feet. We are cautious about advising companies to do this, because we observe that these systems do not appear to succeed. Successful new ventures appear to come about in a much more serendipitous way. They do not seem to be susceptible to a systematic development process. Hence when companies set up a structured support group for new ventures, they normally encourage managers to invest in too many initiatives with low probabilities of success. If it is possible to maintain discipline about the number and quality of new ventures, a system of structured support can be useful.

IBM's Emerging Business Opportunity program, already mentioned in Chapter 7, identified four areas of support that would be given to each EBO—"the extra support and attention needed by young, unformed ventures":

❑ *Leadership*: traditionally IBM had assigned younger managers to lead new ventures, but they proved not to have the organizational clout needed to work across IBM's complex matrix. One of the roles of the EBO program was to ensure that each EBO was led by an experienced IBMer. This had implications for skill building, selection processes, career path processes, and performance evaluation processes.
❑ *Strategy*: IBM's traditional strategy processes presumed reasonably stable strategies for each business. With EBOs the strategy might evolve three or four times in a year. Hence the management teams were given extra support on strategy development.
❑ *Resources*: the traditional funding process did not secure funds for new ventures. The venture leaders had to continuously scramble and "bootlace" resources. EBOs were given secure funding programs and support in finding the people they needed.
❑ *Tracking and monitoring*: IBM's traditional performance metrics

were often unsuitable for new ventures. Hence a separate system of milestone reporting was developed, and finance also ring-fenced the revenues and costs associated with each venture so that the financial picture was clear.

IBM's program is a good example. Even so, we criticize it for being insufficiently tailored to the particular needs of each EBO. In practice, no doubt, the support actually given to each EBO was adjusted based on that EBO's needs. However, the menu of support areas was developed top down rather than bottom up and has become institutionalized rather than driven by the particular needs of the EBOs. It is this presumption that all new ventures need the same kind of support that is dangerous.

One particular issue of support worth special mention involves persuading existing businesses to offer help to a new business. Existing businesses may have specific skills—like product design, customization, low-cost production, or customer relationship building—that could strengthen the new business. Similarly, unique assets and resources, like highly skilled IT professionals or a motivated dealer network, may be owned by one of the other businesses. Making such skills and assets available to a new business is generally very difficult. Even when a new business is linked to an existing business by a common reporting relationship or some shared functions, the natural instinct of each unit is to focus on meeting its own objectives. Any support provided to the new business can be seen as a distraction.

For the new business unit, the ability and willingness to seek and accept help are not automatic either. When a new unit is being built up from scratch, it often lacks some of the disciplines and experts that understand what is needed. In the case of acquisitions, there may be a mixture of arrogance and wounded pride, which discourages managers from seeking help.

Corporate managers have a key role to play to overcome these barriers. While we do not have any foolproof solutions, the following actions can help:

❑ Create some shared objectives for existing businesses, which include building the new business.

❑ Make sure that the progress of the new business is frequently communicated to all the managers that need to be supportive.

❑ Structure incentives such that managers in existing businesses are rewarded for the success of the new business.

❑ Ensure that managers' personal objectives include transferring skills and sharing assets with the new business.

❑ Set up councils or networks of experts to foster the transfer of knowledge and skills to the new business.

In other words, do not leave this crucial source of support to chance. If corporate managers do not actively promote and police the transfer of skills and resources, it will only happen in a patchy way.

MONITORING PROGRESS

Acquisitions of established companies can be assessed by the parent company's normal monitoring processes. Some additional monitoring may be needed to ensure that the cost savings and other synergy benefits that justified the acquisition are fully realized, but no significant change will be required to budgeting and planning processes.

Monitoring new ventures, however, does pose a problem. Not only are these businesses difficult to monitor against plan or against budget, but when performance is unexpectedly poor, there is always a question about whether to pull the plug.

The received wisdom is that new ventures should be monitored against milestones, rather than plans or budgets. One of the few predictable features of a new venture is that in its early years, it will miss budget on a number of occasions and it will need to change plans as a result of new information about competitors, marketplace, or technology. As a result, the best way to monitor progress is to agree milestones that are three to twelve months away and fund the business plan to achieve the milestone. When the milestone is reached, another is set

Box 9.3 Confidence Check for new businesses

Traffic Lights confidence
- ❏ Value advantage
- ❏ Profit pool potential
- ❏ Leadership/sponsorship quality
- ❏ Impact on existing businesses

Execution confidence
- ❏ Sales confidence
- ❏ Technology and operations confidence
- ❏ Partner, supplier, enabler confidence
- ❏ Support-from-core confidence
- ❏ Funding and governance confidence

and funded. If a milestone is missed, a new plan is prepared and the decision about whether to continue to fund the project is revisited.[9]

We agree broadly with this received wisdom. However, it poses some difficult managerial issues. How do managers decide what should be the next milestone? Moreover, when should they decide to stop funding the project?

To help with these issues, we have developed a tool called the Confidence Check (see Box 9.3). Its purpose is to help managers assess their level of confidence that the new venture will succeed. The tool has two sections: confidence about the judgments in the Traffic Lights, the judgments that formed the basis for believing that this would be a success; and confidence about the ability to do what is necessary to make the project work.

The Confidence Check can be applied at any stage as a new business progresses from its beginning to its final stage as a successful division. As each milestone is achieved or difficulties are encountered along the way, corporate managers need a process for confirming their commitment. The Confidence Check can be at the center of this process, which should involve the sponsor, the new business team, and other senior executives such as the chief financial officer, the chief technology officer, and the chief strategist. As a minimum, the process should be applied as the following milestones are approached:

❑ Approval of a detailed business plan, after the exploratory phase of a new business idea.
❑ Development of the technology, prototype product, or service is complete and trial customers are ready to be involved.
❑ Initial scale-up of the offering has been concluded and results from customer trials are available.
❑ First expansion phase has been finished and further investment is required to achieve target profitability.

TRAFFIC LIGHTS CONFIDENCE

The Traffic Lights confidence section involves asking four questions that parallel the four sections of the Traffic Lights: profit pool potential, value advantage, leadership/sponsorship quality, and impact on existing businesses. The four questions are:

❑ Are we confident that the profit pool potential is still sufficient to justify this project?
❑ Are we confident that our value advantage is still sufficient to justify this project?
❑ Are we confident that we have project leaders and sponsors of sufficient quality to justify this project?
❑ Are we confident that the impact on the core businesses is such that this project is still justified?

Just as the Traffic Lights were used in Chapter 3 to help managers decide whether a new business opportunity had a reasonable chance of success, they are used again throughout the early life of the project to confirm that it still has a reasonable chance of success. The analysis carried out before the project started should be revisited and the consequences of any major changes in judgment considered. The easiest way for managers to pull the plug on a project is for them to decide that one or more of the Traffic Lights is red. This may be because misjudgments were made when doing the original assessment or because the world has changed. For example, the original judgment may have overestimated the skills of the new business's leaders. Alternatively, new competitors may have emerged, costs of supplies may have risen, or customer needs may have changed.

EXECUTION CONFIDENCE

The second half of the Confidence Check looks at execution issues. These are the issues for which milestones will be set. Our contribution here is to define the categories and sub-categories of execution that need to be considered. The execution confidence section is a comprehensive list of the execution factors that should be reviewed. Not all factors will be relevant to all new ventures. However, once these factors have been considered, managers can be confident that they have asked all the important questions.

We have defined five execution categories, each of which has a number of sub-categories (Figure 9.5). The arrow in the middle of the

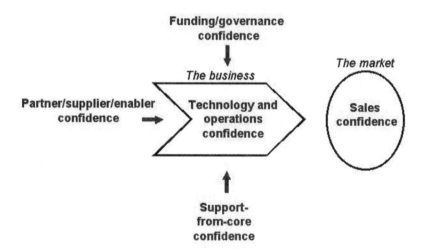

Figure 9.5 Execution confidence

figure represents the new business. The circle to the right represents the marketplace the new business is trying to serve.

One execution category concerns that marketplace. The question we pose is:

SALES CONFIDENCE: Are we confident that we will achieve sufficient sales at the price we need to make an acceptable return (assuming, of course, that we can deliver the product or service at the cost we are planning)?

There are a number of sub-questions that make up the sales confidence question:

1 Are we confident that we have a significant value proposition, a target customer group, and appropriate delivery channels? In other words, do we have a crisp vision for the business?
2 Are we confident that we can identify the target customers and access their decision process?
3 Are we confident that the target customers will buy our offer once we have accessed their decision process?
4 Are we confident that the target customers will pay enough to give us an attractive margin on the cost of goods sold?
5 Are we confident that the target customer group will be large enough to give us the volumes we need to earn a decent return on our fixed costs?
6 And finally, are we confident that we know what sales issues to monitor and what stage gates to set?

The first five sub-questions build on each other. A lack of confidence with any of these is sufficient to create a lack of confidence with the main question. The last sub-question, concerning sales issues and stage gates, is a final reminder that managers need to feel knowledgeable enough about the business to know what aspect of the sales challenge requires attention next.

A second execution category concerns the operations of the business. The question we pose is:

TECHNOLOGY AND OPERATIONS CONFIDENCE: Are we confident that we can produce, deliver, and service our offer and keep abreast of technology at costs that will give us a good margin?

There are a number of sub-questions that make up the technology and operations confidence question:

1 Are we confident that we can overcome the technical challenges involved with this offer?
2 Are we confident that we can overcome the legal, environmental, health and safety, and related challenges involved with this offer?
3 Are we confident that we can produce, deliver, and service this offer in the volumes planned?
4 Are we confident that we can sell, produce, deliver, and service this offer at a cost that will provide an attractive return on capital invested?
5 Are we confident that we can keep abreast of the technology in this area?
6 Are we confident that we know what operations issues to monitor and what stage gates to set?

The first three sub-questions cover the technical and operating challenges. It may be necessary to add additional questions to this list depending on the particular operating challenges facing the business. For example, a high-tech company will have many questions about the technical challenges, such as whether the intellectual property can be protected and whether standards around the new technology can be developed. The fourth sub-question is about whether the costs of providing the offer will, given the likely price and volumes, result in an attractive return. The fifth sub-question is about the longer term. Will it be possible to keep up with likely future technology developments? The last sub-question, concerning operations issues and stage gates, is a final reminder that managers need to feel knowledgeable enough about the business to know what aspect of the technology and operations challenge requires attention next.

A third category concerns partners, suppliers, and enablers. This category covers all organizations external to the company whose support is needed in the success of this venture. The question we pose is:

PARTNER/SUPPLIER/ENABLER CONFIDENCE: Are we confident that we can find and retain the support of the partners, suppliers, and enablers we need?

There are a number of sub-questions that make up the partner/supplier/enabler confidence question:

1 Are we confident that we have or can find partners/suppliers/enablers with the world-class resources and ability to develop that we need from them if they are to help us succeed in this market?
2 Are we confident that our partners/suppliers/enablers will remain committed to working with us despite setbacks or likely other priorities?
3 Are we confident that our partners/suppliers/enablers will allocate sufficient numbers of people in support of our venture and that they will be sufficiently competent and committed?
4 Are we confident that we have or will have good agreements with our partners/suppliers/enablers?
5 Are we confident that we know what partner/supplier/enabler issues to monitor and what stage gates to set?

The first four sub-questions cover the main issues that can lead to problems with partners, suppliers, or enablers. In a specific venture it will be possible to identify different sub-categories of partners, suppliers, and enablers and tailor the questions more precisely to the issues connected to the category. The last sub-question, concerning issues to monitor and stage gates, is a final reminder that managers need to feel knowledgeable enough about the business to know what aspect of the partner/supplier/enabler relationships requires attention next.

A fourth category concerns support from existing businesses. The question we pose is:

SUPPORT-FROM-CORE CONFIDENCE: Are we confident that we will get the support we need from existing businesses?

There are a number of sub-questions that make up this support-from-core confidence question:

1 Are we confident that the existing businesses are motivated to give us the support we need?
2 Are we confident that the existing businesses will remain committed despite setbacks or likely other priorities?
3 Are we confident that the existing businesses have the skills and resources needed to support us?
4 Are we confident that existing businesses will allocate sufficient numbers of people who are sufficiently competent and committed to the project?
5 Are we confident we know what support-from-core issues to monitor and what stage gates to set?

The first four sub-questions cover the main issues related to links with and support from the existing businesses. There are few new ventures that pass the Traffic Lights that do not depend in some important way on support from existing businesses. Thinking through the degree and capability of the available support is important. The last sub-question, concerning issues to monitor and stage gates, is a final reminder that managers need to feel knowledgeable enough about the business to know what aspect of the relationships with existing businesses requires attention next.

A fifth category concerns funding and governance, the support and control that new venture will get from the parent company. The question we pose is:

FUNDING AND GOVERNANCE CONFIDENCE: Are we confident that we have or can set up the funding and governance we need?

There are a number of sub-questions that make up this funding and governance confidence question:

1 Are we confident that the cash-flow requirements and financial outcomes will be acceptable to our parent/sponsors?
2 Are we confident we have sufficient funds (capital and operational) to finance the next stage?
3 Are we confident that there is a governance process in place that will objectively assess the viability of the project, provide funds even in the face of setbacks or competition from existing businesses, and stop the project once the probability of success is too low?
4 Are we confident that we have a governance process that will not impose inappropriate controls, functional policies, or performance requirements on the business?
5 Are we confident that we know what funding and governance issues to monitor and what stage gates to set?

The first four sub-questions cover the main issues related to funding and governance. The parent organization not only needs to be committed to providing funds, but also needs to know when to restrict the flow of funds. As we have seen, some of the most costly failures are due to a lack of control: the parent company becomes as enthusiastic about the new business as the management team running the project. But objective control must not lead to inappropriate constraints and performance requirements. The last sub-question, concerning issues to monitor and stage gates, is a final reminder that managers need to feel knowledgeable enough about the business to know what aspect of funding and governance requires attention next.

These five execution categories have been chosen to direct attention to five of the main causes for new businesses foundering. Research by Richard Leifer and colleagues was instrumental in helping us think through these categories. Leifer led a decade-long research project to track a number of radical innovations. His book, co-authored with five colleagues, is a fascinating read.[10] In it he emphasizes the importance of managing four areas of risk: market risk (related to our sales confidence

Box 9.4 The Confidence Check

Are we confident that:
- ❑ our value advantage is still large enough to justify this project?
- ❑ the profit pool is still good enough to justify this project?
- ❑ the leaders/sponsors of the business are good enough for the project?
- ❑ the impact on existing businesses still justifies this project?
- ❑ we will achieve sufficient sales at the price we need?
- ❑ we can develop the technology and deliver our offer at an attractive cost?
- ❑ we can find and retain the support of the partners/enablers/suppliers we need?
- ❑ we will get the support we need from existing businesses?
- ❑ we have or can set up the funding and governance we need?

category); technical risk (related to our technology and operations category); resource risk (related to our funding and governance confidence); and organization risk (related to our support-from-core confidence). Despite the long time frame of Leifer's research, most of the innovations were still in development or had been abandoned by the time the book was written. Hence his lack of focus on a risk related to our partner/supplier/enabler confidence category may be due to the fact that most of the innovations did not get to the commercialization stage of market development and volume production.

When combined with a reassessment of the Traffic Lights, the full set of questions provides a thorough Confidence Check on a new venture (Box 9.4).

The check can be displayed graphically and, since checks should be made at three to six month intervals, the graphs can plot changes in confidence as well as levels of confidence (Figure 9.6).

The main purpose of the Confidence Check is to help decide what should be the next stage gate. Normally this will be a target that advances confidence along those dimensions where confidence is lowest. If the confidence scores were similar to those in Figure 9.6, the next stage gate might be something to do with the quality of the leaders/sponsors and/or the degree of support being given by the existing businesses. In the example that lies behind Figure 9.6, the problem

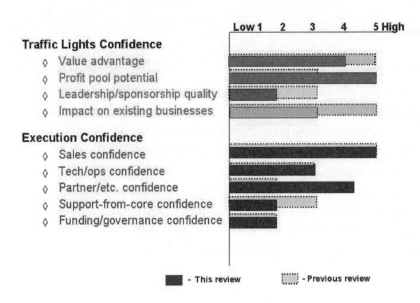

Figure 9.6 Confidence Check: Illustrative example

that had led to the reductions in both the leader/sponsor and support-from-core scores was that a senior manager had moved jobs. This manager had been the main sponsor for the new business, and she had particularly good relations with an existing business (which she had previously run) whose help was needed to release property resources for the new business. Her move meant that she was no longer in a position to help the new business, and her replacement was less likely to be able to deliver support from the existing business or to be a good sponsor to the new venture. The future of the venture was under threat.

WHEN TO KILL A VENTURE

The decision to pull the plug on a new venture is the hardest and yet most important decision that managers face. The Confidence Check helps make the judgment, but does not substitute for it. When one or more of the confidence scores is at 2 or below and there is no obvious stage gate that can be set to raise the score, a reassessment of the project is needed. The Confidence Check does not identify when the plug should be pulled, but it does signal times when a project is in crisis.

The most obvious reason to stop a project is when a number of confidence categories have deteriorated or have remained low despite setting stage gates to improve them. In the case of the project in Figure 9.6, no stage gate was set. Support from the existing business remained good, but started to deteriorate as this business began to face performance pressures of its own. The new manager, however, proved to be an inappropriate sponsor. His reaction to all setbacks was to cut commitment to the new venture and, if the Confidence Check had been used, a gradual deterioration would have been evident on most of the categories. Without the stimulus of the Confidence Check, no crisis was created and the venture did not get closed completely for three years. Careful use of the Confidence Check should have created a crisis after six months, which would either have resulted in immediate closure or some change to the sponsorship of the venture.

Some projects are hard to break into chunk-sized stage gates. When Motorola started the consortium to create a global satellite communication service called Iridium in the early 1990s, it had to launch 66 satellites before it would know whether the service was viable. In the end it turned out that the offering was inherently too expensive compared to cellular networks. It was only of value to a very specialized user group operating in remote areas of the globe.

In other situations, even in high-tech industries, the Confidence Check would be valuable. When Philips developed interactive CD technology starting in the mid-1980s, a Confidence Check process might have helped it pull the plug on the project five years sooner. The project foundered because the internet was a superior technology, but Philips did not close the project until the mid-1990s.

The Confidence Check is not only a tool for cutting back on projects, it can reinforce confidence in further investment. Philips's Navteq project, to develop a navigation service for car users, frequently missed its milestones. However, the strategic case remained strong. Substantial investments and management support finally led to success, creating several billion euros in shareholder value for the company.

Careful analysis, similar to the Confidence Check, at critical points in the development of the venture was key in reaffirming the ultimate potential and reaching the positive decisions.

KEY MESSAGES

In this chapter we have addressed four of the common issues that managers face when developing a new business. We have focused on new ventures rather than acquisitions. Our messages have been:

1 Separate the new venture from existing businesses unless the nine principles of organization design suggest otherwise.
2 Make sure that the new venture reports to a level in the organization where:
   - ❏ the new venture is an important part of the strategy;
   - ❏ there are managers who can be good sponsors;
   - ❏ there are the minimum of layers between the new venture and the "investor";
   - ❏ there is some objective governance of the venture.
3 Use Parenting Opportunity Analysis to decide what guidance and support the new venture needs and limit parenting to these elements.
4 Use the Confidence Check to assess progress, set stage gates, and engineer crises that lead to reassessments.

CHAPTER 10

AN AGE OF REALISM

If the messages from this book become common wisdom, we will have a future that is different from the past.

We will have many companies living comfortably with business plans that are low growth. Since the end of the 1960s, when the first conglomerates began to emerge, such as LTV in the US or Slater Walker in the UK, Anglo-Saxon economies have been living a delusion. The delusion is that good managers can create growth businesses even if they are in low-growth markets. Despite the demise of the 1960s heroes, like Jimmy Ling of LTV and Jim Slater of Slater Walker, there have been enough others who have produce sufficient amounts of temporary magic to feed a belief that anything is possible.

When we started this project we were asked by managers sponsoring the work to study the magicians of the time: Enron, Vivendi, Marconi, and others, which were the LTVs and Slater Walkers of the 1990s. Fortunately, the length of our research period helped us see that these high-growth stars were not exemplars. It helped us become more confident that endless growth is a delusion.

There are still many purveyors of this delusion. Analysts, managers, financial journalists, consultants, and academics have all made contributions. Some spread it when they argue that there is no such thing as a mature business, only mature mindsets. Some reinforce the delusion when they suggest that low growth is a symptom of a lack of innovation and creativity. Low growth, they argue, could be eradicated if managers were only more creative and if they would only invest more in innovation. Some champion technological innovation. Others champion business model innovation. Both are positioned as a pathway to a new economy—an economy where profits are easier to earn and growth is available to all. The delusion fueled the dot-com boom and it has rocket-powered many management teams to their doom.

Arrayed against this delusion are some wise heads, like Lou Gerstner, whose criticism of Wall Street we reported in Chapter 4. He resisted the siren songs tempting him to grow revenue faster by developing into or acquiring into the "new economy." Another wise head is Warren Buffett, the enigmatic leader of Berkshire Hathaway. He has long focused on quality products and market positions rather than growth. He famously declared that he could not understand the "new economy" and, to the huge advantage of his investors, let it and the delusion it rested on pass him by. Another force for good is the rise of share buybacks. Even Bill Gates's Microsoft has joined the stampede to give cash back to shareholders rather than use it for getting into new businesses.

As these forces for sanity receive intellectual support from books like ours, we will enter an age of realism: one where managers are comfortable managing businesses through long periods of low growth, and pension funds are delighted to take home the excellent and dependable returns that these companies are able to deliver. Management teams will no longer feel they have to have a growth plan, and tools like gap analysis will become less influential than the Traffic Lights.

In this delusion-free future there will still be plenty of growth companies. There will be as many management teams capable of developing or acquiring new businesses as there are today. In fact, in the future there may be more than in the past.

This will not be because of more opportunities for growth into new businesses, but because managers who have learned the rules of the game will be better at spotting and developing the opportunities that fit. Today managers are caught in a round of frenetic activity that interferes with their ability to learn about the best opportunities. In the future managers will take a more considered, more strategic approach to new businesses. Rather than squandering money and management time on too many initiatives, often running out of patience and resources to give the support that their really promising opportunities most need, managers will invest only in new businesses that deserve their attention and hence will give each the attention it deserves.

In the age of realism, managers will be more patient. They will recognize that good ideas are rarely good ideas if they do not come to the table with good managers to lead them. They will spend more time examining their value advantage, and considering whether they have sufficient advantage to overcome the unique qualities of their competitors and the costs of learning the new business. They will be more sensitive to the dangers of distraction, and will avoid investing in new projects when their existing businesses are likely to absorb most of their spare resources.

In the age of realism managers will be more creative with their existing businesses. With less distraction from greener grass, more energy will go into exploiting the full potential of existing businesses. The restless, innovative managers who champion new things will not be banished into business development divisions and corporate venturing ghettos, they will be embraced in the core or encouraged to seek their fortunes elsewhere. And if Gary Hamel and his colleagues at Strategos are successful at doing for innovation what Joseph Juran did for quality, the effort managers put into innovation will produce dramatically better returns. While we do not believe that existing businesses can be kept growing for ever, few are given the attention they need to achieve their full potential.

In the age of realism a huge amount of society's wealth will be saved. Predictions that progress will stall and innovation will be abandoned will prove unfounded. Instead, more money will be available for innovation because less will be squandered by overambitious companies. Just as the market system's greater efficiency has made more money available for innovation than the planned economy, the age of realism's avoidance of foolish investments will release more money to support those with good ideas and matching skills.

In today's world our economy takes two steps back for every three steps forward. For every Dell or Samsung, there is a maturing company squandering millions of dollars in failed attempts to enter new businesses, and at the same time letting slip billions of dollars by becoming distracted from optimizing their existing businesses. In fact, we estimate that companies in decline often use up more than half of

265

their market capitalization in unsuccessful attempts to regain their high-growth youth.

In the age of realism, managers will manage low growth or decline when it is appropriate, possibly even without the heavy debt structures of leverage buyouts and private equity deals that seem to be the only way to get managers to focus on their existing businesses in today's growth-addicted world.

The age of realism will still have failures. There will still be projects like Motorola's Iridium, where a promising satellite technology was made uneconomic by the development of cell-based systems. Problems like Philips's difficulties in flat-panel displays, where rising Asian competitiveness made it hard to compete from a European base, will still occur. But they will be less frequent because managers will be more thoughtful about whether they have sufficient value advantage, whether the project leaders and sponsors are good enough, and whether the distraction risks are manageable. There will be less macho and more measured behavior.

In the age of realism strategy will become a more respected discipline. Currently there are still too many managers, consultants, and even academics who believe that strategy is the work you do to figure out how to achieve your objectives. If your objective is to grow at 15% per annum, strategic planning is about figuring out how to do it.

In the future strategic planning will be about defining both objectives *and* action plans. The focus will be on plans that have a good probability of creating value for the organization. Not all organizations will be driven primarily by shareholder value. Some will have employee value, societal value, even environmental value as part of their mission. But whatever value an organization is trying to create, the role of the strategist will be to help form objectives and action plans that are likely to succeed. Gone will be the days when companies tolerate strategies that have a 90% failure rate. Not all strategies will succeed, but the success rate will improve dramatically.

In the age of realism, the strategic business case will have as much status in decision making as the financial business case. This will make optimistic forecasting less necessary and easier to spot. Instead of treating planning as a game of "dare"—I dare you to promise high sales and high margins and I will give you a forfeit if you fail and a prize if you succeed—managers will agree plans for new activities based on their strategic logic.

In the future, the strategy function will develop a harder edge. It will guide management thinking and hold a veto on major decisions. With the power of tools like the New Businesses Traffic Lights, it will act as a gatekeeper, only allowing strategies that pass the test of realism. To achieve this status strategy will need a new power base within the finance function. In fact, the finance function may finally complete its transformation from an accounting and control activity to becoming an evaluator of strategic plans and a monitor of progress.

In the age of realism the finance function will be the keeper of a realistic approach to business. Gone will be crude gap analysis, which has led so many companies into deciding that they need new businesses to fill the gap between their expected growth rate and their top-quartile ambitions. Gone also will be simplistic objectives based on "what the shareholders expect," derived from the investor relations activity. Gone will be stretch targets 10% greater than last year's budget. In their place will be a realistic analysis of what the existing businesses can deliver and how much management attention they need. Added to this will be a sober assessment of the opportunities that exist to enter new businesses and whether any of these opportunities fit with the resources the company has to hand. When combined, these two realistic assessments will help managers define objectives and action plans for the next period.

The age of realism will be a new enlightenment for business, where rational thought has more weight than chief executive ambition, and where managers at many levels have the tools to challenge weak thinking. Managers, customers, and shareholders will all benefit. In the same way that the philosophers of the eighteenth century helped undermine the dogma of churches and a belief in monarchs, the strategic ideas developed over the last 20 years are helping undermine the dogma of growth and a belief in corporate magicians. Fortunately, the transition will be a lot less bloody.

ADVICE FROM OTHER AUTHORS

In this appendix we summarize the advice that we believe other authors might give to McDonald's, taken from a range of excellent books and articles. We chose McDonald's as the focus, rather than Intel or any other company, because we thought that the challenge facing McDonald's in the period covered by this book was particularly interesting: a hugely successful core business that had hit a bump or two, an acknowledged management team, but question marks about the future. We recognize that the authors we have chosen were not writing with McDonald's in mind, hence our summaries are dangerous presumptions. However, this is the advice that we think a manager from McDonald's would have gleaned from a careful study of the authors concerned.

After each summary, we have commented on those aspects of the advice that we think are good and those with which we take issue. These comments are necessarily unfair. With one or two exceptions, we have not given the authors the opportunity to debate the issue with us. However, we include the comments because we believe they provide readers with further insights about where our ideas support those of other authors and where they differ. The exceptions are Gary Hamel and Robert Burgelman. We have had quite a lot of dialogue with both and they have influenced our summaries of their advice.

The order is alphabetical by the last name of the first author. We do not include a section on Clayton Christensen's work because it is covered fully in Chapter 6. Other authors whose books we have studied and been influenced by include Julian Birkinshaw (*Inventuring*), Don Laurie (*Venture Catalyst*), Heidi Mason (*Venture Imperative*), and Michael Treacy (*Double-Digit Growth*). They have not been included because of space constraints.

Merhdad Baghai, Stephen Coley, & David White, *The Alchemy of Growth: Practical Insights for Building the Enduring Enterprise*, Orion Business Books, 1999

These authors are from the consulting company McKinsey. They imply that McDonald's should maintain a continuous pipeline of new business initiatives. They propose that companies should think about three sections of this pipeline: improvements to existing businesses, new enterprises coming on stream, and future options. They refer to these three parts of the pipeline as three horizons.

As a company "under siege"—with challenges in all three horizons—McDonald's, they suggest, needs a structured program:

1 Step 1 is to earn the right to grow by sorting out the core business and divesting any distracting or underperforming businesses.
2 Step 2 is to develop the commitment to grow. It may take two years or more. It may involve management changes. It will involve analysis and debate. But it needs to be a passion accompanied by setting high targets and transformational changes to the culture and systems.
3 Step 3 is to explore new opportunities along seven degrees of freedom: grow share, grow geographically, market existing products to new customers, market new products to existing customers, develop new delivery approaches, consolidate the industry, pursue opportunities outside the industry.
4 Step 4 is to launch a number of exploratory new businesses in a small way. The objective is to create a staircase of steps that will build capabilities and expand the opportunity that has been selected. Capabilities can be competencies, privileged assets, growth-enabling skills, and special relationships.
5 Step 5 is to focus on those new businesses where a competitive advantage can be sustained: where the company has built more capabilities than rivals and has developed a positional advantage.
6 Step 6 is to differentiate the management system for each horizon of the total pipeline in terms of talent management, budgeting and planning, and performance management.

COMMENTS

We find much in *The Alchemy of Growth* that is compelling. The emphases on the core business, on capabilities, on how to build capabilities (the staircase), and on competitive advantage are vital and well addressed. However, we have concerns about the three-horizon concept, about the advice to create different management systems, and about the emphasis on developing a commitment to grow.

The three-horizon concept seems almost tautological: new businesses take five, ten, even twenty years to reach a significant size. Hence, unless your company has some new businesses in the pipeline, growth for the next few years will have to come from existing businesses or acquisitions. However, the advice that these authors give seems to us to be wrong. Moreover, their conclusions do not appear to be supported by their data.

They take their three-horizon concept and combine it with the fact that most new business ideas fail. They then recommend that companies such as McDonald's should have a large nursery of emerging new businesses (horizon 3) in order to have a few fast-growing new divisions (horizon 2) in order to have one significant new core business (horizon 1). This causes them to recommend that the company build three different management systems—one for each horizon. The three different portfolios of businesses (core, growing, and emerging) require different people, performance targets, and planning processes.

We take issue with these recommendations. Only a tiny proportion of our success stories started out as part of a portfolio of new initiatives. Few of the new leg venturing nurseries we studied created new legs. Moreover, we have not found a company that has successfully been able to manage three different management systems for any length of time. Interestingly, the authors make the same observation: "Yet as far as we know, no company, not even those on our list of sustained growers, is using distinct management systems for each horizon. There are no best-practice cases."

So what is wrong with the three-horizon concept? If we think about the growth challenge of some existing businesses, for example a pharmaceutical company, there will be three horizons of new product plans. There will be new products being launched this year, products under development for launching in the next two or three years, and research on new products that may not be launched for five or more years. But these three horizons do not need three management systems. The three horizons work together because they can be managed within the same management system. This is because there is one business model: running a pharmaceutical company.

Unfortunately, the same is not true for portfolios of companies. For McDonald's, the three-horizon concept is not useful. Like almost every other large company, McDonald's will not be able to sustain a different management system for emerging businesses for long enough for them to become new legs to the portfolio. In our view, if McDonald's is to find a new business, it must find one that will fit with its existing management system.

Our final concern is the advice to develop a "commitment to grow." We believe in a more cautious approach. Commitment should develop only after an opportunity has passed the Traffic Lights. Commitment to grow independent of whether there are good opportunities is the prime cause of many expensive failures.

Zenas Block & Ian MacMillan, *Corporate Venturing*, Harvard Business School Press, 1993

Block and MacMillan's book is the oldest of those selected. The authors had been studying venturing at Wharton for a number of years and produced a comprehensive summary of thinking at that time. They published just after the second wave of corporate venturing initiatives and their work shares a sense of optimism for the possibilities and frustration at the failures.

McDonald's, they suggest, will need to make a significant cultural change in order to become more entrepreneurial and create new businesses. The change will take five years or more and is likely to require alterations in top management. Three elements are critical:

❏ Leaders who can articulate a unifying vision and strategy.
❏ A culture that supports initiative and entrepreneurship.
❏ Skills in managing a venturing effort and in developing individual ventures.

The venturing effort will require senior managers at McDonald's to

❏ decide that venturing is going to be an integral part of the corporate-level strategy;

❑ choose between a venturing strategy based on extending existing capabilities into adjacent areas or on developing technology in new fields;
❑ determine the size of the effort in terms of number of ventures and
investment commitment;
❑ lead the development of ideas for new ventures;
❑ develop and disseminate a set of venture selection criteria and explain
decisions to managers involved;
❑ set up each new venture so that it draws on the organization's strengths
and avoids its weaknesses;
❑ prepare for disappointments by using milestones to reset strategies,
"shooting the wounded" early, distinguishing between bad luck and
bad decisions, and setting up a process for learning from success and
failure.

Half-hearted efforts involving a few new ventures or a separate corporate
venturing division are unlikely to succeed. McDonald's needs to "sign up
for the course" and make sure that all of its divisions have a venturing
strategy.

COMMENTS

Block and MacMillan's book is one of the few that covers the tasks of both
senior managers and venture-level managers. Much of what they say is
based on deep research and, rightly, remains unchallenged.

If a company does decide to develop a venturing program, Block and
MacMillan provide plenty of excellent advice. However, our views differ
in some fundamental ways. Our main criticism is that they do not say
which companies should set up venturing programs and which should not.
In fact, they argue that all companies should. We do not think that a venturing program, of the form suggested by Block and MacMillan, is appropriate for most companies. In fact, we do not believe that corporate
venturing programs are a successful way of developing new businesses.
Nor do we believe that most companies are capable of building the skills
that Block and MacMillan argue they will need to succeed. We are also
strongly against advising a company like McDonald's, which has focused
for 50 years on one business, to launch a cultural change aimed at making
every division develop a venturing program.

At a more technical level, Block and MacMillan have observed that companies are more successful when top managers are committed, providing a clear strategy for the effort based on a deep understanding of the company's capabilities and weaknesses. Possibly this is where our views coincide. We also encourage managers to do top-down thinking. They need to identify areas where the company's capabilities will give it an advantage. We then suggest that top managers pick one or two of the most promising investments. Where we part from Block and MacMillan is their suggestion that managers will need to launch many rather than few new investments and that they need to build a generic process and support systems to nurture these ventures.

In our view, the number of new ventures, at any one time and at any one level in the hierarchy, will be so few that it is not appropriate to build a new businesses development capability. Instead, managers should focus on what is required for each of the unique investments that are being supported. We think in terms of a few investments each treated in a unique way, while Block and MacMillan imply a flow of investments processed through an organizational capability.

Even on this point, our differences are more about degree of effort. We support the creation of a small team at the center to help managers screen ideas, set up new ventures, and give support when needed. An analogy might be the M&A team that exists at the corporate level of most companies, whose role is to help screen prospects and assist with the deal. What we are not comfortable recommending to a company like McDonald's is that managers set up a venturing program before they have decided if there are any ideas worth investing in. It is better, we argue, for managers to see if there are any ideas that pass the Traffic Lights. If there are two or three in each of five geographic divisions, then it may make sense to set up a small team at the center to offer support to the division managers responsible for these investments. In this way the capabilities are built to support the immediate task rather than to develop a generic organizational competence.

Robert Burgelman, *Strategy Is Destiny*, Free Press, 2002

Robert Burgelman is a professor at Stanford Business School who has published widely on growth and new businesses. *Strategy Is Destiny* summarizes his thinking using detailed analysis of Intel's attempts to find new sources of growth in the 1980s and 1990s. The implications for McDonald's are as follows:

1 McDonald's top management must view the capability to develop new businesses not as "insurance" against the core business becoming insufficient to sustain profitable growth, but as an integral part of the long-term strategic leadership capability of the company. This will avoid the predictable fluctuations in support for corporate entrepreneurship that lead many companies to go through cycles of "now we need it; now we don't." The consequence of such cycles is that each time a new one is initiated, the company starts from scratch.

2 McDonald's top management must understand that new business development requires a different type of strategic leadership discipline than the strategic leadership discipline associated with the core business. Both disciplines must be pursued simultaneously, for the long term.

3 The key activities necessary to develop a new business involve different levels of management. At the operational level, the activities involve linking technology with customer needs, championing new ideas, and "strategic forcing." At the middle/senior level, the activities are "strategic building," championing organizational solutions, and delineating the boundaries of the new business in the new industry. At the top level, the activities are structuring the organization and engaging in "strategic recognition" and retroactive rationalization. These top management activities are not "reactive." Rather, they require the intelligence to suspend the rules for some time and the tolerance to embrace ambiguity. Only when major uncertainties (technical and commercial) are reasonably resolved and support is building among a number of (though not all) senior executives should senior managers commit the corporation to a new business. Learning to perform these activities on an ongoing basis is part of developing the corporate entrepreneurship discipline.

4 Companies are successful in new businesses when their strengths and weaknesses match well (i.e., better than competitors) the critical success factors in the new business.

5 The first step McDonald's should take is to search for new businesses that have "appropriate" critical success factors. This can be done by managers at all levels, but is only likely to be successful if the screening process includes an accurate understanding of both the strengths and weaknesses of the company and the critical success factors of the new business. Early attempts to enter new businesses may, therefore, be highly educational in terms of helping managers understand their strengths and weaknesses and their ability to judge critical success factors. In other words, managers should not be dogmatic about what the existing corporate strategy says about their strengths and weaknesses. Managers should be prepared to experiment a little.

6 If it is necessary to look beyond businesses with "appropriate" critical success factors, the company is taking on a tough challenge that, if successful, is likely to be as much evolutionary as planned. Progress toward the goal will involve:

❑ leading some top-down strategy work to help develop a new corporate strategy and initiate the building of some new capabilities (but recognizing that top-down initiatives do not have a superior track record);

❑ being sensitive to and maintaining links to the autonomous actions of middle and junior managers who want to grasp opportunities and develop capabilities (but recognizing that these initiatives can often draw the company into major problems);

❑ balancing the dissonance that is likely to arise between efforts to encourage new initiatives and efforts to drive development of the core (particularly hard when the core is performing well and there is little spare resource);

❑ redefining the strategy. This ill-understood part of the new business development process links the new business to the corporate strategy, thereby amending it. Such amendments are intrinsically difficult. They involve the combined activities of middle/senior managers and top managers, as mentioned above.

7 Use a new business development group or internal venturing unit as a transition vehicle for helping new ventures find their "right" degree of autonomy and linkage with the core. This requires viewing new business development as a discovery process and having available an array of organizational options, from locating the activity within an existing business to setting it up as an independent unit with external share-

holders (see Burgelman's *Designs for Corporate Entrepreneurship* framework). As a new business develops and the nature of its interdependence with the core becomes clearer, the appropriate type of organizational design may change. Sometimes the right solution may be to spin off the new business completely. Managerial measurement and reward systems must be flexible enough to continue to reflect the changing interdependence and help maintain the necessary collaboration between the new business and parts of the core business. Ironically, the greatest resistance to this part of new business development often comes from the human resources function. The legal function may also raise concerns about some of the contractual arrangements that may be involved. The greatest impediment to evolving the right organization can be the impatience of energetic top managers, who want to see results right away.

8 Use corporate venture capital to stimulate the exploration of "autonomous" opportunities that are occurring in the external environment. But keep in mind that external ventures will raise integration issues just like internal ventures, which again indicates the important role of the processes of "strategic context" determination.

9 Work on spotting, developing, and deploying middle and senior-level managers capable of nurturing new businesses and envisioning a role for these new businesses in a new corporate strategy. This should be part of the mandate of the executive development function in all established companies.

COMMENTS

Robert Burgelman is one of the few authors who does not focus on the numbers game. He also avoids the rhetoric of optimism that pervades most of the literature. However, he does suggest that all companies must learn the "disciplines of developing new businesses," which is a rather different position from ours. He also encourages more autonomous initiatives (skunk works and experimental ventures) rather than fewer.

Burgelman's work on autonomous initiatives is a huge contribution to the field. We agree with much of what he has found. But we take issue with his implication that managers should encourage more experiments and initiatives rather than fewer. In a debate in the *European Business Forum*,

Burgelman supports his argument by suggesting that new ventures are part of "the irrepressible human spirit." We agree, which is why managing in this environment is difficult. Going with the flow of the human spirit is not necessarily the most value-creating strategy.

Burgelman points out that the disciplines of continuous development are different from those of normal strategic planning. He therefore argues that companies need to learn these additional disciplines, and that they need to learn how to do both these new disciplines and normal strategic planning simultaneously.

We are uncomfortable with this recommendation. There are companies whose business is developing new businesses: Virgin, 3M, maybe Canon, venture capitalists. However, we believe that there are no companies that have the ability simultaneously to run a core business and continuously develop new businesses. Hence Burgelman notes the stop–go behavior of so many companies. This signals to us that he is recommending a solution that he has not observed in practice. Intel's efforts, his main case study, have not been a success.

In our opinion Burgelman is trapped by the seeming tautology that companies must develop new businesses "for the long term" and that bottom-up initiatives are irrepressible. Since existing businesses have finite lives, he argues that a company must develop the skills to harness these bottom-up initiatives if it is to survive. Hence, he makes the seemingly obvious recommendation that companies need to develop the appropriate disciplines.

Our view is that all companies have finite lives. Long-term survival, while a natural desire, is not necessarily a rational or value-creating goal. Developing the ability to create new businesses is not an imperative and may be inappropriate for many companies at certain points in their life cycle. Supporting bottom-up initiatives is often value destroying. McDonald's may be able to develop another significant business, but it is unlikely that it will create value from launching a major effort to develop the skills that Burgelman suggests.

Burgelman believes that most companies cannot solve their growth challenge by top-down analysis. In fact, he argues that initiatives backed by the CEO are dangerous because they garner too much commitment. He believes in a much more organic process in which autonomous actions lower down in the company discover the way forward. The task of top management is to stimulate an organic bottom-up process, suspend normal judgment, and prepare to integrate successes into a new corporate strategy.

Our view is that the problems Burgelman observes in top-down thinking are problems that are easier to cure than he believes. We see them as a failure of top-down wisdom rather than a failure to implement all the disciplines that he suggests. In our shadowing of managers, we observed many occasions where the thinking of the managers and their most senior bosses was strategically flawed in quite elementary ways. Top-down thinking is often poor—as we believe it was at Intel before Andy Grove—but it is relatively easy to change (with models like the Traffic Lights and the Confidence Check). Rather than encourage managers to invest in nurturing a new set of disciplines that require new behaviors at many levels in the company, we believe that encouraging managers to improve their top-down thinking has a better chance of success. In fact, without an improvement in top-down processes, Burgelman's advice, like that of Hamel, will lead companies into supporting too many bottom-up initiatives (as Intel has during much of its past).

Burgelman's use of "critical success factor" fit as a screening device for new business ideas is an advance on the usual "core competence" or "adjacencies" thinking. It recognizes the learning costs of getting into businesses with different critical success factors, a point that we make much of in the Traffic Lights.

Richard Foster & Sarah Kaplan, *Creative Destruction*, Currency and Doubleday, 2001

Dick Foster is a longstanding McKinsey consultant and Sarah Kaplan worked at McKinsey for many years. Foster's thinking is influenced by his past work on technology life cycles and by a remarkable consulting project he did with Johnson & Johnson. The board asked Foster to help it avoid the problems that IBM had run into in the early 1990s. *Creative Destruction* suggests the following:

1 The problem that McDonald's faces stems from failing to change as fast as the market: failing to create new businesses and destroy old businesses fast enough to keep the momentum of value creation going. This failure is common among large companies, especially those with

long periods of success where management's attention is focused on "operational work" rather than "adaptive work."

2 The solution is to focus the top management team on adaptive work in a way that does not take their eyes off the operational demands of their current businesses. This requires them to design a process for doing adaptive work.

3 The process for adaptive work will involve the executive group in different kinds of meetings with different agendas and different conversations. The people attending the meetings are likely to include more than just the top team. Preparation, such as visits to customers or Silicon Valley, is likely to be required so that executives come to the meetings with a visceral understanding of the issues discussed. The key is that the top team decide what the critical issues are and engage wholeheartedly in figuring out how the company can respond, remembering that more creation and more destruction are both likely to be needed.

4 In addition, McDonald's will probably need to change its strategic planning process to encourage more divergent thinking and extended dialogue; its R&D activities to recognize that important developments may rightly happen outside the company; and its corporate venturing to create a more integrated approach to new business development. All three activities need to be focused on exploring the periphery where new technologies and new business models are being created. Rather than treating new business development and R&D as things that happen in a dark corner, the efforts should be central to the strategic planning debate.

5 McDonald's will also need to change the balance between "control" and "permission." The current culture is likely to be killing too many good ideas before they get aired and discouraging managers from taking risks.

COMMENTS

We like Foster's starting point very much. He explains that most value is created by new companies, and most of these are destroyed by the market before they can survive for very long. The ones that do survive underperform the average, because the market changes too fast for companies to keep up. In other words, the process of new companies being created and then destroyed produces more value than that produced by companies who survive for long periods.

We are less certain, however, about his solution, especially since he has no examples of companies consistently outperforming as a result of using his solution. Like so many other authors, Foster is searching for an answer to the riddle of long-term performance, recognizing, at the same time, that he has no exemplars. His solution is logical but probably ineffective. His exemplar case studies are companies like Corning, J&J, and (unfortunately) Enron, but it is clear that his real admiration goes to the private equity industry.

We suspect that his admiration is well placed. The private equity industry is effective at doing something that organizations set up to run a business (like McDonald's) can never do. We draw the parallel with corporate venture capital. Despite three waves of attempts, corporations have demonstrated incompetence in this area for totally predictable reasons. To advise companies to become more like private equity firms is to advise them to copy a game they can never win. If significant creative destruction is needed, is it not better that the company sells itself to a private equity firm than attempts to learn the management skills that these firms have been honing for years?

Maybe this is what Foster should really be recommending to McDonald's. Selling to a private equity firm at a crucial creative/destruction moment later in a company's life could be equivalent to using a venture capital firm to help kick start a company early in its life. We suspect that if McDonald's were bought by a private equity firm, the topic of new businesses would be taken firmly off the agenda, the partner brands would be sold, and all management's attention would be focused on optimizing the hamburger business.

Another part of Foster's proposal with which we are uncomfortable is his recommendation that companies increase "permission" and reduce "control." This suggestion presumes that there are lots of good ideas and good people being suppressed by the current control systems. By giving managers more room to take risks and experiment, companies will uncover a wealth of new value creators. We wish Foster were right. But despite many attempts by many companies to do just what he suggests, there is no evidence that it works. We believe that the good ideas for new businesses and entrepreneurial managers in McDonald's (and there have been examples of both) will force their way into the limelight without much nurturing. Those that need more permission and less control are probably not worth supporting.

The part of Foster's thesis we do like, however, is his view that the new business agenda should be firmly in the hands of the top managers. Strategic planning, R&D, and venturing activities should not promote 1,000 flowers but rather be targeted to explore some carefully chosen avenues. Foster appears to suggest that managers should not abdicate their responsibility to "select" the issues and the solutions. Whereas we believe that managers can use an intellectually rigorous selection process (the Traffic Lights) to guide their judgments, Foster suggests that managers should decide through debate and intuition based on a visceral exposure to the issues.

Gary Hamel, *Leading the Revolution*, Harvard Business School Press, 2000, and discussions with the authors

Gary Hamel needs little introduction: he is the world's leading strategy guru.

"Never has incumbency been worth less. Schumpeter's gale of creative destruction has become a hurricane. Blink and you miss a billion-dollar bonanza." The solution, he believes, is to out-innovate the innovators: to become an industry revolutionary. Radical new business concepts (business models) come from a combination of luck and foresight, and are driven by activists who have the imagination and drive to try the improbable. McDonald's needs to start down a path of creating activists and supporting radical innovations.

McDonald's, according to Hamel, should not focus only on cost reduction or top-line growth or share buybacks or acquisitions. These may be needed but will not provide a sustainable future. McDonald's future will depend on business model innovation, not only in its core business but in new businesses around the core. Sooner or later every business model reaches the point of diminishing returns and McDonald's is probably well past that point.

First, managers need to learn to think about business models. Hamel has an impressive array of tools to help them do this and lock in advantage that will reap high returns.

Second, managers need to focus on what is changing, on trends with implications, and on what is not happening: anything that will help generate a fresh perspective outside the magnetic field of the current business model. Managers then need to engage in a creative, divergent process that generates a range of new business ideas and possible new directions.

The danger at this point is to let 1,000 flowers bloom in an undisciplined way. Hence some choices need to be made about general directions of development rather than specific projects. One, two, or three new "platforms" is plenty. Sometimes experimentation is needed in order to uncover a new platform, but more normally a new platform can be chosen and experimentation channeled within it. Developments outside the chosen direction should not be discouraged, but it is those inside the strategy that are likely to be retained. Incubators as vehicles for experimentation and idea generation do not appear to work.

New business models rarely emerge fully formed. They need to be discovered. This requires a capability to be built: innovation skills, innovation metrics, IT for innovation, and management process for innovation, such as innovation boards.

The key to success is to manage the investment/learning ratio of each project. Managers often overinvest too early or fail to invest in the initiatives that will maximize learning.

COMMENTS

Hamel's work on business models, what he calls business concepts, and on where new wealth comes from—radically new business models—is impressive and right. He parallels and probably led the thinking of Slywotzky. Hamel's advice is also compelling and seems tautological. In support of it he has developed some superb tools for helping managers think about innovation.

Hamel's views on new businesses are more sober than his views on innovation in general. He recognizes how difficult it is for companies to develop into new areas and has concluded that incubators and undirected experimentation rarely succeed. However, he is in something of a dilemma, since his broader work on innovation emphasizes the importance of experimentation and the need for a large "innovation portfolio." This causes him to be less clear about the process of top-down selection. He proposes that managers should commit to general directions of development—platforms—rather than to individual projects. He argues that individual projects evolve as managers discover what business model works. Hence it is better to get commitment to a platform than a project. In this way managers can learn through projects without excessive pressure, yet have the benefit of commitment to a general direction of development.

In our view, individual managers play a huge role in success. The difficulty of committing to a platform is that it is normally not possible to find the unique managers who are needed to pursue the four or five different initiatives required to move a platform forward. More normally a company may have especially talented managers for only one or two initiatives, often in unconnected areas. Better, we believe, to back the talent that exists than to define a platform and try to move it forward with less capable or less passionate managers.

Hamel also suggests that companies need to change the way they manage in order to make more room for new ideas and develop innovation skills. He believes that few companies are good at innovation. "There are no more than a handful of companies that have even begun to build innovation systems that focus on creating a steady stream of new business concepts or new rules within current concepts." But he also recognizes that innovation ghettos, like corporate incubators, do not succeed because they isolate their ventures from the power structure and hence the commitment they need to succeed.

In our view, McDonald's would be foolish to attempt to turn itself into an innovation machine. The company is dominated by operating priorities, appropriately so. This does not mean that McDonald's should spurn innovation. It just means that innovation should have its place in its business model rather than be positioned as a disruptive influence designed to unseat and revolutionize the business model.

There is much overlap between Hamel's thinking and ours. However, we have more faith in the ability to select projects wisely using the Traffic Lights. This makes us more comfortable with top-down processes, and less convinced of the value of stimulating innovative activity.

Rosabeth Moss Kanter, *When Giants Learn to Dance*, Simon and Schuster, 1989, and *Evolve*, Harvard Business School Press, 2001

Rosabeth Moss Kanter is a distinguished professor from Harvard Business School, a guru on strategy before most of us had heard of Gary Hamel. In this summary, we draw on only two of her books. There are also many insights in her other books, such as *Change Masters, Frontiers of Management, Innovation, World Class, The New Managerial Work*, and her latest book, *Confidence!: How Winning Streaks and Losing Streaks Begin and End.*

Kanter suggests the following:

1 "Newstreams" need to be nurtured. "New ideas can easily get lost in the momentum of the mainstream." Companies often have habits and processes that actively (if not intentionally) discourage new ideas. Moreover, efforts to develop newstreams easily lose support. Hence the first thing McDonald's needs to do is to commit to encouraging new initiatives and searching out management processes that are inadvertently discouraging them.

2 McDonald's needs to create the "channels" that will encourage new ideas. "The channels (that support newstreams) need to be dug again and again, the commitment explicitly renewed." There is no best practice here. Each company must develop its own channels. They may be internal incubators, increased encouragement of R&D, external venture funds, special funds, centers for creativity, incentives, planning processes that focus on new ideas, and so on.

3 Once channels exist they should be filled with many ideas by "scouting" for ideas that already exist, "coaching" people with embryonic ideas, and "inspiring" people by example.

4 McDonald's new ideas will come in three types. There will be a small number of big bets that have been carefully selected. There will be a larger number of ventures and experiments of promising, but not proven, projects. The ventures and experiments will mainly be aimed at supporting existing businesses or the big bets. Finally, there will be a much larger number of incremental innovations and ideas at departmental level throughout the organization.

5 Innovation requires improvisation. To aid this improvisation, top management at McDonald's should define some directions and specific ambitions, such as "McDonald's for the health freak" or "another fast-food concept that we can internationalize" (the big bets). This will provide enough guidance for improvisation teams to fire-aim, fire-aim with rapidly developed versions.

Managing newstream projects requires a different approach to that of the mainstream. Managers need to create a different management system from the mainstream culture (e.g., in a venture unit) yet be ready to reintegrate the two management processes as soon as possible.

COMMENTS

We like Kanter's advice that top managers need to set some direction for the search process. We agree with the need for some clarity about corporate development strategy. We differ only on the issue of timing. We believe that clarity about direction should come after ideas have been screened, not before. The process should start with a list of ideas, followed by screening, then a decision is made about the direction of development (the big bets) and in which (if any) projects to invest.

We agree that improvisation is a good word to describe what managers do once a project starts. The initial business model is rarely the one managers end up with. The journey involved in turning a good idea into a successful business is a winding and unpredictable one.

We have more concern about Kanter's enthusiasm for action. She believes that more innovation is good, that the problem lies with the stultifying impact of the processes needed to run the existing businesses, and that the solution is to dig deep channels that encourage new business initiatives. We have already explained why we believe it is a mistake to advise companies to attempt to create a parallel management system for newstreams. We are, therefore, opposed to Kanter's encouragement of incubators and venturing units, and her advice to invest in scouting, coaching, and inspiring. We feel that these efforts will cost a significant amount and lead to many bad projects being sponsored. This will clutter up the agenda and possibly cause management to lose sight of the one or maybe two good projects that McDonald's should be aggressively pursuing.

In her latest book *Confidence!* Kanter reinforces this message with an example about the BBC's efforts to generate new projects. The process evolved into one where 1,000 flowers were allowed to bloom. Whereas we see this as a problem, one that contributed to the 15% cutback and thousands of redundancies announced in December 2004, Kanter is less critical, arguing that companies are only successful at finding new ways forward when they combine top-down bets with bottom-up initiatives.

Our disagreements, however, are more about degree than principle. We acknowledge that most companies have a large number of innovations going on at any time, both bottom up and top down. Most of these innovations are focused on the existing businesses. The big point at issue is how many should be focused on new businesses. In our view a typical company will have three sources of new business ideas. Some come from deliberate choices, hopefully using criteria such as the Traffic Lights. Others come from natural extensions of innovations initiated in support of existing businesses. Still others are generated out of innovation processes designed to come up with new businesses. We believe that the last category needs to be controlled more tightly than Kanter suggests. But our real difference probably lies in the middle category: the natural extensions of sensible innovation projects. We would like this middle category to be put through the Traffic Lights, with the expectation that 90% of the projects will get rejected. Kanter, like Burgelman, sees this middle category as the lifeblood of a company's future.

Richard Leifer, Christopher McDermott, Gina Colarelli O'Connor, lois Peters, Mark Rice, & Robert Veryzer, *Radical Innovation: How Smart Companies can Outsmart Upstarts*, Harvard Business School Press, 2000

Leifer and his co-authors were all from the Lally School of Management. They followed a dozen radical innovations over nearly 10 years.

Leifer's focus on radical innovation is slightly different from our focus on new businesses. "A radical innovation has the potential to produce an entirely new set of performance features: improvements in known features of five times or more; or a greater than 30% reduction in cost." Hence "radical innovation" includes some overlap with "new businesses," but it also includes many projects that would be considered to be part of existing businesses.

The conclusions are the following:

1 All companies should be seeking to upgrade their ability to develop radical innovations.
2 Radical innovations face four kinds of risks: technical, market, resource, organizational.
3 Upgrading McDonald's ability to "do" radical innovation involves making changes that reduce the organizational and resource risks, both of which are largely under the firm's control (the technical and market risks are driven by the project):
   ❑ Set up an "innovation hub" to help evaluate and incubate projects.
   ❑ Educate senior R&D personnel about radical innovation.
   ❑ Provide additional sources of funding, such as a venture capital unit and senior managers with innovation budgets.

❑ Develop the capability of existing businesses and divisions to take charge of projects as they develop and use transition teams to help facilitate the transition.

❑ Ensure that top management has committed to "stay the course."

4 There are seven keys to effective management of a radical innovation project:

❑ Set the expectations of the team.

❑ Identify and track uncertainties.

❑ Develop and implement a learning plan.

❑ Adopt a resource acquisition strategy.

❑ Manage interfaces.

❑ Build project legitimacy.

❑ Get the right person for the job.

COMMENTS

For radical innovations that are part of existing businesses, we agree with most of the points made in *Radical Innovation*. However, for radical innovations that need to be set up as "new businesses" we have some different views.

❑ We do not think it is realistic to expect to significantly reduce the "organizational and resource risks." These exist or not depending on the starting position of the host company. In our view, it is better to screen out projects that have high organizational and resource risks than to attempt to reduce the risks by making changes to the host company. This will lead to fewer projects passing the screen, but those that do will have the lower organizational and resource risks that Leifer has identified as necessary.

❑ We do not think that innovation hubs or venture capital units are appropriate for radical innovation projects that have "new leg" potential. These incubation methods can hide the project from top managers in a way that reduces the need for them to decide whether they are committed or not. As a result, when a funding squeeze occurs or the project hits a setback, it is easily dropped. Incubators and venture capital vehicles often result in a reduction in management's commitment to "stay the course."

❑ We do not believe that top managers should commit to stay the course for a general ambition like radical innovation. As we have explained before, we believe that commitment should be withheld until a project passes the Traffic Lights.

We should not, however, leave the impression that we disagree with much of Leifer's work. Moreover, one aspect of the work had a profound impact on our thinking. Leifer and his colleagues identified and tracked the uncertainties involved in radical innovations. This led them to the categorization of technical, market, resource, and organizational risks. This analysis is a dramatic improvement on the normal matrix of technical and market risks because it acknowledges the effects of the host company as a risk. It was this categorization that led us to develop our Confidence Check, described in Chapter 9. By monitoring the degree of uncertainty and hence degree of confidence in a number of dimensions, managers can more objectively decide which stage gates to set and whether to continue with the project.

Adrian Slywotzky, *The Profit Zone* and *Value Migration*, Harvard Business School Press, 2000 & 2002, and *How to Grow When Markets Don't*, Warner Business Books, 2003

Adrian Slywotzky has written some of the most influential books on strategy in the last 10 years. He is a consultant at Mercer. His books suggest the following:

1 New wealth comes from new business models, such as Starbucks in the coffee market. If McDonald's wants to create a significant amount of value outside its existing business, management will need to build on or innovate into a new business model in some related area. "In fact, even to revive the core, McDonald's probably needs some new business models."

2 The first step is to draw a map of the value patterns in the hamburger industry and related industries. It is important to do this analysis objectively and thoroughly, because organizational memory may screen McDonald's managers from seeing the new value areas.

3 The next step is to choose some markets/products that are in related areas and where the business model is in the expanding and growing stage, what Slywotzky calls the "inflow phase." This can be done by

innovating a new business model or acquiring one that is in early development. One of the most important areas in which McDonald's can look for these new business models is "addressing the hassles and issues that surround the product": additional services for customers or suppliers or channels of distribution. Slywotzky refers to this form of development as "demand innovation." He argues that it generates better opportunities than product innovation.

4   The third step is to build a robust business design starting with the customer, building on business design patterns that are common (Slywotzky lists the common ones), exploiting the company's assets, taking care to acquire the needed new competencies, and thinking about the "hidden liabilities" that the company already has that may get in the way.

5   Finally, new business designs should be kept separate from the core until they have proved themselves and can withstand challenges from existing businesses. At the same time they should get support from senior managers to ensure they are resourced appropriately and fully develop their opportunity.

COMMENTS

We like Slywotzky's top-down approach. Like him, we believe that better top-down strategic thinking can go a long way. We support his advice about defining the value maps and exploring the business models adjacent to the current businesses. We like his use of the term "hidden liabilities" and the importance he gives to this bit of organizational reality. We also like the fact that Slywotzky does not seem to believe that success is a numbers game.

However, we are not confident that companies can easily execute business models with which they are not familiar. In fact, we believe that "hidden liabilities" are often hard to get around. Rather than presuming that there is a solution to hidden liabilities, we presume that they should be part of the screening criteria. Companies should only approve projects where the "hidden liabilities" are small or manageable. In the coffee market, P&G's coffee division would have had many hidden liabilities if it had entered the coffee shop business. Even if P&G had identified the opportunity in time to do something about it, we would not have expected P&G to have been an effective competitor to Starbucks.

Slywotzky's main selection criterion is size. He encourages companies to aim for the largest opportunities with the best ideas. "If the idea is good enough, managers can be bolder about taking on something less familiar." In contrast, our Traffic Lights give little attention to the size of the profit pool. We argue that criteria such as "size of the contribution" and "size of the learning costs" (our term for hidden liabilities) are more important.

We suggest that companies may need to reject all opportunities and decide to stick to the existing business. Slywotzky would consider this to be "sticking one's head in the sand." Moreover, unlike Zook, Slywotzky thinks that there is an equal danger of overinvesting in the core business. He appears to believe that companies have almost a moral duty to try new business models. "If not, it is bad for them, bad for their shareholders and bad for the economy." We are particularly concerned about this moralization of the growth gamble. Managers who believe that they must grow are more likely to harm themselves, their shareholders, and the economy than managers who understand the gamble they are taking on and when big bets are likely to succeed.

Michael Tushman and Charles O'Reilly, *Winning through Innovation*, Harvard Business School Press, 1997

Tushman and O'Reilly are professors at Harvard and UCLA, spanning the East and West coasts of America and the disciplines of organization and business policy. They have done extensive research on the evolution of industries and how companies cope with technological change.

"To succeed both today and tomorrow, managers must play two different games simultaneously. First, they must continually get better at competing in the short term … Managers must also master another game: understanding how and when to initiate revolutionary innovation and, in turn, revolutionary organizational change."

It is hard, they suggest, to drive performance in the existing business while developing the skills to succeed in the next-generation technology or business model. Most fail, like RCA in the move from vacuum to solid state, Swiss watch manufacturers in the move from mechanical to quartz, and Danish hearing aid company Oticon in the move from behind-the-ear to in-the-ear technology. McDonald's will need to be particularly careful as the industry moves from the traditional hamburger business model to the fast-casual model.

During times of change, there is a period of rapid innovation when different technologies and business models compete for dominance. Then, once a dominant new model emerges, there is rapid growth and huge success for the company that can develop the skills, organization, and culture that suit the new model. Companies wedded to an existing model normally find it particularly hard to commit fully to a new model, especially when the new model has rules of thumb or values that conflict with the previous way of doing things.

The first requirement is that McDonald's runs its existing business well. "If an organization is not successful today, there can be no tomorrow." This involves:

❏ Establishing a clear strategy, objectives, and vision.
❏ Identifying gaps between current performance and goals.
❏ Developing an effective problem-solving process for dealing with the gaps.
❏ Building a culture that provides strong social control and includes norms that support innovation—"creativity" and "implementation."

The second requirement is to develop the ability to manage three innovation streams simultaneously—incremental, architectural, and discontinuous.

❏ Incremental can be led by the existing businesses.
❏ Architectural and discontinuous innovations need separate units (one for each project) with the freedom to break the corporate rules.
❏ Senior managers need to be comfortable with multiple competing innovations during periods of "ferment" before dominant new business models emerge.
❏ Vision, team diversity, and good process can be used to keep innovation units separated organizationally as well as integrated into the corporate strategy
❏ Top managers must be ready to "shape the closing of" a dominant new model (i.e., decide when the organization should switch from experimenting with to driving a new model).
❏ The top management team must prepare themselves so that they are ready and able to lead change.

COMMENTS

We agree with almost all of Tushman and O'Reilly's observations about organizations, organizational inertia, and the difficulty of achieving alignment around a new business model or innovation when the organization is already committed to an existing one. We also agree with them that many innovations, and hence all new businesses, require a different combination of mindset, rules of thumb, norms, people, and structures. Their book superbly explains the challenges that new businesses pose. It is matched only by Christensen in its understanding of the realities of organizations.

We also applaud Tushman's advice that companies should focus on putting their existing house in order before they try looking for new things.

We part company, however, on the practical issue of what is possible and on the wisdom of developing a vision before the opportunity for a new "dominant model" becomes clear.

Tushman argues that vision provides one of the critical integrating mechanisms that make it possible for companies to experiment in separated units while keeping some integrated approach to innovation. They are right, but only if top managers are capable of defining a wise vision, before the innovation starts.

Our observation is that this is rare. There are many visions: Intel's "internet" vision, McDonald's "partner brands" vision, AT&T's "computers and communications" vision. The problem is that these visions are often more of a hindrance than a help. Our view is closer to that of Lou Gerstner, who decided not to have a vision for IBM, at least until the path forward was clear. This may be one of the reasons Tushman comments: "Building ambidextrous organizations and initiating revolutionary change is difficult ... only a small minority of farsighted firms initiate discontinuous change before a performance decline."

Our recommendation is different. We suggest that managers review the new business opportunities, choose one or two that pass the Traffic Lights, and invest in them based on the strength of the Traffic Lights logic rather than some predefined vision. As success develops, so also should a new vision. In this respect our view is closer to that of Burgelman. The new corporate strategy should, we believe, emerge as projects succeed.

On the issue of practicality, we have not observed many managers who can handle the ambidextrous organizational requirements that Tushman proposes. For many, creating a cohesive top team is a huge challenge, at least until the new direction has become clear. For others, the ability to maintain competing experiments in separated units and yet integrate them into the corporate-level strategy is too difficult. In fact, Tushman's research demonstrates that the ambidextrous ambition is too difficult for most management teams.

The alternative in our view is to acknowledge the weaknesses: mindset limitations, cultural constraints, and other restrictions of the existing organization and top management. These limitations and constraints can then be used to help screen opportunities. They can be used as part of the Traffic Lights under the headings of "our contribution," "learning costs," and "leadership/sponsorship." New businesses that are difficult because they clash with the constraints are eliminated. Sometimes, especially when the constraints are substantial, all businesses will be eliminated. In this case, focusing on the core or designing projects that eliminate some of the constraints, for example through an acquisition, can be more useful than trying to develop the capability to be an ambidextrous organization.

Like Christensen, Tushman and O'Reilly have produced a superb diagnosis of the problem. But their solution is more theory than practice. There are so few companies demonstrating the capabilities they claim are required that we believe a less ambitious solution is more practical.

Chris Zook & James Allen, *Profit from the Core*, Harvard Business School Press, 2001 and Chris Zook, *Beyond the Core*, Harvard Business School Press, 2004

Chris Zook and James Allen are consultants at Bain & Co. Their work suggests the following:

1 McDonald's needs to focus on its core business and make sure that it is continuing to dominate its industry and produce good financial results. This work may involve some debate about what the core business is. For McDonald's the debate is unlikely to be very protracted, and given the current performance problems it is best to define the core narrowly, at least initially.
2 Careful analysis is needed of the causes of the current hiccup in the core business and appropriate action to be taken. This may require

investments in new products, improved premises, added services, and so on. Revitalizing the core may require significant innovative behavior. The greatest performance improvements, however, are likely to come from growing McDonald's strongest geographic businesses rather than from turning around its weaker businesses. Paradoxically, it is the strongest businesses that are usually underperforming the most.

3 While work is continuing on the core, management should do a full potential analysis of the core business, looking at all the growth opportunities that this strong core provides. It is likely that these opportunities will offer McDonald's good potential. Managers often underestimate the potential for growth from the core.

4 When the core is running smoothly again and plans to exploit its full potential are being executed, McDonald's may want to consider adjacent opportunities. The Bain list of adjacency dimensions suggests that the best prospects might lie in backward integration or in using McDonald's capabilities in similar food formats:

❏ new geographies: part of the core;
❏ new value chain steps: not obvious but if found would be part of the core;
❏ new channels: not obvious, e.g., hamburgers in supermarkets unlikely to be very profitable;
❏ new customer segments: part of the core unless it involves a new retail format;
❏ new products: part of the core unless it involves a new retail format;
❏ backward integration: may offer opportunities;
❏ forward integration: not obvious;
❏ capabilities: most likely if using current fast-food skills in new formats.

5 The list of adjacencies can then be screened against criteria such as impact on core, potential to become a leader, robustness of the profit pool, defensive value, potential for further developments, probability of executing well, and strength of relatedness to the core (number of adjacency steps from the core). McDonald's should be cautious. Adjacency expansion is risky. "The most successful companies at adjacency expansion have some of the most restrictive criteria."

COMMENTS

Zook's thesis, like Peters' "stick to your knitting" before it, is well grounded in fact. We like the emphasis on getting existing businesses into winning market positions before spending time on developing new businesses. We also like Zook's focus on doing a "full potential" analysis of the core business. This helps ensure that companies do not lose faith in their core too early. The fact that Zook's sustained value creators nearly all had strong core businesses is a powerful incentive for companies to try to succeed in one or two businesses before pushing their luck in new areas.

However, Zook does not fully address the very real problem facing many, in fact most, companies: they are number two or three or worse in their existing businesses with little prospect of becoming number one. Hence they are motivated to find something else to work at or some adjacent business to link with that will help them compete. Our solution to this problem is not to actively discourage managers from considering new businesses just because their core is weak, but to equip them with a powerful screening tool—the Traffic Lights—to help them avoid doing anything stupid.

We like Zook's concern that new business efforts may distract managers from the core. We find that managers frequently underestimate the distraction risks.

Zook's focus on adjacencies is also laudable. His definition of what is or is not an adjacency, however, is not very enlightening. An adjacency is different from a diversification to "the extent to which it draws on the customer relationships, technologies or skills in the core business to build advantage." In other words, the company must have something to bring to the party that is important. This is paragraph 1.1 of most books on new businesses, hence it does not add much to common sense. Nevertheless, Zook's adjacency maps do help managers identify a large number of potential adjacencies and his concept of number of adjacency steps away from the core is a practical tool for assessing potential learning costs.

Recognizing that many companies are "awash with adjacencies," Zook provides a list of screening questions. Most of these questions overlap to some degree with parts of the Traffic Lights. In fact, Zook reviewed our Traffic Lights and commented that they are almost identical to the criteria he uses.

However, on close reading of his books we believe that the Traffic Lights are an advance on Zook's thinking in a number of ways. He gives examples of success—Dell into servers—and of failure—Quaker Oats into Snapple—but does not show how their screening process would help managers decide whether a new opportunity is a "server" or a "Snapple." Moreover, Zook does not suggest, as we do, that the screening process may screen out all of the identified adjacencies. His message implies that, once McDonald's has sorted out its core business, there are likely to be plenty of adjacencies to pursue. Our experience suggests that there are plenty of adjacencies, but few that will pass the Traffic Lights.

Overall, we feel that Zook's ideas are the closest to our own and fit our data better than the ideas of the other major authors.

A DATABASE OF
SUCCESS STORIES

This appendix describes the database of success stories we have identified as part of the research. It is not a statistically representative database. Rather, it is a collection of interesting examples of success that we found in the course of our work.

We wanted to create a database of examples of companies that had successfully created a significant new business. The definitions of "business," "new," "significant," and "successful" were:

❏ A separate organization unit rather than merely a new product, channel, or market.
❏ A business model new to the parent and/or requiring new parenting behaviors.
❏ Sales or profits amounting to 20% of the parent company total or shareholder value of $1 billion (whichever was the smaller number).
❏ Considered at the outset to be a permanent part of the portfolio, and successful enough to generate a return on investment equal to or greater than the cost of capital.

As shown in Figure B.1, we have built up information on 66 cases. Some have ended up falling well short of the criteria, even proving considerable failures, like the move of Lattice (when BG Group) into telecoms. Others are better classified as potential or modest successes. Of the 66 cases, 54 meet our criteria to a greater or lesser degree. Of these we have inside information through company interviews on 58% and publicly available information on the remaining 42%.

Of the 54 successes, 9 (17%) have been sold or floated wholly or partially. However, they are included because at the outset the intent was for

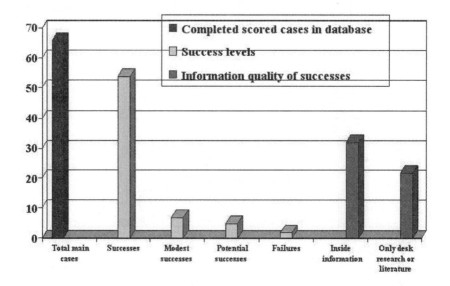

Figure B.1 Success levels and information quality in the database

these businesses to become significant additions to the portfolios of their parent companies.

THE SUCCESSES

Some companies, like Dixons and Whitbread, have had a number of successes. So we have 54 examples from 44 different companies, as listed in Box B.1 overleaf.

In addition to these examples we researched seven companies that have repeatedly created new businesses. These serial developers are 3M, Canon, CP Group, CRH, ServiceMaster, Thermo Electron, and Virgin. Because each of these companies has created many new businesses, we did not include any individual examples in our database.

LOCATION AND MATURITY OF DEVELOPMENTS

Our sample is weighted toward US and UK companies (Figure B.2). It spans over 20 years (Figure B.3), with examples covering a spread of maturities.

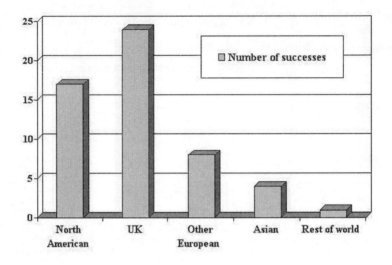

Figure B.2 Location of parent companies

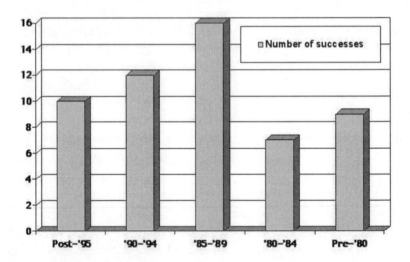

Figure B.3 Timing of initial major commitments

Box B.1 The database of success stories

Corporate parent	Nationality	Development
ABF	UK	British Sugar; a move into sugar refining and distribution through acquisition.
Acer Group	Taiwan	PCs; the creation of a major PC business from a core that produced microprocessors for games manufacturers.
Anglian Water Group	UK	Anglian Water International; the development of an international business following deregulation in the UK.
Anglo American	South Africa	Mondi Europe; move into European forest products, from a core business in minerals and forest products in South Africa
Barclays Bank	UK	Barclaycard; move into credit card business (first in the UK) in the late 1960s from commercial banking.
Bombardier	Canada	Rail cars for mass transit systems; expansion from snow-going equipment for industrial and commercial use (snowmobiles) in 1974.
Bombardier	Canada	Aerospace (regional aircraft and executive jets); move in 1986 through the initial acquisition of Canadair.
Boots	UK	Boots Healthcare International; development of international over-the-counter (OTC) self-medication business (Nurofen, Optrex etc) from remnants of sale of pharma business. Core business is drug stores.
Cardinal Health	US	Pharmaceutical products distribution; a major shift from initial food distribution through acquisition and divestment, and then growth through geographic expansion, followed by forward and backward integration, and moves into adjacent products.
Centrica	UK	Electricity supply; move by British Gas, the UK's leading gas retailer, to sell electricity post-deregulation.

Corporate parent	Nationality	Development
Centrica	UK	Roadside services; diversification through acquisition of the AA, the UK's leading automobile emergency and support organization.
Charles Schwab	US	OneSource; development of the mutual fund supermarket, and subsequent transformation to become a leading e-broking firm.
Diebold	US	ATMs; move into ATMs and ancillary services in the early 1970s by a company then specializing in storage, security and record handling equipment.
Dixons	UK	Freeserve; development of an internet service provider by UK electrical and photographic equipment retailer.
Dixons	UK	PC World; development of UK's largest chain of computer superstores from its inception in 1991.
Dixons	UK	The Link ; development of a major UK chain to retail mobile phones.
DSM	Netherlands	Chemicals; switch by major Dutch mining company out of mining into chemicals.
DSM	Netherlands	Life sciences; move by DSM into to life sciences (pharmaceutical ingredients) leading to decisions to exit parts of the chemicals business.
EMAP	UK	Radio stations; move by UK magazine publisher into radio.
GE	US	GE Capital Corporation; creation of one of the largest global financial services companies by diversified manufacturing company
GE	US	NBC; major move into television through acquisition of NBC as part of larger acquisition of RCA in 1986.
Gillette	US	Braun; move into small domestic electrical appliances through acquisition in 1967.
GrandMet	UK	Move by hotel and restaurant business into drinks through acquisition in mid-1970s of IDV as part of Trumans deal.
GPS	France	GrandVision; transformation of GPS, a French business in one-hour photo processing, into GrandVision, a company focusing on instant and discount optical services.

Corporate parent	Nationality	Development
HDFC	India	HDFC Bank; development of an Indian retail and commercial bank by India's leading specialist housing company.
Hewlett-Packard	US	Computers; HP's transition into a major computing company (emphasizing post-1980 developments).
Hutchison Whampoa	China	Orange; creation of a major UK mobile phone company prior to its sale to Mannesman in 1998.
IBM	US	IBM Global Services; creating the world's largest computer services and consulting business, and now IBM's biggest business.
IBM	US	IBM PC; creation of IBM's PC business.
Irish Life	Ireland	Irish Life & Permanent; move by Irish Life, Ireland's leading life insurer, into retail banking through merger with Irish Permanent Building Society in 1999, and subsequent acquisition of Irish TSB Bank in 2000.
Johnson Matthey	UK	Johnson Matthey Pharmaceutical Materials Division; the development of a significant fourth leg of the specialty chemicals company.
Kelloggs	US	Nutrigrain; entry into the convenience food business in 1970s.
Kelloggs	US	Keebler; creation of a major convenience food business through acquisition of Keebler, a better vehicle for its own convenience products.
Marks & Spencer	UK	M&S Financial Services; move by major UK retailer into financial services.
Maryland National Bank	US	MBNA; creation in 1982 of an in-house credit card business, prior to its float in 1990 to become one of the largest international credit card companies on the basis of serving affinity groups.
Midland Bank	UK	First Direct; a separately branded direct telephone bank launched in 1989 (now part of HSBC).
Neptune Orient Lines (NOL)	Singapore	APL Logistics; transformation of a division of American President Lines (APL), acquired by NOL in 1997, into a global origin-to-destination logistics company.

Corporate parent	Nationality	Development
Nokia	Finland	Mobile phones; transformation of a broadly diversified company spanning rubber products to electronics into a specialist mobile phone company.
Philips	Netherlands	Polygram; creation of a global recorded music company by Europe's leading consumer electronics company
Philips	Netherlands	Navigation Technologies (Navteq); creation of a digital map database company.
Prudential	UK	Egg; creation in 1998 of the UK internet bank and credit card company by Prudential, one of the UK's largest insurers.
Rentokil	UK	Office plants and other services; move by company specializing in vermin control into wide range of businesses providing office support services.
Reuters	UK	Reuters Monitor Dealing Service; transformation of a rather non-commercial but prestigious news agency in 1963 to a major provider of global electronic information and trading services to the financial sector by 1981.
Rexam	UK	Metal packaging business; entered metal packaging as part of a transformation of the widely diversified former Bowater Group through focus on consumer goods packaging.
Royal Bank of Scotland	UK	Direct Line; creation of the UK's biggest direct-selling, general insurance company through an initial move into motor insurance.
Seagram	Canada	Media and entertainment; entry of drinks group into media and entertainment, primarily through acquisition of MCA, owner of Universal Studios, in 1994 and Polygram in 1995, prior to subsequent sale to Vivendi in 2000.
South Staffs Water	UK	HomeServe; creation in 1991 of a domestic emergencies assistance and insurance business by a UK water utility.
SunAmerica	US	Retirement savings; transformation of a mortality-based life insurance company into one specializing only in the retirement savings market.

Corporate parent	Nationality	Development
TRW	US	TRW Automotive; major new business concentrating on automotive safety developed in early 1990s to replace declining space and defense activity (since partially floated by Northrop Grumman Corp).
VNU	Netherlands	Marketing services; transformation of a Dutch publishing company into a major international supplier of business information.
Whitbread	UK	Restaurants; entry of UK pub chain into restaurant business, including Beefeater chain.
Whitbread	UK	Travel Inn; use of Beefeater restaurant locations to set up a budget hotel chain.
Whitbread	UK	Hotel business; initial acquisition of Swallow Hotels transformed through a further acquisition and acquiring the UK Marriott franchise, such that the hotel business has become the largest business in the group.
WPP	UK	Media and communication services; an expansion from the original core of advertising services.

NOTES

CHAPTER 1: THE CHALLENGE OF NEW BUSINESSES

1 Robert Burgelman, *Strategy Is Destiny*, Free Press, 2002.
2 Mats Lederhausen believes that this report was inaccurate: that McDonald's never intended to sell a stake in these businesses. However, the report illustrates the shift in attention that was taking place at McDonald's when Jim Cantalupo took over.
3 Gary Hamel refers to this problem in a slightly different way. He observes that failure with new initiatives is often due to the invisible, untested assumptions that executives make about the environment and appropriate business formula. These assumptions are easy to get wrong because they are the ones made about and appropriate for the existing businesses; whereas our solution is to bias the search for new businesses toward situations where these invisible assumptions will not be a disadvantage. Hamel believes that, by being exceptionally clear about what is known and what is not known, it is possible to manage a learning process that avoids the pitfalls of these untested assumptions.
4 *Business Week*, May 3, 2004.
5 Jay Greene, Microsoft's Midlife Crisis, *Business Week*, April 19, 2004.
6 There is a third way for companies to get into new businesses that does not involve a crisis or finding businesses that fit. Philips's success with Polygram is an example. If the business is far enough removed from the core that there is no attempt to apply the thinking of the existing businesses to the new area, if the management team are given sufficient autonomy, and if there is still a strategic logic that makes sense, success is possible. However, it normally results in the business being sold because it cannot be integrated into the parent company portfolio. Hence it does not really meet our criteria of developing new growth avenues for a company with a declining core. It is also comparatively rare.

CHAPTER 2: BEATING THE ODDS

1 Corporate Strategy Board, *Growth Restarts: Reinvigorating Principled Revenue Growth in Mature Companies*.

2 Chris Zook and James Allen, *Profit from the Core*, Harvard Business School Press, 1999.

3 Gary Hamel (*Leading the Revolution*) gives particular attention to the processes of idea generation, incubation, and "early testing." Mehrdad Baghai (*The Alchemy of Growth*) suggests improvements to incubation processes as a way of filling the pipeline. Rosabeth Moss Kanter (*When Giants Learn to Dance*) recommends improvement to incubation, launch, and business development processes. Clayton Christensen (*The Innovator's Dilemma*) encourages managers to focus on disruptive technologies and greater separation of new businesses as they are being developed. Robert Burgelman (*Strategy Is Destiny*) calls for improvements in bottom-up processes, the role of middle managers, and the ability of corporate-level managers to suspend judgment. Richard Foster (*Creative Destruction*) focuses on the need for richer dialogue between the senior executives at the top of companies.

4 Andrew Campbell, Julian Birkinshaw, Andy Morrison and Robert van Basten Battenberg, The Future of Corporate Venturing, *Sloan Management Review*, Fall 2003.

5 Chis Zook and James Allen, *Profit from the Core*, Harvard Business School Press, 1999.

6 Jim Collins and Gerry Porras, *From Good to Great*, HarperCollins, 2001.

7 In alphabetical order, Mehrdad Baghai, *The Alchemy of Growth*; Zenas Block, *Corporate Venturing*; Robert Burgelman, *Strategy Is Destiny*; Clayton Christensen, *The Innovator's Solution*; Gary Hamel, *Leading the Revolution*, Richard Foster, *Creative Destruction*; Richard Leifer, *Radical Innovation*; Rosabeth Moss Kanter, *When Giants Learn to Dance* and *Evolve!*; Adrian Slywotzky, *How to Grow When Markets Don't*; Michael Tushman, *Winning through Innovation*; Chris Zook, *Beyond the Core*.

CHAPTER 3: THE DIFFICULTIES OF BUILDING NEW LEGS

1 Clayton Christensen and Michael Raynor, *The Innovator's Solution*, Harvard Business School Press, 2003.
2 Richard Foster and Sarah Kaplan, *Creative Destruction*, Currency, 2001.
3 Value destruction here is defined by the cost of capital. Any company that performs less well than the average is destroying value, because the cost of equity is calculated based on the average return that shareholders expect from investments in the capital markets.
4 BG demerged into Lattice and BG Group. Lattice subsequently merged with National Grid and the remaining part of the telecoms activity (SST) was integrated into National Grid's telecoms business (Gridcom). This formed a platform from which National Grid acquired Crown Castle, to become a market leader in telecoms towers in the UK. At the time of writing it is not clear whether this new business for National Grid Transco (the new merged company) is a success. Moreover, it is clear that the attempts by Lattice to build a towers business (SST), although not a financial disaster, were not viewed by management as a success. Within BG Group, two or three of the original new businesses continue with limited support and the main opportunity, domestic combined heat and power, has still not developed a technology at a low enough price point to be commercial.
5 Michael Porter, *Competitive Strategy*, Free Press, 1983.
6 Igor Ansoff, *Corporate Strategy*, McGraw-Hill, 1965.
7 Gary Hamel and CK Prahalad, The core competence of the corporation, *Harvard Business Review*, May 1990.
8 Chris Zook and James Allen, *Profit from the Core*, Harvard Business School Press, 1999.
9 Careful reading of Hamel, Kanter, Slywotzky, and other authors does not reveal sections where they expressly recommend companies to "play the numbers game." Yet the idea that companies need to multiply the number of experiments and ventures pervades their texts. When pushed, most authors reject the "1,000 flowers bloom" strategy, yet encourage companies to be less deterministic, less risk averse, and more experimental.
10 Gary Hamel, Bringing Silicon Valley inside, *Harvard Business Review*, May 2000.
11 Julian Birkinshaw, *Entrepreneurship in the Global Firm*, Sage, 2000.

12 In our discussions with consultants at Strategos and Bain & Co., we were told of research projects both firms had done that confirmed the lack of success of corporate venturing units. It should be noted that there is other research that is more favorable to corporate venturing units. A good summary of this research is contained in *Corporate Venturing* by Zenas Block and Ian MacMillan, Harvard Business School Press, 1993. Our explanation for the contrasting views on corporate venturing is given in Chapter 8.

CHAPTER 4: WHEN LOW GROWTH IS BETTER THAN GAMBLING

1 With growth at around 2–3% and a cost of capital of 12–15%, market capitalization increases by 10% for each 1% increase in growth, using the dividend growth model for valuation. If returns are far in excess of the cost of capital, each 1% increase in growth can have a much larger (25%) impact on market capitalization. As the growth rate approaches the cost of capital, the dividend growth model produces very large valuations.

2 Corporate Strategy Board, *Stall Points*, Corporate Advisory Board, 1998.

3 Arie de Geus, *The Living Company*, Nicholas Brealey Publishing, 1999.

4 Corporate Strategy Board, *Stall Points*, Corporate Advisory Board, 1998.

5 Lou Takes the Gloves Off, *Business Week*, November 18, 2002.

6 David Garvin, Emerging Business Opportunities at IBM (A), Harvard Business School, Case No N9-304-075.

7 Corporate Strategy Board, *Stall Points*, Corporate Advisory Board, 1998.

CHAPTER 5: THE NEW BUSINESSES TRAFFIC LIGHTS

1 After the manuscript was complete, Chris Zook commented that "Figure 5.3 is almost exactly what evolved from our analysis of 12 paired company comparisons where we examined over 500 growth moves one by one and identified the key thematic differences that could have been assessed better by research." As we point out later, the

Traffic Lights are not built on dramatic new theory. There are some new insights and some old ideas presented in new ways. But the main contribution of the Traffic Lights is to pull together the excellent work that has been done by strategy academics over the last 30 years and practitioners such as Zook and Allen at Bain & Co.

2 Michael Porter, *Competitive Advantage*, Free Press, 1986.
3 Richard Foster and Sarah Kaplan, *Creative Destruction*, Currency Doubleday, 2001.
4 Barry Gibbons, *If You Want to Make God Really Laugh Show Him Your Business Plan*, Capstone, 1998.
5 Gary Hamel, Waking up IBM, *Harvard Business Review*, July–Aug 2000.
6 James Mackintosh, Poor quality of Mercedes cars dents profits, *Financial Times*, Oct 29, 2004.

CHAPTER 6: DIVERSIFICATION

1 Tom Peters and Robert Waterman, *In Search of Excellence*, Free Press, 1984.
2 Igor Ansoff, *Cororate Strategy*, New York: McGraw-Hill, 1965.
3 Richard P. Rumelt, *Strategy, Structure and Economic Performance*, Harvard Business School Press, 1974.
4 Gary Hamel and CK Prahalad, The Core Competence of the Corporation, *Harvard Business Review*, May 1990.
5 Michael Goold, Andrew Campbell, and Marcus Alexander, *Corporate-Level Strategy*, John Wiley & Sons, 1994.
6 *Ibid.*, pp. 340–53.

CHAPTER 7: SEARCHING FOR NEW BUSINESSES

1 Mehrdad Baghai, Stephen Coley, and David White, *The Alchemy of Growth*, Free Press, 1998.
2 Gary Hamel, *Leading the Revolution*, Harvard Business School Press, 2001.
3 Rosabeth Moss Kanter, *When Giants Learn to Dance*, Harvard Business School Press, 1988 and *Evolve!*, Harvard Business School Press, 2000.
4 Robert Burgelman, *Strategy Is Destiny*, Free Press, 2002.
5 Clayton Christensen, *The Innovators' Solution*, Harvard Business School Press, 2003.

6 Chris Zook and James Allen, *Profit from the Core*, Harvard Business School Press, 1999.

7 Robert Burgelman, *Strategy Is Destiny*, Free Press, 2002.

8 Julian Birkinshaw, *Entrepreneurship in the Global Firm*, Sage, 2000.

9 Rosabeth Moss Kanter (When Giants Learn to Dance is the author who gives most emphasis to the importance of having a parallel process for developing new businesses. She distinguishes between processes for "mainstream" businesses and processes for "newstream" businesses. She is in good company: most other authors agree with her.

10 In a letter to *Harvard Business Review* in response to Gary Hamel and Gary Getz's article Innovating in an age of austerity, *Harvard Business Review*, July 2004.

11 Michael Goold, Andrew Campbell, and Marcus Alexander, *Corporate-Level Strategy*, John Wiley & Sons, 1994

12 Robert Burgelman, *Strategy Is Destiny*, Free Press, 2002, pp. 368–79.

13 *Ibid.*, p. 368.

14 Clayton Christensen also recommends that managers need to be ready to cut failing projects. His advice, with regard to disruptive innovations, is to be "impatient for profit and patient for sales." Isabelle Royer (in Why bad projects are so hard to kill, *Harvard Business Review*, February 2003) explains why it is so hard to cut projects and offers some remedies: beware of cheerleading squads, establish an early warning system, and recognize the role of the exit champion.

15 David Garvin and Lynne Levesque, Emerging Business Opportunities at IBM (A), Harvard Business School Case No N9-304-075.

16 Robert Burgelman, *Strategy Is Destiny*, Free Press, 2002, p. 373; Rosabeth Kanter, *When Giants Learn to Dance*, Harvard Business School Press, 1989.

CHAPTER 8: IS THERE A ROLE FOR CORPORATE VENTURING?

1 These labels were first used in an article in *Sloan Management Review* titled The future of corporate venturing, Andrew Campbell, Julian Birkinshaw, Andrew Morrison, and Robert van Basten Battenberg, *Sloan Management Review*, Fall 2002.

2 See H. Chesbrough, Making sense of corporate venture capital, *Harvard Business Review*, March 2002, pp. 4–11. See also R. A.

Burgelman, Designs for corporate entrepreneurship in established firms, *California Management Review*, vol. XXVI, no. 3, 1984, pp. 154–66; and *Strategy Is Destiny*, Free Press, 2002. Rosabeth Moss Kanter has also produced a number of important case studies published either in the *Journal of Business Venturing* or the Harvard Business School case series. These cases are discussed in her books from Harvard Business School Press, *When Giants Learn to Dance* (1988) and *Evolve!* (2000).

3 Lucent New Ventures Group is written up in detail by Rosabeth Moss Kanter and M. A. Heskett, Harvard Business School Cases 9-300-085, 9-601-102, and teaching note 5-301-108, also by Henry Chesbrough, Designing corporate ventures in the shadow of private venture capital, *California Management Review*, vol. 42, no. 3, 2000, pp. 31–49.

4 Coller Capital focused on the "secondary" market in which entire port-folios of investments are traded, typically at a substantial discount. Lucent retained a minority stake when it sold NVG to Coller.

5 More specifically, Intel Capital makes four different types of invest-ments: (1) ecosystem investments, to increase demand for the micro-processor, (2) market development investments, such as Ariba Online, to help accelerate technology adoption in a foreign country, (3) gap fillers, which are investments intended to fill a gap in a growing mar-ket, and (4) eyes and ears investments, which are targeted toward new disruptive technologies that Intel might otherwise miss.

6 The idea of separating out certain activities from their normal func-tional management is well established in the literature. See P. F. Drucker, *Innovation and Entrepreneurship: Practice and Principles*, Harper and Row, 1985, and Clayton Christensen, *The Innovator's Dilemma*, Harvard Business School Press, 1997.

7 Christensen (1997) argues that disruptive technologies need to be managed through a separate business unit, though subsequent research has suggested that the decision is contingent on a number of different variables. Venture innovation can be a highly effective way of making the initial investment in a disruptive technology, but we would expect the technology in question to be transferred to a business unit once its commercial potential is recognized.

8 Gifford Pinchot coined the term in his book *Intrapreneuring*, Harper & Row, 1985.

9 The foremost proponent of this idea was Gary Hamel, but many other consultants and academics made similar arguments. See G. Hamel,

Leading the Revolution, Harvard Business School Press, 2001, and R. Foster and S. Kaplan, *Creative Destruction*, Doubleday, 2001.

10 It is worth noting that the statistical evidence collected in the London Business School questionnaire showed that venture innovation often fails because of excessive autonomy. That is, there was a strong, statistically significant correlation between venture unit performance and operating autonomy, and between venture unit performance and operating budget independence.

11 The success of GE Equity up to 2000 is well documented in Don Laurie, *Venture Catalyst*, Nicholas Brealey Publishing, 2001.

12 See M. Maula and G. Murray, Corporate venture capital and the creation of US public companies: The impact of sources of venture capital on the performance of portfolio companies, in M. A. Hitt, R. Amit, C. Lucier, and B. Shelton (eds) *Strategy in the Entrepreneurial Millennium*, John Wiley & Sons, 2001.

13 See G. Hamel, *Leading the Revolution*, Harvard Business School Press, 2001, and C. Markides, *All the Right Moves*, Harvard Business School Press, 2000.

14 Ralph Biggadike studied corporate diversification in the 1970s and concluded that a major cause of failure was management's timidity. See R. A. Biggadike, The risky business of corporate diversification, *Harvard Business Review*, May–June 1979; or R. A. Biggadike, *Corporate Diversification*, Harvard Business School Press, 1979.

CHAPTER 9: POSITIONING AND SUPPORTING A NEW BUSINESS

1 Zenas Block and Ian MacMillan, Corporate Venturing: Creating New Businesses within the Firm, *Harvard Business School Press*, 1993.

2 Clayton Christensen, *The Innovator's Dilemma*, Harvard Business School Press, 1997.

3 Charles O'Reilly and Michael Tushman, The Ambidextrous Organization, *Harvard Business Review*, April 2004.

4 Clayton Christensen and Michael Raynor, *The Innovator's Solution*, Harvard Business School Press, 2003, Chapter 7.

5 Robert Burgelman and Leonard Sayles, *Inside Corporate Innovation*, Free Press, 1986.

6 Tushman, Smith, Wood, Westerman and O'Reilly also emphasize the importance of separation in Innovation Streams and Ambidextrous Organization Designs, submitted to *Academy of Management Journal*, July 2004. They provide compelling data on the advantages of separation.
7 Michael Goold and Andrew Campbell, *Designing Effective Organizations*, Jossey-Bass, 2002.
8 Robert Burgelman, *Strategy Is Destiny*, Free Press, 2002.
9 Zenas Block and Ian MacMillan, *Corporate Venturing: Creating New Businesses within the Firm*, Harvard Business School Press, 1993, Chapter 9, Controlling the Venture.
10 Richard Leifer, Christopher McDermott, Gina Colarelli, Lois Peters, Mark Rice, and Robert Veryzer, *Radical Innovation: How Mature Companies Can Outsmart Upstarts*, Harvard Business School Press.

INDEX

organization design
accountability test 236, 238, 241
difficult links test 236, 238, 241
feasibility test 236, 237, 241
flexibility test 236, 238, 241
market advantage test 236, 237, 240
nine tests for 235–40
parenting advantage test 236, 237, 240
people test 236, 237, 240
redundant hierarchy test 236, 238, 241
specialist cultures test 236, 237, 240
Otellini, Paul 14–15
overvaluation trap 78–80, 83–4

Palmisano, Sam 90, 194
parenting new businesses 205–6
Parenting Opportunity Analysis 246–50, 262
Parenting Theory 1, 3–4, 64, 156–66, 176
link with Traffic Lights 163–69
Parker, Gerry 14
Partner Brands 13, 15–16, 144–6
Patrick, John 135
PC Plus 14, 80
PC World 50
Pearson, Michael 219
Peters, Lois 287–9
Philips 2, 5–6, 17, 70, 123, 141, 180–81, 199, 206, 214, 261, 266
Pizza Hut 46, 191
PLM 138
Polygram 5
PortalPlayer xi
Porter, Michael 56–7, 98–9, 122–4
positive thinking 39
potential, releasing 37
potential/fit matrix 95–6
Prahalad, CK 155

Pret A Manger xii, 13, 15, 144
PricewaterhouseCoopers 89
private equity venturing 209, 218, 221–4, 229
Procter & Gamble 3, 43, 71, 155
product/market matrix 59–60, 154–5, 159, 161–2
profit pool potential 97–8, 117–30, 164–5, 167, 169, 202
Prudential 4, 32, 40, 134, 145, 186, 235, 242
purposeful accidents 37–8

rare games 26–7, 117, 119–20, 129, 165, 166, 168–9, 178–9
relatedness 154–5, 157, 233
Rentokil 28–9
Rentokil Initial 66
research project 3–6, 21–4
resource-based view of strategy 155
Rexam 138
Rice, Mark 287–9
Rio Tinto 1, 156
risks, inherent in new businesses 46–50
Royal Academy of Arts xv
Royal Bank of Scotland xi, 2, 23, 46–50, 134, 175
Royal Sun Alliance 207
Rumelt, Richard 154
Ryanair 29

Samsung 265
saplings 30–31, 166–8, 178–9
Savelsberg, Rene 214
Schreuder, Hein 3, 68
Sheffey, Forrest 187
Shell 2, 21, 59, 115, 218–19
Siemens 141, 217
skills, humility about 29–31
Slater Walker 151, 263
Slater, Jim 263
Slywotzky, Adrian 289–91

ACKNOWLEDGMENTS

I n putting this book together there are many people who deserve our thanks. Most important are the large number of managers who gave us their time and who trusted us to treat their confidences with respect.

Julian Birkinshaw, Robert Burgelman, and Gary Hamel have been particularly useful discussants. Chris Tchen shared his consulting experience. Lucy Campbell did some excellent research on McDonald's. Angela Munro helped assemble the text and exhibits. Michael Goold provided editorial guidance.

Nicholas Brealey, our publisher, insisted on some structural changes that have made the book much more accessible. He also worked tirelessly on the title and provided the sort of relationship every author would most want with his or her publisher.